overy of Buddhism

SCHOOL OF ORIENTAL

The British discovery
of Buddhism

Philip C. Almond

**Reader in Studies in Religion
University of Queensland, Australia**

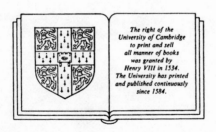

The right of the
University of Cambridge
to print and sell
all manner of books
was granted by
Henry VIII in 1534.
The University has printed
and published continuously
since 1584.

CAMBRIDGE UNIVERSITY PRESS

Cambridge

New York   New Rochelle   Melbourne   Sydney

Published by the Press Syndicate of the University of Cambridge
The Pitt Building, Trumpington Street, Cambridge CB2 1RP
32 East 57th Street, New York, NY 10022, USA
10 Stamford Road, Oakleigh, Melbourne 3166, Australia

First published 1988

British Library cataloguing in publication data
Almond, Philip C.
The British discovery of Buddhism.
1. Buddhism – Great Britain – History
– 19th century   2. Great Britain –
Religion – 19th century
I. Title
294.3′0941   BQ709.G7

Library of Congress cataloguing in publication data
Almond, Philip C.
The British discovery of Buddhism / Philip C. Almond.
p. cm.
Bibliography.
ISBN 0 521 35503 6
1. Buddhism – Study and teaching – Great Britain – History – 19th
century.   2. Great Britain – Religion – 19th century   I. Title
BQ162.G7A45 1988
294.3′0941 – dc 19   87-35506 CIP

ISBN 0 521 35503 6

Transferred to digital printing 2003

WS

To Monmana

Contents

Preface

The student of religion has been well served by a number of volumes devoted to the history of Christian thought in the nineteenth century. But very few studies have been devoted to the nineteenth-century interpretations of non-Christian religions, or to the role that these played in the shaping of Victorian culture. This volume is intended partly to fill that gap by examining the creation and interpretation of Buddhism in Great Britain during this period. It is to be hoped that the examination of the way in which Victorian thinkers made sense of the East, and of the means by which Victorian Christians came to terms with an alien tradition both complementary to and opposite to their own, will cast some new light on a period which was seminal for the development of contemporary Western religious pluralism.

To a large extent, I have allowed the interpreters of Buddhism to speak for themselves. At one level, this is a means to show forth the subtle and complex connexions between the network of texts which comprise Victorian discourse about Buddhism. But at another level, a deeper one, it is intended to evoke in the reader not only a cognitive apprehension but a sense of, and a feeling for, those aspects of the discourse that are uniquely Victorian. My intention has been to supply as much detail as space allowed to enable the reader personally to encounter Victorian Buddhism.

I should like to express my thanks to a number of people: to Professor Charles Long for a number of stimulating conversations; and to my colleagues Dr Richard Hutch and Mr Rod Bucknell who read earlier drafts of this study and made many helpful suggestions. I am grateful too to Mrs Roni Hawkins for typing the manuscript.

P.C.A., Brisbane, April 1987

Introduction

Ah! Blessed Lord! Oh, High Deliverer!
Forgive this feeble script, which doth thee wrong.
Measuring with little wit thy lofty Love.
Ah! Lover! Brother! Guide! Lamp of the Law!
I take my refuge in thy name and thee!
I take my refuge in thy Law of Good!
I take my refuge in thy Order! OM!
The Dew is on the Lotus! – Rise, Great Sun!
And lift my leaf and mix me with the wave.
Om mani padme hum, the Sunrise comes!
The Dewdrop slips into the shining Sea!

With these words, Edwin Arnold concluded his *The Light of Asia*, a blank-verse life of the Buddha in eight books. Without doubt, it was one of the most popular long Victorian poems. First published in 1879, it went through at least a hundred editions in England and America. It was translated into numerous foreign languages, and in 1884 *Trübner's Record* announced that it was to be published in Bengali and Sanskrit.[1] Christopher Clausen remarks that, 'Largely on the strength of it, the hitherto obscure Arnold achieved fame, a knighthood and an ultimately disappointed expectation of the laureateship.'[2]

As a result of its popularity, there was an enormous upsurge in awareness of, and interest in, Buddhism in late Victorian England, along with which went a polarization in attitudes towards it. Christmas Humphreys was later to write, 'It is little exaggeration to say of this great work that it obtained for the Dhamma a hearing which half a century of scholarship could never have obtained ...'[3]

1

George Cobbold, an Anglican clergyman, described *The Light of Asia* in 1894 as the book which 'probably more than any other work of the day has been the means of drawing the attention of English-speaking people to Buddhism ...'; but this itself drew a protest from this surprisingly liberal Anglican: 'Men and women have risen from perusal of the *Light of Asia* [*sic*] with a sense of damage done to their Christian faith, and with a feeling ... that in Gautama Buddha they have been confronted with a formidable rival to Jesus Christ.'[4]

This combination of attraction to *The Light of Asia* and a Christian rejection of its subject was powerfully expressed in a meeting of the Victoria Institute towards the end of the century. The address was given by the Reverend Richard Collins, from 1854 to 1878 a missionary in India and Ceylon. He drew a distinction between Arnold's Buddha and the historical Buddha, and claimed that the Buddha of *The Light of Asia* 'is no more a picture of the genuine and real Buddha, than Alfred Tennyson's King Arthur is a picture of the actual King Arthur ...'[5] Such sentiments were expressed much more forcibly in the subsequent discussion. W. H. Robinson applauded the style, talent, and construction of the book. But he went on to declaim, 'I say Sir Edwin Arnold's book is one of the most mischievous, and is chargeable with having given currency to the opinion among shallow, or uninformed thinkers, that the Buddha was at least as great a man as He whom Christians adore, and his religion in some respects preferable to Christianity.'[6] Mr Robert Moncrieff, a visitor to the Institute, was moved to exclaim even more harshly:

having read *The Light of Asia* very soon after it was published, I said, 'how can that be Light which has produced darkness of the grossest kind?' ... Sirs and ladies, I venture to ask you if any people on the face of the earth seem to be more utterly indifferent to the shedding of blood and to human suffering than the followers of Buddhism. At the same time, with all this wretched, horrible disregard for human suffering and human life, they show the greatest care for animal life ... These contradictions are parts of the darkness proceeding out of *The Light of Asia*, which we are asked to accept in preference to *The Light of the World* (*applause*).[7]

The polarity exemplified by the reaction to Arnold's poem was part of a much more general polarity about Buddhism that was embedded in mid and late Victorian culture. It was a polarity stimulated by *The Light of Asia*. But it had been present in Victorian

England, at least among the educated middle and upper classes, since the 1850s. Indeed, it was precisely this polarity, or rather the positive side of it, that had made possible such a literary creation as *The Light of Asia* and guaranteed its success. In the Victorian fascination with Buddhism, Arnold found a ready market for his work. Buddhism had been culturally potent and surprisingly pervasive for some twenty years before the appearance of his work; and it remained so for some twenty years after.

In 1869, for example, Max Müller not without a hint of irony remarked, 'Now it has been the peculiar fate of the religion of Buddha, that among all the so-called false or heathenish religions, it almost alone has been praised by all and everybody for its elevated, pure, and humanizing character. One hardly trusts one's eyes on seeing Catholic and Protestant missionaries vie with each other in their praises of the Buddha; ...'[8] In 1890, the anonymous author of a review of several major works on Buddhism foreshadowed, albeit a little prematurely, the waning of enthusiasm for it. But he did nevertheless give a clear picture of the impact it had made on the Victorian imagination:

The enthusiasm for Buddhism, which has been aroused of late years among us, has probably passed its highest point. A few years ago the magazines were full of it; and every young lady, who made any pretensions to the higher culture, was prepared to admire 'such a beautiful religion and so like Christianity' ... The daring reformer, who stood up alone against a dominant caste to proclaim the brotherhood and equality of man; the isolated thinker, who struck out a whole system of philosophy and morals, independent of or opposed to all that had preceded it; his heroic career of self-sacrifice and life laid down for his friends; – that vast literature pervaded by love and purity, rich in proverb and parable, moving in such high regions of philosophy; – that world-wide community, in whose romantic monasteries, under rock-temple and leaf-hut, through all those silent centuries men rapt above the world had lived the calm life of meditation; – all these are seen now, by any one who cares to know the truth, in forms more commonplace, less original, less complete.[9]

The slightly tongue-in-cheek tone of this passage does signify, as its author claims, the passing of the high point of enthusiasm for Buddhism; it is a tone rarely heard in the literature prior to this time. But in spite of this, it indicates vividly those heroic qualities of the Buddha, and the romantic ambience of Buddhism, that attracted so many Victorians.

Even at this time, however, many of its detractors remained vehement. The *London Quarterly Review* for 1888 – 9 harshly asserted that 'European admirers of Buddhism are as great an anachronism as an adherent of Egyptian or Chaldean astronomers.'[10] Monier Monier-Williams, one of the least sympathetic of Oriental scholars to Buddhism, in an address given to the World's Missionary Conference in London, declared somewhat disingenuously that, 'It is one of the strange phenomena of the present day, that even educated persons are apt to fall into raptures over the doctrines of Buddhism attracted by the bright gems which its admirers cull out of its moral code and display ostentatiously while keeping out of sight all the dark spots of that code, all its trivialities, and omitting to mention precepts, which, indeed, no Christian could soil his lips by uttering.'[11]

It is this hitherto virtually neglected aspect of Victorian culture that this work intends to examine.[12] In the first place, I want to argue that there was an imaginative creation of Buddhism in the first half of the nineteenth century, and that the Western creation of Buddhism progressively enabled certain aspects of Eastern cultures to be defined, delimited, and classified. In the second place, I want to analyse the discourse about Buddhism that was created and sustained by the reification of the term 'Buddhism', and which, in its turn, defined the nature and content of this entity. I hope to show the way in which 'Buddhism' was created, and discourse about it determined, by the Victorian culture in which it emerged as an object of discourse.

In so doing, something of the history of Buddhist studies in the West, and especially in Great Britain, will be thrown into relief. But two qualifications need to be made. First, this work does not pretend, either in terms of its content or its method, to be a history of Buddhist scholarship. Buddhist scholarship is important in the context of this work only in so far as it contributed to the creation and maintenance of Buddhism and a discourse about it. Second, part of the purpose of this book is to demonstrate as precisely as possible the way in which the scholarly analysis of Buddhism was influenced by the object it created, and the discourse that defined that object. Buddhist scholarship was not only the cause but also the effect of that which it brought into being – Buddhism.

An important point of method is connected with the above. How are we to determine from the enormous amount of scholarly material

4

which was produced those parts of it which contributed to the development of a discourse about Buddhism? In effect, I determined to restrict the scholarly material I wished to consult to that which was cited, reviewed, or quoted in the serious but more popular literature about Buddhism. On the one hand, this may have resulted in my ignoring some works which, with our historical hindsight, are of importance in the history of Western scholarship on Buddhism. On the other hand, as will become apparent, this decision enabled me to examine a large number of texts which, however unlikely they would be to be included in a contemporary history of Buddhist scholarship, were seen by their contemporaries as significant contributions. On the same principle, I have generally consulted American, German, or French sources only where they have been similarly cited, reviewed, or quoted.

A further point of method: I proceed from the assumption that Victorian discourse about Buddhism is part of a broader discourse about the Orient such as has been brought to light by Edward Said in his book *Orientalism*. Discourse about Buddhism did have a different flavour to that which Said discerned by virtue of his concentration upon Islam and the Middle East. But I, like Said, am concerned with the internal logic, the structure of views about Buddhism apart from the question of how Buddhism '*really*' was. That is to say, I am not concerned with the extent to which Victorian interpretations of Buddhism correctly or incorrectly perceived, selected, reflected on, and interpreted the congeries of texts, persons, events, and phenomena in various cultures that it classified as Buddhist. My concern is rather with how these were presented by the West, in the West, and primarily for the West. Said's words are as relevant for Buddhism as for the Orient of which it was seen as forming a substantial part:

The value, efficacy, strength, apparent veracity of a written statement about the Orient ... relies very little, and cannot instrumentally depend on the Orient as such. On the contrary, the written statement is a presence to the reader by virtue of its having excluded, displaced, made supererogatory any such *real thing* as 'the Orient' ... that Orientalism makes sense at all depends more on the West than on the Orient, and this sense is directly indebted to various Western techniques of representation that make the Orient visible, clear, 'there' in discourse about it.[13]

Central to my argument, then, is the presupposition that the construction and interpretation of Buddhism reveals much about nineteenth-century concerns and can be read as an important sign of crucial socio-cultural aspects of the Victorian period. Victorian interpretations of Buddhism, whether of its founder, its doctrines, its ethics, its social practices, or its truth and value, in constructing Buddhism, reveal the world in which such constructing took place. Consequently, in the chapters which follow, discourse about Buddhism has been examined not only with a view to discerning the way in which the image of an alien religiosity was constructed, but also with the aim of demonstrating the way in which the discourse thus constructed illuminates the broad socio-cultural context in which it was created. Discourse about Buddhism provides, as we shall see, a mirror in which was reflected an image not only of the Orient, but of the Victorian world also.

1

The discovery of Buddhism

INTRODUCTION

Buddhism was 'discovered' in the West during the first half of the nineteenth century. It was at this time that the term 'Buddha' ('Buddoo', 'Bouddha', 'Boudhou', etc.) began to gain currency in the English- and French-speaking worlds, and that the term 'Buddhism' first made its appearance in English in the scholarly journals which appeared, in part at least, as a consequence of the developing imperial interests of both England and France in the Orient.[1]

This is not, of course, to deny that, as is now well known, there had been periodic encounters between the West and what we now understand as Buddhism. Pieces of information had filtered through to the early Christian world. From A.D. 1000, a version of the life of the Buddha in the form of the legend of Barlaam and Josaphat influenced the Western Christian ascetic ideal. And from the thirteenth to the eighteenth centuries there had been a succession of contacts: William van Ruysbroeck, Marco Polo, John of Monte Corvino, Dominican, Jesuit, Capuchin, and Franciscan missionaries to Japan, China, and Tibet, had all encountered Buddhism and reported their findings to a curious West.[2]

But for the greater part of the nineteenth century, these early encounters made little impact on the understanding of Buddhism in the West. The various reports of travellers, missionaries, diplomats, and so on, with a few notable exceptions, did not form a significant part of, or play an important role in, the network of texts about Buddhism that began to develop at the end of the

7

eighteenth century. Certainly, they are seldom cited. Moreover, the possibility of these various discrete and unconnected references to Buddhism forming part of the emerging discourse about Buddhism was only there after the middle of the nineteenth century when 'Buddhism' had been constructed. Only then was it possible to see such encounters, *in historical retrospect*, as the earliest contacts of the West with Buddhism; and only then was it possible to classify them within discourse about Buddhism. Until that time they remained in Western consciousness merely as disparate accounts of the encounter of the West with indistinct aspects of the Orient – but not of the *Buddhist* Orient.

A crucial part of the process of the formation of Buddhism was the recognition that there were various culturally diffuse religious phenomena which had apparent relationships with each other. As early as 1693, Simon de la Loubère, an envoy of Louis XIV on the third French mission to Siam, surmised that the religion of Siam had come from Ceylon, for the Siamese 'averr for truth, that the Religion of the *Siumeses* [*sic*] came from those quarters because that they have read in a *Balie* Book, that *Sommona-Codom* whom the *Siameses* adore, was the Son of a King of the Island of *Ceylon*'.[3] Further, on information gained from the Chinese, he also hazarded the opinion that the Chinese 'bonzees' gained their doctrine from Thailand. After a number of etymological comparisons between the languages of Japan, China, and Siam, he concluded:

I find therefore some reason to believe, that the *Chineses* having received the Doctrine of the *Metempsychosis* from some *Siamese Talapoin*, they have taken the general name of the Profession, for the proper Name of the Author of the Doctrine: and this is so much the more plausible, as it is certain that the *Chineses* do also call their *Bonzees* by the name of Che-kia [Sákya] as the Siameses do call their *Talapoins* Tchaou-cou. 'Tis therefore impossible to assert, from the testimony of the *Chineses*, that there was an *Indian* named *Che-Kia*, Author of the Opinion of the *Metempsychosis*, a Thousand years before Jesus Christ: seeing that the *Chineses* who have received this Opinion since the Death of Christ, and perhaps much later than they alledge, are forced to confess, that they have nothing related concerning this Che-Kia, but upon the Faith of the Indians; who speak not one word thereof, not thinking that there was any first Author of their Opinions.[4]

Loubère's opinions on the Siamese origin of Chinese Buddhism and his dismissal of its Indian origin had little influence in the early nineteenth-century creation of Buddhism. But his general description of the religion of Sommona-codom was to do so, through the agency of William Chambers. In the first volume of *Asiatick Researches* in 1788, he drew together the information in Loubère and in Robert Knox's *An Historical Relation of Ceylone*, the first edition of which was published in 1681. 'From Knox's history of *Ceylone*', he wrote, 'it appears, that the impression here spoken of is upon the hill called ... Adam's Peak. And that the natives believe it to be the foot-step of their great idol *Buddou*. Between the worship of whom, as described by Knox, and that of Sommona-codom, as related by M. de la Loubère, there is a striking resemblance in many particulars ...'⁵ Chambers's identification is reflected in an article in 1801 by M. Joinville on the people of Ceylon. 'It has been justly observed', he remarked, 'that the SAMONOCODUM of the people of *Siam*, is the same as the BOUDHOU of the *Singalese*.'⁶ And Captain Mahony, in his account of Ceylon in the same year, observed that 'GAUTEMEH BHOODDHA is acknowledged by the *Singhalais*, to be the same holy character termed by the *Siamese*, SOMMONOKODOM, and BOOTISAT.'⁷

Even so, such connexions often remained unrecognized. Thus, for example, in *The English Encyclopaedia* of 1802, we read only of

BUDUN, one of the Ceylonese gods, who is fabled to have arrived at supremacy, after successive transmigrations from the lowest state of an insect, through the various species of living animals. There are 3 deities of this name, each of whom is said to reign till a bird shall have removed a hill of sand, half a mile high, and six miles round, by carrying off a single grain once in 1,000 years.⁸

And this entry is repeated in the *Encyclopaedia Perthensis* in 1807, in the *Encyclopaedia Britannica* in 1810, 1817, and as late as 1854, in the *Pantologia* in 1813, and in *The London Encyclopaedia* in 1829.⁹ As late as 1833, Charles Gutzlaff, the Protestant missionary to China, could still wonder whether Sommona Kodom, whom he knows as the founder of Buddhism in Laos, Cambodia, and Siam, 'was a disciple of Budha himself ...'¹⁰

Still, although there was uncertainty at the popular level, at the scholarly level, the links were clearer. In 1697, the Jesuit Louis le Comte declared that 'all the Indies have been poysoned with his pernicious doctrine'. And he identified the Buddhists of Siam with those of Tartary, Japan, and China.¹¹ A century later, the Abbé Grosier drew on his recollections: 'The priests attached to the worship of *Fo* are called *Talapoins* by the Siamese, *Lamas* by the Tartars, *Ho-chang* in China, and *Bonzes* in Japan.'[12] And Michael Symes in his account of an embassy to the Kingdom of Ava in 1795 reported that 'The Cingaleze in Ceylon are Boodhists of the purest source, and the Birmans acknowledge to have originally received their religion from that island. It was brought say the Rhahaans, first from Zehoo (Ceylon) to Arracan, and thence was introduced into Ava, and probably into China; for the Birmans assert with confidence that the Chinese are Boodhists.'[13] From his experience of the Burmese context, at the turn of the century, Father Sangermano of the Catholic mission at Rangoon observed:

... all the nations comprised in the Burmese Empire, the Pegùans, the Aracanese, the Sciam, etc., join in the adoration of Godama, and the observance of his laws. And not only here, but likewise in the kingdom of Siam this is the established religion. Godama is besides adored in China under the name of Fò, and in Thibet under that of Buttà. His worship also prevails in many places along the coast of Coromandel, and particularly in the island of Ceylon, which is the principal seat of the Talapoins.[14]

And statements of this sort were to continue to appear periodically throughout the first two decades of the nineteenth century.[15]

Generally, around the 1820s, this congeries of religious phenomena throughout Asia is being classified as the religion of Buddha or Buddhism. William Ward, a Baptist missionary in India, inquired whether 'the religion of Booddhū, now spread over the Burman empire, Siam, Ceylon, Japan, Cochin-China, and the greater part of China itself, be not in reality the ancient religion of India, and the bramhinical [*sic*] superstition the invention of later times ...'[16] According to James Mill, 'The religion of Buddha is now found to prevail over the greater part of the East; in Ceylon, in the farther peninsula, in Thibet, in China, and even as far as Japan.'[17] John Davy in 1820 in his account of Ceylon went as far as to claim that Buddhism was more widely extended than any other religion: 'It appears', he wrote, 'to be the religion of the whole of Tartary, of China, of Japan, and their dependencies, and of all the countries between China and the Burrampooter.'[18]

There were however no clear conceptions of the historical connexions between the Buddhisms of these various countries. Lieutenant-Colonel William Francklin of the East India Company saw Buddhism, not unlike Loubère, as having reached China and Japan from Ceylon via Ava.[19] In contrast to this, John Crawfurd in his journal of an embassy to Siam and Cochin-China, and following notes on Buddhism supplied to him by Horace H. Wilson, concluded that the Buddhism of Siam

has no direct connexion with the worship of that name as it originated in Tartary, of which the Siamese appear to know nothing – that it is derived from the reform or regeneration of that religion, which originated in Magadha, the modern Behar, in the sixth century before the birth of Christ ...[20]

This uncertainty aside, by the mid-1830s, 'Buddhism' had come to define the religious beliefs and practices of most of Asia. *The Penny Cyclopaedia* of 1836 began its account of Buddhism by remarking that it had 'become the religion of the great majority of the inhabitants of the high table-land to the north of the Himālaya, as far as the boundary of Siberia, and it is the prevailing creed of China, of the Peninsula of India beyond the Ganges, of Ceylon, and several islands of the Indian archipelago, and of the empire of Japan'.[21] The *New Englander* of 1845 saw Buddhism as having contributed more than any other religious system to the creation of the civilization of Eastern Asia.[22] By 1854, when it was as we shall see more or less established that India was the birthplace of Buddhism, the fact of its wide expansion led Joseph Edkins of the London Missionary Society to the almost heretical opinion that, in spite of its present indolence and decadence, the India of the past was not in need of the revivifying powers of British colonial policy. 'The very existence of Buddhism', he wrote,

is sufficient evidence of the energy of the Indian race as it was long ago. The Mongols, Thibetians, and Ceylonese, with the inhabitants of the Indo-Chinese peninsula combine with the Chinese and Japanese to prove by the faith they still maintain in Buddhism, the enthusiasm of its first missionaries and their power to influence mankind. Buddhism was not always that decrepid and worn out superstition that it now appears.[23]

Corresponding to this containment of the East within the object 'Buddhism', there was an imaginative awareness of the multitudinous numbers of its adherents. As early as 1799, Francis Buchanan maintained that it was the feature of it which demanded the attention of the West: 'However absurd the tenets of this religion may be, yet as influencing the conduct of so large and proportion of mankind, it becomes an object of great importance in the history of the human race.'[24] But it was only in the 1820s that the sheer enormity of the numbers of adherents of Buddhism became evident to the West. The religion having been 'created', there came the ensuing realization that its adherents outnumbered those of Christianity. For the remainder of the century, the number of believers would constitute the most commonly cited feature of Buddhism that necessitated the discussion of it. Its adherents would be variously estimated to be between three hundred and five hundred millions. Often, it was conceded that Buddhism had more followers than any other religion. And this became a commonplace in spite of the fact that, for example, Monier-Williams objected in 1889 that this claim was based on an 'utterly erroneous calculation',[25] and that many Chinese missionaries argued that not all Chinese could be considered *only* Buddhists, or even Buddhists at all.

THE BEGINNINGS OF DISCOURSE

Throughout the preceding discussion, I have tried carefully to avoid giving the impression that Buddhism existed prior to the end of the eighteenth century: that it was waiting in the wings, so to say, to be discovered; that it was floating in some aethereal Oriental limbo expecting its objective embodiment. On the contrary, what we are witnessing in the period from the later part of the eighteenth century to the beginning of the Victorian period in the latter half of the 1830s is the *creation* of Buddhism. It *becomes* an object, is constituted as such; it takes form as an entity that 'exists' over against the various cultures which can now be perceived as instancing it, manifesting it, in an enormous variety of ways. During the first four decades of the nineteenth century, we see the halting yet progressive emergence of a taxonomic object, the creation of which allows in turn the systematic definition, description, and classification of that congeries of cultural 'facts' which instance it, manifest it, in a number of Eastern countries.

The creation of Buddhism took place in two more or less distinct phases. The first of these coincided with the first four decades of the nineteenth century. During this period, Buddhism was an object which was instanced and manifested 'out there' in the Orient, in a spatial location geographically, culturally, and therefore imaginatively *other*. Buddhism, as constructed in the West, made

12

manageable that which was encountered in the East by travellers, diplomats, missionaries, soldiers, traders, and so on. Buddhism as a taxonomic object organized that which the Westerner confronted in an alien space, and in so doing made it less alien, less other. The locus of Buddhism was the Orient.

This would subtly change in the first twenty-five years of the Victorian period. Originally existing 'out there' in the Oriental *present*, Buddhism came to be determined as an object the primary location of which was the West, through the progressive collection, translation, and publication of its textual *past*. Buddhism, by 1860, had come to exist, not in the Orient, but in the Oriental libraries and institutes of the West, in its texts and manuscripts, at the desks of the Wetern savants who interpreted it. It had become a textual object, defined, classified, and interpreted through its own textuality. By the middle of the century, the Buddhism that existed 'out there' was beginning to be judged by a West that *alone* knew what Buddhism was, is, and ought to be. The essence of Buddhism came to be seen as expressed not 'out there' in the Orient, but in the West through the West's control of Buddhism's own textual past. To an examination of these two phases in the creation of Buddhism we may now turn.

We have seen how, by the beginning of the Victorian period, Buddhism had become a taxonomic object. But the uses to which it could be put in the tasks of description and classification remained very limited. Still, for some fifty years, information had been collecting; guesses had been made, some informed, some not so informed. In 1777, for example, John Stewart in a letter to Sir John Pringle described Tibetan religion as a corrupted version of Enlightenment Deism: '... the religion of Thibet, from whence-ever it sprung, is pure and simple in its source, conveying very exalted notions of the Deity, with no contemptible system of morality; but in its progress it has been greatly altered and corrupted by the inventions of worldly men ...'[26] Robert Percival, in his account of Ceylon at the turn of the century, remarked that neither the Europeans nor the Ceylonese themselves seem to have formed any clear idea of their religion. Some have asserted, he went on to say, that the religion of the Ceylonese is merely a variation on that of the Hindoos, though 'it appears to me to be founded on a different system of idolatry from that practised among the Hindoos'.[27] And like Stewart, he also suggested that the religion of Ceylon is a corrupted rational religion: 'It gives us a striking proof of the wonderful confusion of their ideas with regard to religion, when we find that the same people who adore one Supreme Being more powerful than all others, should at the same time offer up their devotions to devils, animals, and the very productions of the earth.'[28] William Chambers also, like Percival, argued for the distinction between what he called the religion of the *Chingelays* and that of the Hindoos.[29]

The relation of contemporary Buddhism to its own past remained opaque into the 1820s, as did its relation to Hinduism. John Crawfurd, for instance, in 1820 in his *History of the Indian Archipelago*, argued for a distinction between the religion of the Burmans, Siamese, and Cingalese and an original, genuine, and pure Buddhism; and one which, moreover, bore an intimate relation to the religion of Brama, i.e. Hinduism. From evidence of the relics of Hinduism in the principal temples of Java, he perceived 'a proof that the religions of Brama and Buddha are essentially the same, the one being, as for some time suspected by oriental scholars, nothing but a modification of the other'.[30] This opinion was reflected in Edward Upham's 1829 volume, *The History and Doctrine of Budhism*, a book which bears the distinction of being, however eccentric, the first book in English to include the word 'Budhism' in its title. Of the relation of the religion of the Buddhists to that of the Hindus, Upham wrote:

Budhism has a vein of doctrine which breathes of ambrosial odours and ambrosial flowers, when both its services and altars stood side by side with those of the Hindoo gods, and the worshippers of Brahma were delighted to honour the bright star of Budha in the planet Mercury. The records of history are for the present wanting to enable us clearly to trace out the period ... of that deadly struggle which took place between two great sects ... Without assuming any pretension to an intimate or thorough knowledge of Budhism, or arrogating ought beyond an anxious and long protracted study of the complex, and even chaotic elements of that system, the conviction has powerfully struck my mind, and become an essential point to state, that in Budhism there is mixed up a germ of intellectual motion, 'a seed not swallowed up and lost in the wide womb of uncreated night', which speaks of moral responsibility, and responds to the realities of eternity, ...[31]

THE BUDDHA: A HINDU GOD?

Part of the confusion in determining the relation of Buddhism to
the religion of India and in ascertaining a clear picture of Buddhism
was the reliance of many early investigators on information related
to them by Hindu pundits. George Turnour in the introduction to
his edition of the first twenty chapters of *The Mahawanso*, a history
of Ceylon from 587 B.C. to A.D. 236, remarked that European
scholars in India towards the close of the eighteenth century, by
virtue of the expulsion of Buddhists from India, came into contact
exclusively with Hindu pundits. They were not only interested in
confining the researches of Orientalists to Sanskrit literature but also
'... in every possible way, both by reference to their own ancient
prejudiced authorities, and their individual representations, labored
to depreciate in the estimation of Europeans, the literature of the
buddhists ...'[32] The *New Englander* in 1845 pointed out that George
Faber's work on *The Origin of Pagan Idolatry* and Ward's *A View of
the Hindoos* were vitiated in their accounts of Buddhism by their
reliance on Brahmanical authority. Francis Wilford, who set out
in 1805 to prove that the Sacred Isles of the Hindus were, 'if not
the *British* Isles ... at least some remote country to the North-west
of the old continent ...',[33] came to regret the trust he had placed in
his Hindu assistants.[34] As the *New Englander* put it, Wilford
'became the dupe of Brahmanical subtlety, and penned his
"laborious absurdities" respecting the Holy White Island of the west,
which brought on him a severe fit of illness, when he discovered the
cheat imposed on him by the Brahmans who made erasures in the
MSS'.[35]

Of particular importance in this issue was the Hindu view of the
Buddha as an avatar, or incarnation of the god Vishnu. In 1821,
John Davy questioned the identification of the Buddha with Vishnu,
but remained uncertain on the problem of whether Buddhism was
a heresy of a Brahmanical tradition that originally included the
Buddha: 'Is Boodhoo an incarnation of Vishnu? Is the religion of
Boodhoo grafted on, and a heresy of the Brahminical? Several
Oriental scholars of eminence maintain the affirmative. The
Boodhists themselves are positive in holding the negative. Where
all is probably fiction, one assertion may be opposed to another.'[36]
Vans Kennedy was adamant in 1831 that there was no connection.
In no instance of researches into Hindu mythology, he declared,

'has this propensity to prefer imagination to the labour of research been more singularly exemplified, than in the speculations which have been published respecting Buddha, and his religion; because, from the simple coincidence of names, it has been at once concluded that the ninth incarnation of Vishnu, and the alleged founder of Buddhism, were one and the same person'.[37]

The importance of the position of the Buddhists themselves on this issue was recognized in 1823 by William Erskine. He maintained the indispensable necessity of judging the doctrines of Buddhism by 'the accounts given of them by themselves, and not by the representations of their rivals'.[38] But the Hindu view of the Buddha was to retain its position of primacy until the end of the 1830s. In 1827, for example, Michael Symes concluded, 'After what has been written, there can be little necessity to inform my readers, that the Birmans are Hindoos: not votaries of Brahma, but sectaries of Boodh, which latter is admitted by Hindoos of all descriptions to be the ninth Avatar, or descent of the Deity in his capacity of preserver.'[39] According to the *Oriental Herald*, in its review of Upham's *The History and Doctrine of Budhism*, there were three Buddhas, the first of whom founded the system, the latter two of whom were reformers of it. And it was the first of these that was to be regarded 'as the ninth avatar or incarnation of Vishnoo'.[40] Even as late as 1842, the *Encyclopaedia Britannica* began its entry on Buddhism by defining 'Buddha or Buddhu' as 'one of the two appearances of Vishnu, assumed for the purpose of deluding the enemies of the gods, and effecting their destruction by leading them to profess heretical opinions, and thus to reject the Hindu religion';[41] and this is repeated in the 1854 edition.[42] Yet, in spite of this Hindu-inspired definition of the Buddha, both the 1842 and 1854 volumes recognized that by failing to distinguish Buddhism from the Hindu view of it, 'all the writers on the subject whose works we have consulted have entangled themselves in the mazes of inextricable perplexity and contradiction, and thickened the darkness which they laboured to dispel'. As a consequence, the 1842 volume concluded, 'all that has been written concerning him [the Buddha] with reference to the religion of India is wholly irrelevant and foreign to the subject'.[43] And by 1847, the Hindu view of the Buddha and the Buddha of Buddhism had become so taxonomically distinct that it was possible for James Bird, then Vice-President of the Calcutta branch of the Royal Asiatic Society, to entertain the doubt – incorrectly as it turned out – whether the Brahmanical Buddha of the *Puranas* was the same being as Gautama or Sakya Muni of the Buddhists.[44]

HISTORICAL BUDDHAS

The whole matter was further complicated by the question of the existence and nature of Buddhism prior to Gautama. Specifically, the issue turned on the question of the existence of historical Buddhas prior to the last Buddha, Gautama. One way in which the problem could be resolved was by the postulation of two Buddhas, one the founder of Buddhism referred to by the Hindus, the other a later reformer of it. This was the solution adopted by Sir William Jones in 1790. '*The Brahmans*', he wrote,

universally speak of the *Bauddhas* with all the malignity of an intolerant spirit; yet the most orthodox among them consider *Buddha* himself as an incarnation of Vishnu. This is a contradiction hard to be reconciled unless we cut the knot, instead of untying it, by supposing with *Giorgi* that there were *two Buddhas*, the younger of whom established the new religion, which gave so great offence in *India*, and was introduced into *China* in the first century of our aera.[45]

This two-Buddha theory was to recur throughout the first half of the nineteenth century. Friedrich Creuzer, for example, in his *Symbolik und Mythologie* at the beginning of the 1820s saw the Buddha as the reformer of the sect of Vishnu in 1600 B.C., some thirty-six years after the death of Krishna.[46] And Faber concluded that

The primeval Buddha is the same as Vishnou, or Siva, or Osiris: while the Buddha, who is reprobated as a heretic and who is denied by the Brahmenists to be an incarnation of the great father, was a religious adventurer; who assumed the title and character of the god, who claimed to be one of his numerous terrestrial manifestations, and who as such made certain obnoxious changes in the old Buddhic theology.[47]

Although Jones's postulation of two Buddhas was rejected as early as 1823 by Erskine,[48] it persisted – although not in quite so fanciful a form as suggested by Faber and Creuzer. Upham, for instance, concluded that Buddhism 'is in fact two systems of different eras wrought into each other, at some period of the revival of the faith, by an ambitious and zealous teacher – that there is an ancient and modern system of Buddhism, the ancient recognizes the dogma

17

of fate, the modern of free will'.[49] *The Calcutta Review* for 1845 referred also to Ritter's claim that there was an ancient and a modern Buddhism, and to Colonel Sykes's assertion that Gautama was a reformer of a previously existing Buddhism, in the light of all which it concluded that Sakya must be regarded, not as the preacher of a new religion, but as the reformer of an old.[50] In 1830, John Crawfurd endorsed Horace Wilson's two-Buddha theory. According to the latter, the original Buddha had been of Scythian or Tartar extraction; but the real founder was Gautama who, he claimed, flourished in Behar in the sixth century B.C.:

This personage might have borrowed the anti-vedaic notions of the elder *Buddha*, and the tenderness for animal life ... Very great confusion has been occasioned in all discussions relating to *Buddha*, by identifying these two persons, – an error originating with the Hindoos themselves ... They ... mixed up the two, and blended, obviously, in a very awkward manner, the *Buddha*, the ninth Avatar of Vishnu, who appeared shortly after *Crishna*, with the Prince of Magadha, the son of *Sudhodan* and Máyá Devi.[51]

It is difficult to be certain why there was such an insistence on the historical existence of a Buddha prior to Gautama. In part, it may be the result of the date accorded to the *Puranas* which saw them as extant well before Gautama. In part, too, it could be the consequence of a commitment, incipient or otherwise, to a euhemerism that entailed that any divine being was originally a human hero. However that may be, by the mid-1830s, it was being mooted in several places that the existence of Buddhism prior to Gautama was historically doubtful. Thus, in 1831, Kennedy concluded that there was no evidence 'which will satisfactorily attest the historic existence of these two Buddhas; while, on the contrary, the historic existence of Gautama, and his institution of the Buddhist religion, seem to be substantiated by every proof which the case admits of'.[52] In 1836, Jonathan Forbes, on service in Ceylon with the 78th Highlanders, was aware of the theory of Buddhas prior to Gautama. But he would admit only the latter to genuine historical existence since it was he whose moral doctrines were the rule of conduct, whose name was invoked as the present Buddha, and whose life and ministry were credibly recorded in the existing records.[53] In the same year, George Turnour similarly argued that before Gautama, all the historical data, whether of Hindu or Buddhist origin, were doubtful:

the mystification of the buddhistical data ceased a century at least prior to B.C. 588, when Prince Siddhato attained buddhohood, in the character of Gótamo Buddho. According to the buddhistical creed, therefore, all historical data, whether sacred or profane, *anterior to Gótomo's* [*sic*] *advent*, are based on *his* revelation. They are involved in absurdity as unbounded, as the mystification in which hindu literature is enveloped.[54]

The assertion of the historical existence of Buddhism prior to Gautama was to occur for another twenty years. William Knighton, in 1845, for example, was undecided about the historical veracity of most of the Buddhas that allegedly preceded Gautama. But, on the assumption that Buddhism had extended to China before the appearance of Gautama, he argued that 'we can scarcely doubt of the humanity and substantiality of the two last – Kassapo and Gotamo ...'[55] Knighton is cited by Henry Sirr in his account of Ceylon some five years later. Though he maintained that the beginnings of Buddhism cannot be dated,[56] he none the less asserted that the last two Buddhas were men and mortals, this being 'fully proved from history'.[57]

Some were willing to argue not only for the historicity of Kassapa and Gautama but also for the historicity of the two Buddhas preceding them. In 1849, for example, Lieutenant-Colonel J. Low dealt with the question of the relative antiquity of Buddhism and Brahmanism. Following on from Eduard Roer's review of Eugène Burnouf's *Introduction à l'histoire du Buddhisme indien*, he argued that Buddhism originated at some indefinable period and was re-established by the ministry of Gotama Buddha.[58] But he did go on to suggest that the period of the first Buddha was some three to four thousand years ago, though he admitted that 'we have not sufficient means for tracing the changes which the Indian mind underwent from the period of the 1st Indian Buddha ... up to the 4th Buddha, or how many theological theories may have been alternately accepted and rejected during that period'.[59] In 1854, it is still possible to write as though the existence of Buddhas prior to Gautama was a historical likelihood. Brevet-Major Alexander Cunningham of the Bengal Engineers argued that there was, prior to Sakya Muni whose death he dated in 543 B.C., a more ancient Buddhism which prevailed in India and in the countries populated by the Aryans; and that consequently, 'The belief in *Krakuchanda, Kanaka*, and *Kāsyapa*, the three mortal Buddhas who preceded *Sākya Muni*, was in India contemporaneous with the worship of the elements inculcated in the *Vedas*.'[60]

BUDDHISM: ITS PLACE OF ORIGIN

This question of the existence of Buddhism prior to Gautama was also connected with that of the place of origin of Buddhism. While the possibility of a Buddhism that pre-existed Gautama remained, the possibility of a non-Indian place of origin was present too. Two general areas were most frequently suggested: first, Africa; second, Persia or Mongolia.

It was William Jones who, it appears, was the first scholar in the English-speaking world to connect Egypt and Buddhism, although as early as 1724 La Croze in his *Histoire du Christianisme des Indes* was of the opinion that the ancient Indies had been colonies of Egypt. Jones argued that Sa'cya or Si sak, either in person or through a colony from Egypt, imported 'the mild heresy of the ancient *Bauddhas*'[61] into India; and he based his opinion partly on the Ethiopic character of the features of the Buddha in statuary.[62] Robert Percival, at the turn of the century, also noted an African character in representations of the Buddha. 'Buddou is always represented', he remarked, 'with thick, black frizzled hair like an African Negro',[63] although he went on to point out that the Ceylonese do not allow that this reflects an African origin, and are horrified at the mention of any resemblance. In 1810, Edward Moor in his *The Hindu Pantheon* remarked that there was something mysterious and still unexplained in the fact that some statues of the Buddha 'exhibit thick *Ethiopian* lips; but all, with woolly hair',[64] and he quoted Wilford to the effect that in all of the images and statues of the Buddhas 'there is an appearance of something *Egyptian* or *Ethiopian*; both in features, and in dress, differing from the ancient *Hindu* figures of heroes and demi-gods'.[65]

By 1819, Jean Abel-Rémusat had argued in the *Journal des Savans* that the physical characteristics of the Buddha described in Sanskrit Buddhist texts counted decisively against his African origin and, on the contrary, pointed to a central Indian origin for Buddhism.[66] But in spite of this, the perception that the features of the Buddha were African and the judgement that Buddhism was therefore of African origin, appeared regularly in the literature through the 1820s and into the 1830s, here as an opinion accepted, there as one which had to be refuted. In 1821, for example, John Davy pointed out that the question of the birthplace of Buddhism was still a matter of considerable obscurity. The majority of oriental scholars maintain, he suggested, that it was probably derived from Ethiopia, while very few argue for its Northern Asian origin; and the principal argument for its Ethiopian origin is the appearance of some of the images of the Buddha: 'It is said, they show that Boodhoo was an African, having marked on them the short woolly hair, the flat dilated nostrils, the thick fleshy lips, and indeed every feature of the African countenance.'[67] Davy himself remained unconvinced of the resemblance, maintaining that it is either accidental or fanciful. In his experience, he wrote, the features of Tibetan, Burman, and Chinese figures are more or less Tartar, and those of Ceylonese figures, Ceylonese. In imitation of Percival, he too questioned the Sri Lankans on this matter; and, like Percival, received the reply that even the supposition is an insult. On the matter of the Buddha's hair, 'they say it was like their own, and that the object of artists is not to represent curly, woolly hair, but hair cut short, as Boodoo's [*sic*] was when he became priest; ...'[68]

The image of the African Buddha was an extremely widespread one, and was carried by Europeans to all parts of the Orient. In 1820, John Crawfurd is moved to refer to it, if only to reject it, in remarking on the figures of the Buddha at the temple of Borobadur in Indonesia: 'There is no appearance of the wooly [*sic*] hair of the African.'[69] In the following year, there appeared Hiram Cox's *Journal of a Residence in the Burmhan Empire*. In the entry for 22 October 1797 Cox speaks of a visit to a Burmese Pagoda, in the principal niches of which were four colossal erect images of the Buddha. 'It is remarkable', he commented, 'that these have all crisped hair! The poonghees deny that they have any affinity with Caffres, but say that when Godoma assumed the religious habit, he cut off his hair with his sword, leaving it rugged or furrowed, and the features of a genuine Burmhan have a good deal of the Caffre cast.'[70] Francklin, having visited the caves at Elephanta in India, reflected the same imaginative vision:

His woolly and frizzled hair, thick lips and Herculean form, are cogent reasons for believing this shape of the divinity to have been of foreign importation. The aquiline or straight nose forms one objection to the generally received opinion of his being copied from the European [?] or African negro ... The coincidence, in the sculptured details of Egypt, Persia, and Hindoostan, are everywhere perceptible, and seem to have had one common origin.[71]

21

African Buddhas were perceived to be even in China. In 1834, the pseudonymous missionary Philosinensis visited the island of Poo-to off the Chinese coast. Of some of the idols, he wrote, 'We perceived a great number of *blue beards* among them; but were unable to ascertain what these strange representations meant. In all these colossal statues, the negro features were predominant. This corroborates the opinion that Budha sprung from some Ethiopic tribe; whether aborigines of Hindostan, or originally from Egypt, the cradle of monstrous absurdities, is uncertain.'[72] Even into the 1840s, the vision of the black Buddha was carried by Gutzlaff to China. The three Buddhas of the past, present, and future, he wrote, 'are often represented in colossal forms, with negro features, curled hair dyed a light blue, thick lips, and flat broad noses'.[73]

Another recurrent if less popular view of the birth place of Buddhism was Asia, Western and Central. The *Oriental Herald* for 1829 followed 'an obscure tradition' that saw Tartary as the original home of the system. And it cited Jean-Sylvain Bailly's view that this region was the cradle of the whole human race from which the various tribes 'issued as from a fountain'.[74] The *Calcutta Review* for 1845 referred to Horace Wilson as favouring the ex-Indian origin of Buddhism. According to Wilson, 'It is not unlikely that a colony of Sacae or Scythians settled in India, that they brought with them the faith of Buddha, and communicated it to India, whence it returned improved by the scholarship of learned converts: Buddhism is still widely cultivated throughout Central Asia, and that part of Asia is most probably its ancient and original seat.'[75] A decade later, Low put forward the proposal that its origin was to be sought in Persia.[76] He argued that the Buddhists preserved the gods and genii that they and the brahmans had mutually worshipped in Persia; while the latter diverged into polytheism, the former added hero-worship to their own original faith. Opposed to Rémusat's view that Buddhism travelled from India to central Tartary, he asked, 'was there not a germ, if not a fully expanded blossom of this religion existing long before away towards Persia and Turkistan?'[77]

By the late 1840s it was generally considered that India was the place of origin of Buddhism: 'It is generally admitted', wrote James Bird in 1847, 'that the dogmas of this faith had their rise in India ...'[78] Edward Salisbury, Professor of Sanskrit and Arabic at Yale College, in a paper read before the American Oriental Society in

May 1844, affirmed that it could be taken for granted that Buddhism was of Indian origin. There was a time, he continued,

when from the want of sufficient materials, out of which to form a correct judgement, and from the force of ingenuity seeking to supply that want by theorizing upon fancied etymologies and the like, men of great learning could differ on the question, whether the originator of this religious system was a native of Hindustan, or of Scythia, or a negro. But there is no longer any ground for such disputation.[79]

Though there was still room for doubt to be expressed as late as 1850 in the case of Tennent,[80] and later in the case of Low, the Indian origin of Buddhism was firmly established by this time.

It had had, of course, no shortage of supporters from the beginning of the century, indeed, even earlier. At the end of the seventeenth century, Engelbert Kaempfer, physician to the Dutch Embassy to the court of Japan, traced its origins to India: 'I have strong reason to believe,' he reported, 'both from the affinity of the name, and the very nature of this religion, that its author and founder is the very same person, whom the Brahmines called Budha and believe to be an essential part of Wisthnu ...'[81] Francis Buchanan in 1799, using the texts of the Burmese Buddhists collected by Father Sangermano,[82] argued for the northern parts of Hindustan as most probable on account of the topographical details contained in them. From the reports of the mountains, snow, seas, and rivers, he concluded that the Buddha was a near neighbour of Tibet, and that he lived on the banks of a river whose source was that place.[83] Buchanan's opinion was cited by Davy in 1821; he affirmed also, after conversation with a 'learned native', that its birthplace was to the north-east of Ceylon. In support of this, Davy drew attention to a number of climatic details in the religious books to which his Sri Lankan informant had referred. Of particular interest to Davy were certain directions of the Buddha regarding woollen robes and times for bathing. In Kosol (Kosala), he allowed his disciples to bathe only once in fifteen days but in hot countries once daily – 'a most convincing proof that the climate of Kosol must have been at least cool and not tropical'. Further, it was reported that in September at noon when the sun was at its zenith, the shadow of a man was six times the length of his foot; and therefore, Davy concluded, 'it is evident that Kosol was pretty far north'.[84]

But it was textual evidence that finally shifted the weight of argument in favour of India. In 1836, Hodgson argued that the fact that the 'original records' of Buddhism were in Sanskrit was decisive. Hodgson was later to be proved wrong in his assumption that the Sanskrit Buddhist texts were the original ones, but he was correct in perceiving that the Buddhist texts themselves would leave no feasible alternative to India. 'Formerly', he wrote,

we might be pardoned for building fine-spun theories of the exotic origin of Buddhism upon the supposed African locks of Buddha's images: but surely it is now somewhat too late, in the face of the abundant direct evidence we possess against the exotic theory, to go in quest of presumptions to the time-out-of-mind illiterate Scythians ... The Buddhists make no serious pretensions to a very high antiquity: never hint at an extra Indian origin.[85]

The definitive word was given by Eugène Burnouf in 1844 in his *Introduction*. Burnouf maintained that, although information was yet limited, it was conclusively demonstrated that the greater part of the books held sacred by the Buddhists of Tibet, Tartary, and China were translations of Sanskrit texts. Consequently, the Sanskrit texts are the originals of which the others are only copies; and this, he concluded 'restores to India and to its language the study of a religion and philosophy of which India was the birth-place'.[86]

BUDDHISM AS A TEXTUAL OBJECT

By the beginning of the 1850s, a discourse about Buddhism had developed. 'Buddhism' by this time described and classified a variety of aspects of Oriental cultures. Moreover, it had been distinguished from the religion of the Hindus, and had come on the whole to be viewed as having begun with Gautama (at some as yet unspecified time), and as having originated in India. Most of these opinions of it were only able to gain a foothold as a result of Buddhism having come to be viewed as an object determinable primarily by the collection, and editing, of its own texts. By the 1850s, the textual analysis of Buddhism was perceived to be the major scholarly task. Through the West's progressive possession of the texts of Buddhism, it becomes, so to say, materially owned by the West; and by virtue of this ownership, ideologically controlled by it.

At the beginning of the Victorian period, there was a clear recognition that remarkably little was known about Buddhism. In 1836, for example, *The Penny Cyclopaedia* reported that, although

24

much had been written upon Buddhism, a critical investigation of its origin, system of doctrines, and the history of its diffusion, still remained a desideratum. In the light of the fact that hardly any of the original documents had been fully examined and that knowledge of Buddhism was almost exclusively derived from non-Buddhist sources, it warned its readers 'not to receive with too implicit faith the statements respecting Buddhism which we shall endeavour to condense within the limits of the present article'.[87] But it did go on to recognize that textual analyses of Buddhist documents were in hand, and that these might well alter present perceptions of it.

This was certainly to be the case. The work of Klaproth, Schmidt, Rémusat, and Landresse on Chinese and Mongolian texts; of Hodgson on the Sanskrit and Tibetan texts, of Alexander Csoma of Körös on the Tibetan bkaḥ-ḥgyur, were seminal in establishing the Buddhism of Northern Asia as a textual object. It was to become progressively less a living religion of the present to be found in China, Nepal, Mongolia, etc. and more a religion of the past bound by its own textuality. Defined, classified, and understood as a textual object, its contemporary manifestations were seen in the light of this, as more or less adequate representations, reflections, images of it, but no longer the thing itself.

The textual reification of Buddhism reaches its highest exemplification in 1844 in Burnouf's *Introduction*. This work was recognized from the time of its publication as the single most important work in the field up to that time. *Chambers's Encyclopaedia*, some thirty years later, was to point out that 'this book may be said to have been the beginning of anything like correct information on the subject among the western nations'.[88] At the time of its publication, Eduard Roer reviewed it for *The Journal of the Asiatic Society of Bengal*. He wrote:

As a fortunate combination of circumstances had concentrated at Paris all the first and secondary sources for the history of Buddhism, a man was required who united to a profound knowledge of the ancient languages of India, an acquaintance with the modern languages and literature of the Buddhists, the critical tact of the philologist and historian, and the comprehensive grasp of the philosopher, qualities which in E. Burnouf are most happily blended together.[89]

What Roer is here expressing is precisely the realization that in Burnouf's work, 'Buddhism' had become primarily an object the nature of which was to be determined by reference to a rich textual base.

Although Burnouf had concentrated on the northern texts of Buddhism – the Tibetan, Chinese, Mongolian and their Sanskrit sources – he was also aware of the importance of the Pali sources. Since the 1830s, the textual base of the Buddhism of Sri Lanka, and consequently of Burma, and of Thailand also, had been progressively selected, translated, and interpreted. The work of George Turnour, and of the Wesleyan missionaries Daniel Gogerly and R. Spence Hardy, was seminal. From the 1850s onwards, Buddhism was an object determined both by its Sanskrit and its Pali sources.

To be sure, one must not overestimate the availability of primary Buddhist sources during the latter part of the nineteenth century. As Rhys Davids indicated in 1876, the number of published sources was small. But the increasing presence of Buddhist manuscripts in Europe during the Victorian period did make possible significant textual work in the last quarter of the century. J. W. de Jong in his 'A Brief History of Buddhist Studies in Europe and America' has made it quite clear that there was a significant upsurge in the editing and publishing of many Pali works from 1877 onwards, especially after the creation of the Pali Text Society by T. W. Rhys Davids in 1881. And from that same year, there was a significant increase in the editing and publishing of Sanskrit Buddhist texts.[90] Thus, during the nineteenth century as a whole, we can discern clearly the process of the textualization of Buddhism.

The question of the comparative antiquity of the Pali and Sanskrit texts, and therefore the question of to which to refer for information about early Buddhism, was to remain an obscure one until well after the end of the century. Loubère in his *A New Historical Relation* was the first European to mention Pali, and he drew attention to the similarity of the terms for the days of the week in Pali and Sanskrit. But it is to William Chambers that credit must go for discovering their connexion. He found words in Tamil 'from the *Shanscrit*, common to both that and the *Balic*'; and he noticed that the *'Shanscrit* word *Mahá*, which signifies *great* is constantly used in the *Balic* language in the same sense'.[91] And, like Loubère, Chambers also remarked on the similarity in the terms for the days of the week in Pali and Sanskrit.

It was not until 1824 that the first Pali grammar was published in Columbo by the Wesleyan missionary Benjamin Clough, completing the work begun by W. Tolfrey of the Ceylon Civil Service. Although this was known and presumably used in Ceylon (by George Turnour, for example), it seems to have had a minimal impact on European Orientalists. In January 1832, A. W. von Schlegel reported in a letter to Christian Lassen that only two copies of Clough's work had arrived in Europe.[92] More significant was Burnouf and Lassen's *Essai sur le Pali*, the first Pali grammar to be published in Europe. As early as 1826, Burnouf and Lassen were aware that there existed Buddhist texts in both Sanskrit and Pali; and they argued for the priority of the former: 'In effect, the long duration of Buddhism in India is sufficient to explain the formation of Pali, and subsidiarily, its adoption by the Buddhists of the South. When the religion, or rather the new philosophy, was born, Sanskrit had to be the language of its followers.'[93]

This whole issue of the comparative antiquity of the Pali and Sanskrit Buddhist texts was influenced by the different though related question of the absolute comparative antiquity of Pali and Sanskrit, itself an issue that remained unresolved until much later. But leaving that to one side, the conviction of the comparative antiquity of the Buddhist *Sanskrit* texts, first proposed by Burnouf and Lassen, was to have a considerable influence well into the second half of the century.

The *Allgemeine Deutsche Real-Encyclopädie* for 1833 declared that it was at the time of Christ that the Sanskrit books of the Buddhists were 'translated into the languages of Pali, Tibetan, Chinese, and Mongolian'; and this was repeated in the ninth, tenth, and eleventh editions in 1843, 1851, and 1864 respectively.[94] *The Penny Cyclopaedia* for 1836, citing Hodgson, suggested that Sanskrit was the language in which the Buddhist sages first committed their writings; and that they were only subsequently translated into Pali. Consequently, it maintained, it was the Buddhists of Nepal who 'seem to have preserved the antient [*sic*] doctrines of the sect with the greatest purity ...'[95] Turnour, on the other hand, was inclined to the priority of the Pali texts.[96] This was a division between Turnour and Hodgson that was still a matter of lively debate in 1847. James Bird, for instance, on the grounds that the tantric portion of the Buddhist scriptures and the mantras of Nepal and Tibet assimilate Buddhism more to the followers of Shiva than to the Buddhists of Ceylon, Burma, and China, argued for Turnour's position against Hodgson, 'that the body of scriptures in Ceylon is more ancient than that now met with in Nepal'.[97]

Still, there remained no shortage of support for Hodgson's position. Edward Salisbury, for example, in his review of Burnouf's *Introduction* in 1849, pointed out that it was still undetermined whether the Sanskrit texts had a higher antiquity than the Pali books of Ceylon, and farther India. But, he continued, until a determination is reached, 'the former are the most original of all sources which can be consulted, for the purpose of acquiring a knowledge of the system from its beginnings'.[98] Five years later, William Knighton in his *Forest Life in Ceylon* declared that the world was yet ignorant of the precise relation which Pali bore to Sanskrit.[99] Horace Wilson in 1856 was less reticent. For him, the Pali texts were from a period considerably later than the Sanskrit Buddhist texts, more specifically, from the fifth century A.D. He argued for this remarkably late dating on internal grounds. The Pali texts, he asserted, 'bear the characteristics of a later and less intellectual cultivation, in their greater diffuseness, and the extravagant and puerile additions they frequently make to the legendary matter'.[100] The vast majority of commentators were to reject judgements of this sort, seeing in the Pali materials a simpler, purer, and more intellectual Buddhism. This was, at least in part, the result of the fact that by the mid-1870s, the priority of the Pali material was the received opinion. This is reflected, for example, in the first edition of Robert Childers's Pali dictionary in 1874. He declared that the Pali version of the Buddhist scriptures was the only genuine and original one. To Brian H. Hodgson, he continued,

is due the discovery in Nepal of an extensive Buddhist literature in the Sanskrit language, which at one time was generally considered to present Buddhism in its oldest form. This view is even now not without adherents of deserved reputation, but our increasing familiarity with South Buddhism is rapidly rendering universal the belief that the North Buddhist books have no claim to originality, but are partly translations or adaptations of the Pali sacred books, made several centuries after Gautama's time, and partly late outgrowths of Buddhism exhibiting that religion in an extraordinary state of corruption and travesty.[101]

BUDDHISM AND BRAHMANISM

Crucial to the formation of Victorian discourse about Buddhism was the problem of the comparative antiquity of Buddhism and Brahmanism. As with those issues we have already examined that were closely connected with it, it was the middle of the century before it was generally accepted that the priority belonged to Brahmanism. To be sure, much confusion existed during this period as to relative and absolute dating of various aspects of Brahmanism. But overall, the general drift of opinion is from uncertainity in the 1830s to the assertion of the priority of Brahmanism in the 1850s.

As early as 1801, Joinville had recognized the similarity between the two religions, and the importance of determining their chronological priority. There could be no doubt, he wrote, that the one is the child of the other, 'but it is hard to know which is the mother'.[102] He suggested that the issue could not be decided on historical grounds but rather on the grounds of doctrinal differences between the two religions; and in the light of these, he argued for the priority of Buddhism. His first argument concerned the less developed nature of the notions of the soul and the origin of the world in Buddhism. He wrote:

The religion of BOUDHOU having extended itself in very remote times, through every part of *India*, was in many respects monstrous and unformed. An uncreated world and mortal souls, are ideas to be held only in an infant state of Society, and as Society advances such ideas must vanish – a fortiori, they cannot be established in opposition to a religion already prevailing in a country, the fundamental articles of which, are the creation of the world, and the immortality of the soul. Ideas in opposition to all religion cannot gain ground, at least cannot make head, when there is already an established faith; whence it is fair to infer, that if *Boudhism* could not have established itself among the *Brahmins*, and if it has been established in their country, that it must be the more ancient of the two.[103]

This essentially Enlightenment argument is reinforced by several others, the one based on variations in their respective astronomical systems, the other on differences in dietary habits. The former of these, although not without interest as an example of eighteenth-century a priori reasoning, does not merit detailed discussion. The latter, however, is a delightful example of the way in which the comparative antiquity of two ancient religious traditions could be determined almost sylogistically from the proposition that 'The *Boudhists* eat animals; the *Brahmins* do not':

29

All reformers attempt to throw a slur on the individuals professing the religion they wish to reform: Now if the *Boudhists* had been the reformers, they could not have reproved the *Brahmins* for eating rice, as they eat it themselves; nor for eating rice only, for when the religion allows eating both meat and rice, it is in every person's choice whether he will eat only one of these. But if, on the contrary, the *Brahmins* had been the reformers, they could throw blame on the *Boudhists*, by prohibiting meat to themselves. These reasons make me believe that the religion of the *Brahmins* is not so ancient as that of the *Boudhists*; ...[104]

Although *The Edinburgh Review* rejected Joinville's claim in 1807,[105] it was still finding support in 1816 in Faber's *The Origin of Pagan Idolatry*.[106] But, by the 1830s, the confident resolutions of Joinville have been replaced by a much more general uncertainty. Charles Coleman in 1832 gave the following summary of the issue:

As in most cases where much obscurity prevails, conjecture is correspondingly active ... By some it has been urged, in favour of the Buddhas, that, as man in a primitive state of society would be more likely to entertain a belief that the universe was the effect of chance, or of some natural operation, rather than the creation of a divine power, it will follow, that such being the creed of the Buddhas, that portion of the people of India who had adopted the Brahminical faith must have done so, and have departed from an earlier belief, in consequence of an advance of knowledge among them, which other parts of the same country did not experience; and that, therefore, while the Brahmans, who first amog them acknowledged and worshipped a supreme Being, were departing afterwards from the unity of worship, and erecting idols as symbols of his power and attributes, the Buddhas remained stedfast [*sic*] in their disbelief of a first divine cause ... The religion of Buddha must then, they say, be the most ancient ... Others again, the advocates of the priority of the Brahmans, either urge the ninth *avatar* of Vishnu, or allege that the sect of Buddha has been founded by good and virtuous men, who were disgusted at, and dissatified with the idol worship of the Brahmans, and who, running into contrary extremes, introduced ... a love and adoration of virtue and justice, and a benevolent regard towards the most minute of sentient animals. The major part of these learned theorists have, however, concurred in making Egypt the fountain-head from which one of these sectarial streams first issued, but they have not agreed on the main point – which of them had that honour; as it is by one given to the Buddha atheist, and by the other to the Brahminical polytheist.[107]

To be sure, *The Penny Cyclopaedia* in 1836 noted the arguments in support of the priority of Buddhism, but went on to claim that this 'may at present be considered as almost out of date, and all who have inquired into the subject seem to agree in the adverse opinion that Buddhism grew out of Brahmanism ...'[108] But this judgement was a little premature, for the question of the priority of these two religions remained a lively issue throughout the 1840s.

In 1845, for instance, *The Calcutta Review* cited Klaproth and Hodgson as favouring the priority of Brahmanism. Hodgson did so in terms formally similar to Joinville, albeit to the opposite effect: 'Buddhism is monastic asceticism in morals; philosophical scepticism in religion; and whilst ecclesiastical history all over the world affords abundant instances of such a state of things resulting from gross abuse of the religious sanction, that ample chronicle gives us no one instance of it as a primitive system of belief.'[109] In favour of the priority of Buddhism, Joinville, Tytler, and Francklin were cited. Tytler in his *Inquiry into the Origin and Principles of Budaic Sabism* in 1817 had argued for the priority of Buddhism on the ground of its relative simplicity: 'The *simplicity* discernible in Buddhism, the genuine principles of disinterested humanity, and piety which pervade the whole of the system, clearly demonstrate the originality of this admirable and unadorned fabric over the *complicated* structure, decorated under false notions of embellishment with meretricious ornaments of all kinds which are visible in the multifarious tenets peculiar to modern Hindus.'[110] This Enlightenment motif of simplicity was the essence of Francklin's argument also: 'Buddhism is in many respects a creed *simple* and unformed, while Brahmanism is the very reverse: the presumption therefore is, that the latter is the more finished exhibition of the former; and consequently that Buddhism is more ancient than Brahmanism.'[111] These rationalistic arguments in favour of the priority of Buddhism must even then have been of some cogency. For, far from rejecting them out of hand, *The Calcutta Review* concluded that the safest decision to arrive at was 'Sub judice lis est.'[112] Even in 1850, this uncertainty remains, at least for some authors. Tennent, for example, in his *Christianity in Ceylon* found doubts still hanging 'over its origin and its chronological relation to the Brahmanical religion'.[113]

There remained supporters of the priority of Buddhism throughout the 1840s. Knighton in 1845 was still persuaded that few who have considered the respective claims of Buddhism and Brahmanism to priority could 'rise from the investigation without being convinced that the former is the more ancient of the two',[114] though one must note that he includes the post-Buddhist Puranas under Brahmanism. Burnouf's *Introduction* was undoubtedly to have an important effect on claims such as these, and this work could not be ignored in the debate. Roer, in his review of the *Introduction* in 1845, pointed out that the priority of Buddhism or Brahmanism had yet to be decided to general satisfaction, though he went on to say there should not be any doubt about the comparative antiquity of Brahmanism among those who have studied Indian antiquities. Interestingly, he suggested a number of reasons for the predilection for the antiquity of Buddhism – 'the *apparent* depth of some [Buddhist] opinions, combined with the apparent want of historical documents, throws it back also into the depth of time'; and consequently, an event that disappears into such temporal mists has, for some persons, 'an enchantment which the most excellent historical statement of the real connexion of cause and effect would fail to excite, as it thus would be encompassed in the notion of everyday phenomena'.[115] He himself, however, has no doubt that in Burnouf's work is 'established beyond doubt the higher antiquity of Brahmanism; ...'[116]

Even Roer's support of Burnouf did not go uncontested. Low, in 1849, remarked a little snidely that although Roer may have convinced himself that the priority of Brahmanism had been firmly established, 'he can scarcely hope that everybody will be quite prepared to follow his example'.[117] Even in 1858, *The Christian Remembrancer* could point out that there were 'not wanting authorities for the hypothesis that Buddhism is more ancient than Brahmanism'.[118] But, it went on to call it an hypothesis scarcely worth notice, a comment borne out by the fact that it played virtually no role in discourse about Buddhism from the mid-1850s onwards.

In summary, by the middle of the century, Buddhism had been 'discovered'. It had been distinguished from Brahmanism, primarily classified in terms of its own textuality, and recognized as existing in India from the time of Gautama, and as manifesting itself to a greater or lesser degree of purity in various Oriental contexts. The parameters were established for the development of a rich Victorian discourse about Buddhism.

2

Buddhism and the 'Oriental mind'

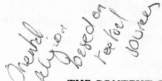

THE CONTEXT OF VICTORIAN BUDDHISM

By the middle of the nineteenth century, the foundations for a Victorian Buddhism had been laid in the evolving in the West of an ideal Buddhism, a Buddhism constructed from textual sources increasingly located in and therefore regulated by the West. As a consequence, for the remainder of the century, a uniquely Victorian perception of Buddhism was to emerge. Buddhism developed as a 'something' primarily *said* in the West, delimited and designated by virtue of its ideological containment within the intellectual, political, and religious institutions of the West. Buddhism as it manifested itself in the East could only there be *seen* through the medium of what was definitively said about it elsewhere.

In the middle and late Victorian periods, there were conditions – both material and ideological – that were congenial to the development of the scholarly study of Buddhism. More importantly, for our purposes at least, they were conducive to the flowering of an interest in Buddhism among the middle and upper classes of Victorian England, and, although certainly to a much lesser extent, among the literate of the working class also.

One considerable influence on the emergence of Victorian Buddhism was the mounting interest in reading in the 1850s, among the middle class especially. The appearance during this decade of a cheap and popular literature combined with a social climate of increasing prosperity, improving education, and an expanding population combined to produce an enormous demand for reading materials. Of the middle-class population of England and Wales, Thomas Heyck writes:

This class, growing in economic and social power as well as in numbers, had a voracious appetite for literature of all kinds. Middle-class people wanted entertainment, diversion, information, social instruction, moral guidance and spiritual reassurance. As members of a relatively new social order, the middle class lacked the traditions and connections that might have satisfied some of these needs, and they turned instead to publications for satisfaction and guidance. Religious literature, fiction, encyclopaedias, newspapers, political commentary and criticism of many varieties were ground out of the presses to meet the new market.[1]

Without doubt, the most important works on Buddhism give the appearance of having been produced for an educated but none the less non-specialist wide-reading public, rather than for a scholarly elite. Only towards the end of the century was academic specialization and professionalization to alter the ambience of works on Buddhism. Certainly in England, the writings of Spence Hardy, Thomas Rhys Davids, Monier Monier-Williams, of Bishops Copleston and Bigandet, had a decidedly more popular flavour than their European counterparts. To be sure, the works of, for instance, Vasily Vasil'ev, Emil Schlagintweit, Carl Koeppen, Christian Lassen, and Eugène Burnouf did become part of the network of intra-scholarly references to Buddhism; and the English translations of Oldenberg's *Buddha: Sein Leben, seine Lehre, seine Gemeinde*[2] in 1882 and Barthélemy St Hilaire's *Le Bouddha et sa religion*[3] in 1895 had a significant impact within the English context, at the scholarly and popular level. But they were essentially part of a scholarly discourse which was grounded in the European academic world.

The enormous growth in periodical literature also played a significant part in the burgeoning interest in Buddhism in the latter half of the nineteenth century. As Heyck points out, the journals were to become crucial institutions in nineteenth-century high culture. Large numbers were founded each year, some five hundred between the years 1830 and 1880.[4] It was, of course, an age of rapidly increasing knowledge. The staple journal format, the review-like essay or the essay-like review, provided the major means by which a sometimes bewildered reading public could learn about, assimilate, and interpret syntheses on a large variety of subjects. Walter Bagehot, nineteenth-century economist and journalist, pointed out a little dourly that the need to instruct so many persons required a form long enough to cover a large subject and short enough to make any laborious analysis conveniently impossible: 'The modern man must be told what to think; shortly, no doubt, but he *must* be told it. The essay-like criticism of modern times is about the length which he likes. The *Edinburgh Review*, which began the system, may be said to be, in this country, the commencement on large topics of suitable views for sensible persons.'[5] Certainly, it was through the pages of *The Academy, British Quarterly Review, The Nineteenth Century, Fortnightly Review, The Edinburgh Review, London Quarterly Review*, and so on, that most Victorians were to learn of Buddhism. They remained content with brief synoptic essays that offered everything necessary for a Victorian familiarity with Buddhism, or were motivated by the journals to read in full the large number of accounts of Buddhism reviewed in them.

Emergent Victorian Buddhism was also served by the ideological pluralism of the period. The Victorian period was, as Walter Houghton has made clear, an age of doubt: 'As one prophet after another stepped forward with his program of reconstruction, the hubbub of contending theories, gaining in number as the century advanced, and echoing through lectures, sermons, and periodicals as well as books, created a climate of opinion in which quite apart from any specific doubts, the habit of doubt was unconsciously bred. One had an uneasy feeling, perhaps only half-conscious, that his beliefs were no longer quite secure.'[6] As we saw in the *Introduction*, Buddhism was to play a not insignificant role in this ideological ferment. It was one of those numerous '-isms' in Victorian society upon which one needed to have an opinion.

It benefited too from the Victorian penchant for religious literature.[7] Victorians could not fail to be at the most horrified or enchanted by, at the very least interested in, a religion so different from Christianity and yet in some ways so decidedly similar; for it was generally recognized to be, even by those least sympathetic to non-Christian religions, as *The Times* aptly put it, 'the grandest and purest, after Christianity, of all Eastern religions'.[8] Buddhism had an appeal to those who saw the need for a religious world view but were increasingly unable to shoulder the intellectual and emotional burden of belief in a Christian tradition that, on the face of it, was becoming increasingly effete both in precept and in practice. It served as a showcase for what was best in the flexible and tolerant religious

35

mind of the time, and it provided as a consequence an ideal *bête noire* for the imprecations of the religiously conservative.

All this is not meant to imply that there were large numbers of Victorians who converted to Buddhism. On the contrary, even in those few cases where one gets a suggestion that this would be desirable, an overt commitment was socially difficult and, in the absence of an organized Buddhist group, practically impossible. The pressure of public opinion acted as a powerful deterrent to the expression of any opinions that might be conceived of as socially deviant or socially destructive. Walter Houghton remarks, 'Even if the thinker himself believed that the service of truth was worth any actual, or supposed, ill consequences to society, he was often deterred by the fear of social stigma and its potential threat to his public career, especially if the truth ran counter in any way to Christian orthodoxy.'[9] Only at the end of the century do we have any clear cases of conversions to Buddhism, though even here it is generally to the somewhat eccentric spiritualistic Esoteric Buddhism of Madame Blavatsky and her Theosophical Movement.[10] Not until 1907 were there sufficient persons, either as Buddhists or as students of Buddhism, to form a Buddhist Society in Great Britain and Ireland.[11]

There was also a culturally much more deep-seated reason for the failure of Buddhism to make converts, even amongst those most intellectually and emotionally attracted to it. This was the inability of Victorian England and, I suspect, of nineteenth-century Europe and America as a whole, to appreciate and appropriate the East *as* East, to value it or to evaluate it *qua* Eastern. There was, one might say, an a priori incapacity to treat it on equal terms. Rather, the West was able only to deal with it from the position of its own *essential* and unquestionable superiority. The greater value of the West over the East, indeed over all those it variously perceived as backward, uncivilized, or degenerate, was not a conclusion reached on the basis of an argument. On the contrary, it was the rarely-challenged premiss in any argument on the truth or value of Eastern philosophy and culture. Ideologically powerful within writings about India for the greater part of the nineteenth century, particularly as a result of James Mill's *The History of British India* in 1817, this rigid sense of fundamental difference between East and West, Occident and Orient, was to permeate most nineteenth-century studies not only of Buddhism,

36

but of other Eastern religions too – of Hinduism, of Islam, of Confucianism and Taoism, and so on.

BUDDHISM AND DECADENCE

In the case of Buddhism however, this bifurcation of the world did not entail its wholesale rejection. In large part, this was because, as we have seen, Buddhism had become by the middle of the nineteenth century a textual object based in Western institutions. Buddhism as it came to be ideally spoken of through the editing, translating, and studying of its ancient texts could then be compared with its contemporary appearance in the Orient. And Buddhism, as it could be seen in the East, compared unfavourably with its ideal textual exemplifications contained in the libraries, universities, colonial offices, and missionary societies of the West. It was possible then, as a result of this, to combine a positive evaluation of a Buddhism textually located in the West with a negative evaluation of its Eastern instances.

From that time when Buddhism is for the West primarily delineated from its texts – that is from the middle of the nineteenth century – contemporary Buddhism in the East is seen as being in a general state of decay. This is in marked contrast to the first half of the century. During this period, the beginnings of a Western discourse about Buddhism did not hint of Buddhism as a decaying, degenerate religion. In the absence of an ideal textual Buddhism with which to compare what was encountered in the East, it *could* not. In contrast, those who saw Buddhism in the East in the second half of the century could not but measure it against what it was textually said to be, could not but find it wanting and express this in the language of decay, degeneration, and decadence.

This contrasting of an ideal textual Buddhism in the West with its instances in the East is often manifest, generally latently present, but rarely absent. Joseph Edkins, a missionary of the London Missionary Society, as early as 1854 demonstrates clearly the way in which a latent image of an ideal Buddhism was carried to the East by Victorian travellers and used to measure what was found there. In China at the time of the Taiping Rebellion, Edkins wrote of Buddhism:

37

The deep interest excited by the revolution now in progress will lead to inquiries as to why this Indian religion has sunk into such helplessness and decay as the traveller observes. It will be asked why it has no power to cope with Christianity, its new and mighty adversary, and why after so many centuries of successful domination over the Oriental mind it has not only lost its proselyting power but even that of saving itself from the destructive attacks of its enemies.[12]

For Major Alexander Cunningham, Buddhism had become decadent by the middle of the seventh century A.D. Already by this time, he claimed, the monks had become an indolent and corrupt body content to spend their lives in the monotonous routine of monastic life. Compared with those of more ancient days whose 'bodily abstinence and contemplative devotion, combined with practical exhortations and holy example, excited the pious wonder of the people',[13] the corrupt practices of later Buddhists countenanced the idea that the more useless they became in this life, the more suited they were for the next.

Such very general claims abound in Victorian Buddhism. Fannie Feudge, one of the few women to have commented on Buddhism at this time, was fascinated by the tradition but scathing of its corruptions in Siam: 'With each successive generation', she concluded, 'new corruptions have crept in, till now almost all of good that ever existed in this wondrous creed has been swept away in the strong tide of clerical corruption, and there remains but the putrid carcase, meet for destruction – a whited sepulchre, fair and beautiful without, but inwardly full of dead men's bones and all uncleanness'.[14] The Reverend Samuel Beal, erstwhile Chinese missionary, described the practical teaching of the Buddha as 'to a great extent effaced in China by the later growth of Pantheism and mystic fancies'.[15] In 1890, the Reverend Archibald Scott argued that the history of Buddhism revealed a long process of degradation 'without having manifested any power as yet to recover and to reform itself according to its original and essential principles'.[16]

In a number of instances, the decay of Buddhism was seen as the direct result of the growth of idolatry. *The Christian Remembrancer* for 1858 described the degeneracy of Buddhism into idol-worship as the necessary development of its teaching; necessary, since no system can survive which admits of no supreme god and aims for the annihilation of its votaries.[17] Similarly, Jonathan Titcomb, Bishop of Rangoon from 1877 to 1882, found that 'the true glory of Buddhism has departed. It is now a crude mass of semi-idolatry and silly superstition; encrusted by dead formalism, and sunk in apathetic ignorance'.[18] Buddhism in Ceylon also found its critics; the *London Quarterly Review* bemoaned the fact that 100,000 Buddhist pilgrims visited the footprint of the Buddha at Adam's Peak annually. But it found Tibetan Buddhism even worse: 'Buddhist degeneracy touches its nadir in the prayer-cylinders of Tibet ... We do not know another religion in the world which has undergone such deep debasement as is witnessed in the Buddhism of Central Asia.'[19]

For a number of late nineteenth-century Liberal Protestant theologians, the decay of Christianity began after the death of Jesus. Analogously, although as early as the 1860s, the degeneration of Buddhism was seen as having begun shortly after the death of the Buddha. To J.M.M., the author of 'Buddhism' in the *Journal of Sacred Literature* for 1865, the simple creed of the Buddha was adulterated by his later followers: 'much of which its founder never dreamed was introduced into the system, and which, had he heard it, he would have treated as foolishness or presumption. Simple as his teaching was, his disciples have spun it out into an affair so lengthened and prolix, that it requires the labour and patience of years to disentangle its intricacies.'[20] The same point was made by Bishop Bigandet, Roman Catholic vicar apostolic of Ava and Pegu. He admitted, at least with some show of reluctance, that the 'high religious sense' of the Buddha that was communicated to his immediate followers 'has almost vanished away, in all Budhist [*sic*] countries'.[21]

The same theme was to recur throughout the latter part of the Victorian period. Margaret Child-Villiers, Countess of Jersey, waxed enthusiastic over the Buddha and his version of Buddhism but nevertheless alleged that 'Buddhism, *as he taught it*, is not the religion of the five hundred millions who are said to reverence his shrines',[22] and Richard Collins maintained that 'Nothing would have astonished or disgusted the founder more than to find himself adored as a God and his simple teaching converted into an ecclesiastical ritual of the most superstitious character.'[23] The religion of the Buddha revealed textually was almost universally contrasted favourably with Buddhism as it was in reality. Only very rarely was the cause of the contemporary decadence of Buddhism seen to be the religion of the Buddha himself, although George Grant for example surmised, in what was generally a sympathetic though somewhat condescending account of Buddhism, 'that there must be something radically wrong with the root, when the fruit has been so poor for centuries'.[24]

This image of the degeneration of Buddhism could also be contrasted with that of an unalloyed Christianity advancing hand-in-glove with an enlightened, progressive nation. The *Dublin University Magazine* for 1839 proclaimed, 'England, the most highly enlightened and civilized nation upon earth, enjoying the knowledge of the sublime truths of the Christian revelation in its purest form, freed from the errors and corruptions which human devices introduced, has from her wealth more power of diffusing truth than ever fell to the lot of any nation.' England's duty was clear, it continued, 'to preach the Gospel among nations, to dispell [*sic*] the darkness that still pervades so large a portion of the globe, to spread abroad the light of Christian truth, and to teach to millions of her grateful subjects the knowledge of that God who died for their salvation'.[25] Less vociferously, some fifty years later, *The London Quarterly Review* for 1888 – 9 suggested that the religions of the East were one and all effete. Their development had ceased and they were no longer productive and aggressive. Consequently, after their inevitable demise, there could only be one successor: 'The greater than Buddha has come to claim his own.'[26] Archibald Scott went as far as to admit that the Christian Church had often travestied Christianity but, he argued, it never fell from the faith so fearfully as Buddhism had from the original doctrine of the Buddha. The Buddha intended his system to supersede religion and worship but 'now his name is employed to support the grossest of all superstitions, a religion with more idols in it than that of the most idolatrous of peoples, a worship founded on the efficacy of magical incantations, and of prayers rendered by machines'.[27]

In sum, the image of decay, decadence, and degeneration emerged as a result of the possibility of contrasting an ideal textual Buddhism of the past with its contemporary Eastern instances. Simultaneously, this provided an ideological justification for the missionary enterprises of a progressive, thriving Christianity against a Buddhism now debilitated. The Victorian creation of an ideal textual Buddhism was a key component in the rejection of Buddhism in the East. But, at the same time, this same creation enabled the appropriation and assimilation within Victorian culture of a Buddhism of sorts, grounded in the past, ideally conceived, and textually constructed.

THE ORIENTAL MIND: INTELLIGENCE AND IMAGINATION

It would however be a mistake to suggest that even an ideally construed Buddhism could be embraced completely. There remained numerous aspects of an ideal textual Buddhism that were not capable of positive evaluation, that remained essentially Oriental, essentially *other*. On the other hand, there were numerous features of Buddhism that could be positively esteemed, that were unequivocally in harmony with various and varied Victorian ideals. Permeating Victorian discourse about Buddhism we find a persistent polarity of acceptance and rejection, of sameness and otherness. Most often, that which is inherently incapable of assimilation in the West and that which is most at odds with Victorian values is described as a feature of or ascribed to the Oriental mind. In contrast to its Occidental counterpart (though this term was rarely used, the first person plural pronoun substituting for it), the Oriental mind was less intelligent, more fanciful, childish and simple, prone to exaggeration, generally indolent, and lacking in originality.

In all respects, the Oriental mind was inferior, a fact the blame for which was often laid at the door of Buddhism. In 1830, John Crawfurd asserted that all the Buddhist nations, among Asiatic nations as a whole, are only of secondary rank: 'not one of them has ever attained the first rank in arts or arms, or produced individuals known to the world as legislators, writers, warriors, or founders of new forms of worship'.[28] There was the suggestion too that the Oriental mind was destined to remain inferior in spite of the best efforts of the Western colonial powers. Jules Barthélemy St Hilaire; French philosopher and *homme politique*, lamented the fact that Buddhism, excellent as it was in some respects, remained unable to reform the political institutions of those countries that received it. 'Our most benevolent and liberal efforts', he wrote,

must remain ineffectual against these deplorable institutions which have been sanctioned not only by time, but also by the inveterate habits of the people, their indifference, and their incurable superstition ... The worth of religions can in some degree be valued by the social institutions which they have inspired or tolerated, and it is one of the glories of Christianity, that it has produced free societies and governments, which ... advance each day to new progress and new perfection. Nothing of the kind is to be seen in Buddhist societies ...[29]

Robert Spence Hardy, a Wesleyan missionary in Ceylon and, in spite of his intense dislike of Buddhism, a crucial figure in the emergence of Victorian Buddhism, was not only convinced of the benevolent nature of the British rule in Ceylon but also certain of the Ceylonese appreciation of it. According to Hardy, 'no land ever shone upon by an eastern sun had greater reason to rejoice in its Government, than the people of Ceylon in the beneficent aspect of the British rule ... The natives at large see their privilege, and are grateful for the boon.'[30]

Hardy was undoubtedly an imperialist of the most ardent kind. Still, not only for him but for many Victorians, the benevolent rule of England over those who were not fortuitously but rather necessarily ordained to be subject peoples, was seen as a responsibility ordained by God. Rather disingenuously, Hardy inquired of his readers, 'Why have India, Burma, Ceylon, the fastnesses of southern Europe, many of the tribes of Africa, extensive tracts of country in New Holland, the Canadas, the fairest isles of the Western Indies, and numerous other places of no mean importance been placed under the control of the British sceptre?'[31] The answer was ineluctably clear – to bring about the conversion of the world to Christianity. The *London Quarterly Review* for 1854 – 5 concurred. 'We believe', it declared in an article on the relation between the British Government and Buddhism in Ceylon, 'that we have been raised up to civilize the savage, to colonize the uninhabited, but habitable, portions of the globe, and to diffuse the blessings of the Gospel amongst mankind.'[32] The ruggedly individualistic Samuel Baker, later known for his exploits in African exploration, was in no doubt. It was not chance but the 'mighty will of Omnipotence, which, choosing His instruments from the humbler ranks, has snatched England from her lowly state, and has exalted her to be the apostle of Christianity throughout the world'.[33] Certainly, Baker – never the most humble of men – thought of himself as having had apostolic status thrust upon him.

The Oriental mind was assuredly, according to the Victorians, less intelligent than its Western equivalent. In matters cerebral, the Oriental was, like other non-Western people, considered backward, degenerate, or retarded. Loubère, for example, at the end of the seventeenth century, saw the Siamese as having a quick and clear imagination most suitable for mathematical studies. But, he went on to say, 'they cannot follow a long thread of Ratiocinations, of which they do foresee neither the end nor the profit'.[34] Still, Loubère, it must be noted, does excuse the Siamese incapacity as the result of their hot climate. Indeed, 'the very *Europeans* could hardly study there, what desire soever they might have thereunto'.[35] The climate renders the Siamese unfit for warfare also; but he again emphasized that Europeans are not exempt from this for 'everyone born in the Indies is without courage; although he is born of European parents ...'[36] In Loubère then, the binary opposition of West and East has yet to harden into the more characteristically nineteenth-century typology of advanced versus backward cultures, societies, or races. Still, the correlation of climate with various human abilities was much in vogue in debates about Asia in the late seventeenth century and remained fashionable in the eighteenth century.[37] It recurred here and there during the nineteenth century, though in support by then of the binary typology mentioned above.

Loubère's judgement on the acumen of the Siamese reappeared in Davy's opinion of the Ceylonese in a clearly more hard-headed way. Although he admitted to being reluctant to pronounce on the degree of civilization and moral character of the Singhalese, and prefaced his remarks with the comment that he was more favourably disposed towards them than a number of his colleagues, he none the less saw the Singhalese as incapable of comparison with any European nation: 'In intellectual acquirements, and proficiency in arts and sciences, they are not advanced beyond the darkest period of the middle ages. Their character, I believe, on the whole, is low, tame, and undecided: with few strong lights or shades in it, with few prominent virtues or vices ...'[38] For Barthélemy St Hilaire, the Oriental mind is, on the face of it, not far removed from the animal realm. The horizon of the Oriental is limited to the sensory realm; he drags out his existence with a limited and inaccurate view of self and world impaired by an intelligence 'not sufficiently developed to attain the source from which he himself, as well as the world, has emanated'.[39] In a similar way, Reginald Copleston, sometime Bishop of Calcutta, revealed to his readers that the Buddhist theory of the universe had a solemn charm for the Indian mind albeit boundless nonsense. To appreciate the appeal of such a cosmology for a Singhalese, the Bishop suggested that 'One has only to remember what satisfaction is given to the feelings of a half-educated English-man, when the lecturer tells him there are probably "some stars whose light has not yet reached us".'[40]

Corresponding with the Oriental's lack of intelligence was an over-active imagination. A Buddhist cosmology that indicated for one the low intelligence of those who believed it, signalled to another the Oriental tendency to the fanciful, the fantastic, and the grotesque. Sir Lepel Griffin, Resident at Hyderabad from 1888, believed that the representations of the Buddhist hells cast Dante into the shade: 'Every description of torment which the ingenious Oriental mind, nourished on despotic cruelty, could devise are inflicted on the criminal, not eternally, but through unimaginable ages.'[41] William Bryant declared that it is well known that the Hindus have been characterized from the earliest times by an excess of imagination. Rejecting the traditional image of oriental despotism, he cited over-whelming natural forces as the cause of 'an uncontrolled fancy which never ceased to revel in the creation of grotesque, monstrous imagery'.[42] Moreover, since there was no place in the Hindu mind for reflection, careful testing and criticism, it was overwhelmed 'with uncontrollable terror in presence of monstrous beings which it had itself unconsciously called into phantasmal existence'.[43]

This implicit half-formed projection theory of religion, according to which the religious entities of the Indian traditions are the imaginative and therefore fictive constructions of the Oriental mind, appeared in various accounts of Buddhism. Hermann Oldenberg, for instance, whose influential work on Buddhism is less culturally determined than those of most of his contemporaries, nevertheless combined elements of this projection account with that of the theory of climatic effects to appraise the fanciful religious world of the Indian. 'Whatever is,' he suggested,

appears to the Indian worthless compared to the marginal illuminations with which his fancy surrounds it, and the images of his fancy grow in tropical luxuriance, shapeless and distorted, and turn eventually with terrific power against their creator. To him the true world, hidden by the images of his own dreams remains an unknown, which he is unable to trust and over which he has no control.[44]

This combination of the role of the imagination with the imagery of a tropical climate occurred also in Fannie Feudge's 'The Mammouth Religion of the World'. For her, imagination stimulated the growth of idolatry. All forms of idolatry, she declared, 'have been alike nursed and cradled by the glowing imagination and ardent fancies of the natives of these sunny climes'.[45] Frederika MacDonald in a warm account of Buddhism that emphasized its rationality and morality felt compelled to apologize for the first impression of Buddhism that might be gained by the adventurous student: 'grotesque fables, monstrous and sometimes puerile, tales concerning all manner of mythological personages and fantastic legends, where the wild imagination of the East plays lawlessly amidst fine poetic dreams and mere barbarous absurdities!'[46]

As we shall see in the next chapter, the Buddha was accorded virtually universal admiration throughout the Victorian period. Less admirable for many Victorians was the mythology with which accounts of the life of the Buddha abound. For this too, the excesses of the Oriental imagination could be held responsible. William Knighton, for instance, wrote quite consciously against the tradition of disdain for all things Oriental fostered in the minds of many by the numerous editions of James Mill's *The History of British India*. But even Knighton cannot avoid attributing the legendary aspects of the life of the Buddha to the immoderacy of the Oriental mind: 'the oriental warmth of imagination of his followers has not been content to allow this grand historical picture to stand forth ..., they must even colour it highly to make it more gaudy; they must overlay it with ornament to make it more glittering and captivating to small minds'.[47] In a review of Oldenberg's *Buddha*, Colinet remarked that no Hindu would have imagined that the Buddha could have been conceived except to the accompaniment of signs and marvels;[48] Agnes Machar saw accounts of the Buddha's enlightenment as utilizing 'every extravagance of oriental imagery' to celebrate the event.[49] Samuel Kellogg, one of the most acerbic of all writers on Buddhism, suggested that, on the battle between the Buddha and the spirit of evil Mara, the Buddhist writers 'have exhausted their powers of description and have lavished all the resources of Oriental imaginations'.[50]

One of these resources often cited by Victorian writers was the Oriental propensity to exaggerate. After an account of the Buddha's life shorn of its legendary accretions *The Westminster Review* for 1856 declared that the legends themselves 'are amplified into the most extravagant and tedious productions of Oriental exaggeration'.[51] Barthélemy St Hilaire found that the legends had drowned the realities of the Buddha's life in a mass of fabulous and excessive details; but only thus, he reflected, could the 'superstitious and extravagant imagination of Indian races' be satisfied.[52] Even the eirenic Thomas Rhys Davids, who thought Barthélemy St Hilaire's study to be 'a thoroughly erroneous and unreliable view of early Buddhism',[53] agreed unwittingly with him that the miraculous incidents in the life of the Buddha appeared to be due 'entirely to the love of exaggeration and of mystery universal among rude peoples'.[54] Doubt was also expressed about the number of the Buddha's followers in the light of the Oriental inclination to exaggerate, for Oriental fancy delights in the embellishing of a narrative with extravagant figures;[55] and the Buddhist claim to antiquity was the result of an 'Oriental love for piling up the ages and dating everything from infinity to infinity'.[56] For Monier-Williams, every sentiment in the East was exaggerated,[57] a proclivity he assigned to the Indian environment. While periodical outbursts of unbelief and agnosticism had taken place in both Europe and India, 'the tendency to run into extremes has always been greater on Indian soil and beneath the glow and glamour of Eastern skies'.[58]

THE ORIENTAL MIND: INFANTILE AND INDOLENT

The aspects of the Oriental mind discussed thus far – its intellectual inferiority, over-active imagination, and inclination to exaggerate – were part of a more general conviction that the Oriental mind like that of other non-Western peoples was essentially and fundamentally primitive. This was a view not original to the nineteenth century. The opinion that there was a distinctive primitive mentality had been gaining ground in European thought since the seventeenth century; and the Oriental mind was assimilable with the more general category of the primitive mind. More specifically, the metaphors of the child and the infant expressed powerfully the Western view of both the primitive and the Oriental mind as being in a state of backwardness that might none the less be remedied by the benevolent care and attention of Occidental parents.

The Christian Remembrancer for 1858, in despair over a Buddhist cosmology in conflict with modern science, admitted that it had no clue to its interpretation. It suggested however that the reader might probably get an idea of it only by analogy with 'the efforts of children rivalling each other in the extravagance of stories invented to amuse each other, or to display the ingenuity of their fancy'.[59] Eitel, a quarter of a century later, was to complain that many Buddhist

doctrines were misunderstood by being taken literally and in-
appropriately classed 'among antiquated notions and infantile
babblings'.[60] Moreover, he claimed, humanity was in its infancy
when Buddhism began. And therefore, 'it was not only natural, but
educationally wise, when it chose a crude, imperfect, infantile mode
of expressing its thoughts, when it spoke to those rude tribes of Asia,
children as they were, in the language of children'.[61] Such a subtle
distinction between a sophisticated adult Buddhism with an exoteric
message suited to the needs of its more childlike adherents was rare
in Victorian Buddhism. Walter Medhurst's position was much more
typical. While admitting that in Chinese religion there is none of
the cruelty or impurity that mars the religion of India, he yet found
what he called a childishness unexpected in a people so shrewd and
intelligent. To Medhurst, China falsified the eighteenth-century
deistic notion of knowledge of God by reason alone: 'Let them go
to China,' he exclaimed, 'where little or no assistance has been
derived from supernatural discoveries, and they will then see, how
the wisest drivel in divine and eternal things, and how far they fall
short of even children in Christianity.'[62] Barthélemy St Hilaire was
also to invoke eighteenth-century discussions, specifically the contest
between Bayle and Voltaire on the existence of godless nations. He
remarked that the existence of Buddhist nations had resolved the
question in favour of Bayle. Even so, Buddhist atheists were not to
be considered on a par with those Europeans who professed not to
believe in God. On the contrary, atheistic nations have not yet
attained to the idea of God, to the great detriment of their organization, dignity, and happiness. Bayle was right, averred Barthélemy
St Hilaire. But he still went on to suggest, 'Perhaps ... we ought
to add with Voltaire, "These nations neither deny nor affirm God;
they have never heard of him ... They are, in fact, children, and
a child is neither an atheist nor a deist; he is nothing."'[63]

The supposedly obedient and imitative nature of children was
invoked to explain the success of Buddhism. James Alwis, a British-
educated Singhalese whose eventual discovery of his own language
and of Pali led him to see in Buddhism a crucial source of Oriental
civilizations, failed withal to see Asians as cultural adults. The people of the East 'at the first dawn of Buddhism', he asserted, 'had,
as they still have, much in common with children. Like children they
cling to their parental kings. Like children they listened to their
parental advice. Above all, they imitated their example, and

embraced Buddhism.'[64] Such traits may have been seen as positive ones, certainly by a ruling elite whether British or Singhalese. But the purported Oriental lack of veracity could not be construed other than negatively. J. Dyer Ball, for example, was inclined to see Buddhism as a preparation for rather than a hindrance to Christianity. But he severely criticized Buddhism for this childish characteristic:

As to the want of veracity, a state of mind more or less inherent in all Orientals in their childlike state; for it is well known that, in the child, the line of demarcation between fact and fancy is very indistinct – may we not indite Buddhism as having fostered and encouraged such an attitude of the conscience, owing to its countless fables believed as truths and the carelessness in the way it has its fancies play about the stern realities of life ...?[65]

In contrast to this, there were however certain, so to say, childlike qualities among certain Oriental people that were admired. In a review of Harold Fielding's (Hall's) rather idiosyncratic *The Soul of a People*, William Metcalfe, then editor of the *Scottish Review*, accepted Fielding's view of the Burmese as 'simple as children of Nature, kind towards man and beast and creeping things, easily pleased, courteous to the last degree ... contented and peaceful, and devoted to the faith of the Buddha ...'[66] But he rejected Fielding's assertion that the Burmese character was the result of their attachment to the Buddhist faith. On the contrary, Metcalfe maintained, Buddhism had had an effect neither deep nor great. In language redolent of the image of the noble savage, he surmised that, with some cultural modification, they are children of nature whose life 'is that of the natural man as effected by the physical conditions in which they have been born and bred ...'[67]

Like children, Orientals are also simple, credulous, and lacking in originality. Sandberg, for example, maintained that the Buddhists borrowed their doctrine of rebirth from the Brahmins, who in turn received it from the Greeks. No Indian philosopher, he judged, can be anything but a plagiarist: 'Give him a striking thought, yielding scope to his talents for innumerable and useless re-arrangements, and he can indeed go on twisting a hideous chain of ingenious workmanship, reaching to infinity. But he cannot originate. He will *go on* without stopping; but *start* he cannot.'[68] Further, to George Bettany, accounts of the life of the Buddha lacked the touches that would mark him out as an individual. Somewhat extraordinarily, he went on to claim that, unlike the Hebrews and Europeans, the Hindus and the Chinese failed to develop individuality. 'Their civilization', he claimed, 'created types rather than individuals, accustomed continually to do the same thing, feel similarly, and think alike.'[69]

Another characteristic of the Oriental mind, closely related to the above, was its indolence. Descriptions of the laziness of Orientals had been common in the seventeenth and eighteenth centuries, though they were to reach their acme in the Victorian period as a contrast to the Victorian beau ideal of work and activity. Loubère in 1693 saw the Siamese as capable of accomplishment in the highest arts and sciences, 'but their invincible Laziness suddenly destroys these hopes'.[70] A hundred years later, Father Sangermano described the Burmese in a similar way: incorrigibly idle, 'instead of spending their time in improving their possessions, they prefer to give themselves up to an indolent repose, to spend the day in talking, smoking, and chewing betel, or else to become the satellites of some powerful mandarin'.[71] The Singhalese fared no better. In 1850, James Tennent described them as having remained torpid and inanimate under the influence of Buddhism.[72]

The indolence of the Oriental in contrast to the vivacity of the European suggested the effeminacy or unmanliness of the former. The active, vigorous, aggressive, and progressive European stood erect over the passive, unchanging, and recumbent Asian. For *The Prospective Review* in 1850, 'The attitude of the European is sword in hand – half wild with excitement, to meet an enemy, or to utter his tragic "Jaire [*sic?*] vous pleurez." The slow and steady pace of the Hindoo seems unmanly to such a character.'[73] For Monier-Williams, the natives of India are far too apathetic to trouble themselves about any form of religion other than their own and far too ignorant and dull of intellect to be capable of questioning its veracity. Moreover, their environmental circumstances render them incapable of having *any* precise religious beliefs. Indolence is the result of the sheer effort to survive: 'Their faculties are so enfeebled by the debilitating effect of early marriages and so deadened by the drudgery of daily toil and the sheer necessity of keeping body and soul together, that they can scarcely be said to be capable of holding any definite theological creed at all.'[74]

The indolent Oriental mind was also thought of as the cause of the Buddhist doctrine of Nirvana, conceived of as a passionless, emotionless rest where the tired soul dreamlessly slumbers. Nirvana, wrote Fannie Feudge, 'is the *summum bonum* of the Buddhist, the very *ne plus ultra* of the indolent East Indian's ideas of happiness here or hereafter'.[75] The desire for rest among Orientals was for Sandberg the reason for Buddhists fixing upon the ideal of Nirvana. Clearly without any fear of contradiction, he felt able to declare that anyone with experience of Oriental peoples

will confess that the one idea of the highest degree of happiness they possess is that of rest – absolute immovable rest. Let a Hindu lie as a log and sleep, he is then deliciously, intensely, happy … With the natural tendency of the Hindu philosopher to imagine nothing logical unless pressed forward to the utmost extremity, even though it involve the *reductio ad absurdum*, the Sanskritic Buddhist made Nirvana his acme of absolute painlessness and rest.[76]

Indolence, laziness, inactivity had therefore their spiritual counterparts – Nirvana, mysticism, contemplation. *The Christian Remembrancer* stressed the necessity for its readers to 'ever bear in mind the distinction between the keen, subtle, logical, discriminating intellect of the West, and the vague, thoughtful, comprehensive, mystical turn of mind that prevails among the nations of the East',[77] and Agnes Machar saw the *Angst* of the Buddha as the result of his being born 'in the dreamy contemplative East rather than in the energetic West'.[78]

As Oriental indolence was contrasted with Western energy, so also was Oriental pessimism with Western optimism. George Grant, for example, reminded his readers that Orientals and Hindus especially 'are prone to take a pessimistic rather than our optimistic view of life'.[79] Oldenberg, with delightful naïvety, epitomized the combination of industry with optimism, indolence with pessimism. 'Of this life,' he wrote, 'which promises to the cheerful sturdiness of an industrious struggling people, thousands of gifts and thousands of good things, the Indian merely scrapes the surface and turns away from it in weariness.'[80] *Chambers's Encyclopaedia* suggested that the basis of the Buddhist notion of universal suffering is the pessimistic disposition of the Indian mind. It attributed this chiefly to the comparatively feeble physical organization of Easterns generally. For the author of the article on Buddhism, the Indian 'has little intensity of animal vitality; and therefore, bodily existence, in itself, has to him little relish ... So far, again, from finding activity a source of enjoyment, exertion is painful, and entire quiescence is, in his eyes, the highest state of conceivable enjoyment.'[81] To Unitarian Richard Armstrong, the Indian climate was the immediate cause of pessimism: 'The perpetual, implacable, scorching sun flared down on the glorious verdure it had created; and if it made the palm and the sal lift their heads to the skies, it forced men to crouch enervated on the ground and curse their lives.'[82] Ernest Eitel similarly laid the blame for Oriental pessimism on the Eastern climate. To the Westerner, he suggested, transmigration holds no fear, for life is a blessing. But, he continued, 'it is a different thing altogether with the sons of hot climates, with the indolent native of India, with the sedentary Chinaman. To him life itself has no particular fascination. He counts death – if he may rest after that – a blessing.'[83]

Indolence was a feature not only of Oriental individuals but of Eastern cultures as a whole. Static, unchanging, immovable, conservative, they remained relics of the past. To Adam Ferguson in 1767, 'The modern description of India is a repetition of the ancient and the present state of China is derived from a distant antiquity to which there is no parallel in the history of mankind.'[84] John Richardson, author of *Dissertation on the Languages, Literature and Manners of Eastern Nations*, declared, 'the least attention to oriental manners will clearly show that the characteristic habits of these people, even at this hour, are in every respect, similar to the most remote accounts'.[85] James Tennent in the middle of the nineteenth century asserted that the Buddhism of Ceylon had remained unchanged for upwards of two thousand years. The Singhalese are consequently 'the living mummies of past ages'. In their immovable characteristics, he continued, they realize 'the Eastern fable of the city whose inhabitants were perpetuated in marble'.[86]

However that may be, during the second half of the century, Buddhism was often cited as a counter to the generally accepted belief in the stagnation of Oriental societies. *The Calcutta Review* of 1845 remarked that the history of Buddhism shows that 'the Hindus are not those *unchangeable* beings that some would represent them to be';[87] and it therefore gives hope to the presently discouraged philanthropist for the eventual successful outcome of his plans. To James Bird, the very fact that Buddhism was able to break down the Brahmanical pretension of superiority and deeply rooted religious prejudice showed that 'Brahmanical prejudices and Hindu customs are not of that unchangeable character so long and erroneously ascribed to them', a fact that would not be lost on those concerned with what Bird called 'the dissemination of true religion and the subversion of error'.[88] Buddhism provided a useful device to overcome the language of unchangeability, fixity, or immutability that was no longer congenial to the colonialist philanthropist, whether religiously inspired or otherwise motivated. A benevolent colonial policy demanded at least the possibility of innovation and change among Orientals themselves. As *The Intellectual Observer* put it in 1867:

Railways, irrigation works, better pay for labour, and the opening prospects of personal advancement to those who are intelligent and industrious – these are the circumstances which seem likely to raise the Oriental mind when they can be brought to bear upon it. The superstitions of Buddhism and Brahminism belong to particular conditions of society and experience seems to show that extensive changes in speculative thought can only be effected when other changes have prepared the way ... No amount of European benevolence can be a substitute for self-action, and the conservatism of Eastern nations can only be overthrown by movements that develop new interest and create new wants.[89]

Moreover, the language of changeability, of development, of possible growth and progress dovetailed with the discourse of decadence and decay rather than with that of unchangeability and immutability. Both the notions of a degenerate East and of a changeable one entailed European hegemony in a way that the image of a static East never could. Both ideas come together in 1854 in Joseph Edkins. He pointed to the very existence of Buddhism as sufficient evidence of the energy of the Indian race as it was long ago. The Mongols, Tibetans, Ceylonese, Chinese, Indo-Chinese, and Japanese prove by their present faith in Buddhism the enthusiasm and influence of its first missionaries. The Indian was not always the indolent being he now appears to be, and moreover, invoking the image of decay, 'Buddhism was not always that worn out superstition that it now appears.'[90]

Only on rare occasions was the existence of a qualitatively distinct Oriental way of being called into question. On the contrary, as we have seen, it provided a fundamental and governing mode of organizing the East. More specifically, it provided a filter through which those aspects of Buddhism acceptable in the Victorian context could be assimilated, and by means of which those aspects essentially unassimilable could be rejected. This polarity of assimilation and rejection of Buddhism expressed latently and manifestly through the image of the Oriental mind was to underlie much of the discourse on Buddhism that developed in the Victorian age.

3

The Buddha – from myth to history

THE BUDDHA AND THE GODS

Can we despise him, or revile his creed,
Or curse his greatness? Whatsoe'er his meed,
He surely does not merit our contempt,
Tho' he may have our censure, and we empt
The Vials of our wrath upon his head,
Because he wandered from the truth and led
The East astray: yet tho' his crime be great,
He seems more worthy of our love than hate ...

We will not hate him, but shall we be blamed
If we admire and love the man who shamed,
By love and gentleness in word and deed,
The harsh disciples of a nobler creed?
Or shall we feel the hasty bigot's rod
Because we deem him like the Son of God?
Howe'er it be, his name shall be enrolled
Among the foremost of the great of old.[1]

'More worthy of our love than hate', 'Among the foremost of the great of old': these are the sentiments that epitomize the Victorian view of the Buddha. Throughout the latter part of the nineteenth century, especially, the Buddha met with almost universal acclaim – not so much for his teaching as for his character. Esteem for the historic founder of Buddhism is clearly discernible in the epic poem of Richard Philips, *The Story of Gautama Buddha*, from which the above verses come. But such an attitude of veneration towards the Buddha was shared not only by sympathizers like Philips and of course Edwin

Arnold but even, remarkably enough perhaps, by those who had least sympathy for Buddhist teachings. Barthélemy St Hilaire was the doyen of Buddhism's critics, a fact recognized by its supporters and opponents alike. None the less, he felt compelled to remark that 'with the sole exception of the Christ, there does not exist among all the founders of religion a purer and more touching figure than that of the Buddha. In his pure and spotless life he acts up to his convictions; and if the theory he propounds is false, the personal example which he gives is irreproachable.'[2]

By the middle of the 1870s, some fifteen years after the above words had been penned, an overall picture of the life of the Buddha had emerged in the West. So it was possible for evaluations of the Buddha to appear. But the very positive assessments made at this time are quite surprising in light of the fact that, even in 1875, the number of sources available that related to the life of the Buddha were very few in number. This is made clear in the article on Buddhism for *The Encyclopaedia Britannica* of 1876. Its author, T. W. Rhys Davids, by this time the most renowned of British scholars on Buddhism, listed only five principal sources. All of these had appeared comparatively recently, in the years between 1848 and 1875. They were Spence Hardy's *A Manual of Buddhism*, Bigandet's *Legend of the Burmese Buddha*, Fausböll's edition of the Pali text of the Jataka commentary, and finally the work upon which Arnold was to base his *The Light of Asia*, Foucaux's French translation of the *Lalita Vistara*.[3]

The impact that the Buddha made on Victorian England in the second half of the nineteenth century is yet more striking still when it is recognized that, until well into the 1840s, the identity, the life, and the date of the Buddha were shrouded in what seems, at least from our perspective, an almost impenetrable haze. This is because, for the first three or so decades of the century, the Buddha was not, in any modern sense of the term, an historical figure. Rather, he was one aspect of a complex comparative mythology and chronology, part of an Enlightenment predilection for all kinds of systematic classifications. To be sure, the 'mythological' Buddha of the early part of the century was linked to the historical Buddha of the later Victorian age by the network of texts in which he figured, texts that appeared throughout the century. Consequently, at one level, there is a unity of discourse by virtue of which we can identify the Buddha of William Jones with, say, the Buddha of Hermann Oldenberg.

But at another level, a deeper one, these Buddhas are not contiguous objects.

The Buddha of mid and late Victorian times is locatable in history through his contemporary textual presence. He is an object conceptually related to a developing naturalistic view of the universe, to an emergent critical view of the Bible, to an India under British hegemony, to a world view increasingly determined by a geologically and biologically based chronology and progressively less by a Biblical chronology and cosmology. The Buddha is very much a human figure; one to be compared not with the gods, but with other historical personalities – with Jesus, Mohammed, or Luther.

In contrast to this very human image, the Buddha of pre-Victorian times was located, primarily, not in history but in a realm beyond – a realm populated by the gods of India, of Greece, and of Egypt. Sometimes, he was more mundanely located; but even then it was in a place and time the parameters of which were determined by interpretations of biblical cosmology and biblical chronology.

Influenced in part by members of the French Academy, British scholars towards the end of the eighteenth century were beginning to identify the Buddha with a variety of mythological and historical, divine and human figures. The technique found most useful in this endeavour was etymology. In both the seventeenth and eighteenth centuries, it served as the primary tool in making identifications between figures divine and human. As a result, a complex inter-religious taxonomy developed. Most importantly for our purposes, as early as 1693, the Buddha had begun to have a part in this complex exercise within the context of Loubère's conjectures on the etymology of Sommona-Codom and the nature of the Pali language. He wrote:

I must not omit what I borrow from Mr. *Harbelot.* I have thought it necessary to consult him about what I know of the *Siamese*; to the end that he might observe what the words which I know thereof, have in common with the *Arabian, Turkijh* and *Persian*: and he informed that *Suman*, which must be pronounced *Souman* signifies *Heaven* in *Persian*, and that *Codum*, or *Codom*, signifies *Ancient* in the same Tongue; so that *Sommona-Codom* seems to signify the *eternal*, or *uncreated Heaven*, because that in *Persian* and in *Hebrew*, the word which signifies Ancient implys likewise *uncreated* or *eternal* ... Add that the word *Pout*, which in *Persian* signifies an *Idol*, or *false God*, and which doubtless signified *Mercury* amongst the *Siameses*, as I have already remarked.[4]

Such recondite techniques were still in vogue a century later. Loubère's identification of Sommona-Codom or Pout with Mercury was directly cited by William Chambers in 1788. In addition, Chambers went on to forge an identity between the Buddha and the Scandinavian god Woden. After a number of etymological comparisons, he concluded:

From all which it should appear that *Pout*, which among the Siamese is another name for *Sommonacadom*, is itself a corruption of *Buddou*, who is the *Mercury* of the Greeks. And it is singular that, according to M. de la Loubère, the mother of *Sommonacadom* is called in *Balic* [Pali] *Maha-mania*, or the *great Mania*, which resembles much the name of Maia, the mother of *Mercury*. At the same time that the *Tamulic* termination *en*, which renders the word *Pooden*, creates a resemblance between this and the *Woden* of the *Gothic* nations, from which the same day of the week is denominated, and which on that and other accounts is allowed to be the *Mercury* of the *Greeks*.[5]

Although he was shortly afterwards to change his mind on the issue, in 1786 William Jones was in no doubt that 'WOD or ODEN, whose religion, as the northern historians admit, was introduced into *Scandinavia* by a foreign race, was the same with BUDDHA, whose rites were probably imported into *India* nearly at the same time.'[6] These identifications of the Buddha with Woden and with Mercury were to occur regularly, albeit with increasingly less frequency for the next sixty or so years. In 1816, for instance, to George Faber, author of *The Origin of Pagan Idolatry*, it seemed impossible not to conclude that Woden and the Buddha were identical. Moreover, he argued, since the Goths and Saxons had emigrated from the Indian Caucasus, 'the theology of the Gothic and Saxon tribes was a modification of Buddhism'.[7] Even in 1854, for Major Cunningham, if not (as he suggested) for the general reader, 'The connection between Hermes, Buddwãs, Woden, ane [*sic*] Buddha is evident.'[8]

A whole variety of other identifications were mooted. In 1799, Francis Buchanan remarked that the Buddha had been identified with Noah, Moses, and Siphoas by different learned men, and with Sesac or Sesostris king of Egypt by William Jones. In spite of the similarity of the words Sesac and Sakya, a similarity that he saw as having given rise to Jones's suggestion, he nevertheless concluded that 'no two religions can be well more different, than that of the *Egyptian* polytheist, and that of the *Burma* unitarian'.[9] This identification of the Buddha with Hebrew figures on the one hand, and Egyptian gods on the other appeared also in Faber: 'Thoth is certainly the eastern Buddha', he exclaimed; 'and Buddha or Menu, in his different successive manifestations, is at once Adam and Enoch and Noah.'[10] Faber was not without his supporters. William Francklin, for example, in 1827, saw Faber's numerous identifications as part of a 'never-failing key in unfolding the intricate mysteries of ancient mythology'.[11] For Francklin himself, the Buddha was not only Noah, 'the great transmigrating Father',[12] but also, if we follow his table of Indian, Greek, Roman, and Egyptian deities, Neptune and Osiris; and the latter of these is also to be identified with Jupiter, Brahma, Pan and Apollo, Crishna and Siva.[13] James Mill, too, in the first edition of *The History of British India* in 1817, did not confine the Buddha to Asia. 'There was', he claimed, 'a Butus, or Buto of Egypt, a Battus of Cyrene, and a Boeotus of Greece ... One of the primitive authors of the sect of Manicheans took the name of Buddas ...'[14] It is not without interest to see how Mill's comments fared in later editions of the work when it came under the editorial control of Horace Wilson. In his editorial remarks in the 1840 edition of Mill, in a delightful understatement of the case, he noted, 'Some knotty mythological points are here very summarily disposed of.' He went on to inquire, 'What reason is there to suppose the Buddha of the Hindus related to Butus, or Buto of Egypt?'[15] By the time of the fifth edition in 1858, his previously expressed doubts have been replaced by an implicit but none the less clear rejection of such claims. Since Mill wrote, 'Much additional information has been collected ... and the history of Buddhism is clearly made out', the suggestion that his readers should see 'Burnouf Histoire de Bouddisme, and Harvey's [i.e. Hardy's] Eastern Monachism and Manual of Buddhism'[16] makes it clear that Mill's conjectures are invalid. But more importantly, for our purposes, Wilson's remarks show that the rejection of Mill's claims is not simply the result of additional information but of a radically fresh reorientation of the conceptuality in which the Buddha had found a place. A human Buddha, the Buddha of Burnouf and Hardy, has supplanted a divine one.

To be sure, doubts had been cast on the identifications of the Buddha with the gods well before this time. But the objections were made on quite different grounds. For example, as early as 1795, Michael Symes in his account of the embassy to the Kingdom of Ava questioned the identity of two religions so substantially different in nature: 'etymological reasoning', he asserted, 'does not, to my mind, sufficiently establish that Boodh and Woden were the same ... The deity, whose doctrines were introduced into Scandinavia, was a god of terror, and his votaries carried desolation and the sword throughout whole regions; but the Ninth Avatar brought the peaceful olive, and came into the world for the sole purpose of preventing sanguinary acts.'[17]

Such arguments as the above were sufficiently common to demand rebuttal by those who favoured the identity theory. Faber had to admit that it may 'naturally be objected' that there is no great resemblance between the ferocious and military Woden and the mild and philosophic Buddha. Even so, he argued, we are not bound to suppose that the very ancient theology of the Buddhists was always as it is now; and moreover, even if the theology of the Buddhists had not changed, 'that the military tribes of Cuthic extraction ... should have transformed the mild Indian deity into the god of battles, is nothing more than might have been obviously anticipated from their peculiar circumstances'.[18] This was a not unreasonable argument. But the die was cast and a series of scholars were to question the identity of the Buddha and Woden. In 1821, for instance, John Davy was to ask:

What are we to think of the opinion of those eminent men, who have imagined its [Buddhism's] extension over all Europe as well as Asia, and have identified Boodhoo with Fro, Thor, and Odin, the gods of the Scandinavians? What analogies are there between the Boodhaical, and the Scandinavian systems? The points of resemblance, if any, are certainly very few, whilst those of dissimilitude are innumerable.[19]

And of the alleged etymological similarity? 'The argument from the name of a day, on which the analogy between Boodhoo and Odin or Woden is chiefly founded, is hardly worth noticing', he peremptorily declared.[20]

As late as 1868, one can still find discussions of the identity between the Buddha and Woden in etymological terms. Though already, by this time, they have an air of quaintness, even of antediluvianism.[21] In fact, by the 1840s, more as a result of a decline in comparative mythology and its attendant etymology than as the consequence of the emergence of the historical Buddha, such identifications are effectually *passé*. The *Encyclopaedia Metropolitana* in 1845 expressed its indignation at the French antiquary who 'in terms that betray a flippancy and arrogance too common among his countrymen' condemned those who identified the Buddha with Odin. But this must be taken as an expression of national pride rather than as a commitment to the identity theory, for the article did go on to recognize that doubt could be entertained over their identity.[22] In the same year, though, *The Calcutta Review* made it unmistakably clear that the day of the identity theory was gone. The use of a gentle irony in the following passage demonstrates that, whether one is for or against the identity theory is irrelevant. It no longer plays a role in the contemporary *episteme*:

Todd, Franklin [sic], Faber and many others, thought that *Woden* the god of the Saxons and Buddha were the same personages. Much learned labour has been bestowed in tracing out this analogy by our old Mythologists, a class of men who will hunt up the etymology of every word to the tower of Babel and fix on its derivation with as much precision as some of the Welsh genealogists do, in pointing out the exact line in which a Welsh family descended from Adam. Happily the day of this knight errantry in ferreting out obscure derivations has nearly passed away, and though Woden may be twisted into Buddha, by the change of a *w* into a *b*; yet the voice of history declares that ... *the genius of the two systems is widely different*.[23]

THE HISTORICAL BUDDHA

Although the issue of the Buddha and the gods was fading towards the middle of the nineteenth century, the question of the existence of Gautama, the Buddha to be, remained in some doubt. In 1856, Horace Wilson admitted that various considerations cast doubts on the accounts of the life of the Buddha and 'render it very problematical whether any such person as Sakya Sinha, or Sakya Muni, or Sramana Gautama, ever actually existed'.[24] In *The Times* for April 1857, Max Müller remarked that little was known of the origin and spread of Buddhism and, in an allusion probably to Wilson, that 'The very existence of such a being as Buddha, the son of Suddhodana, King of Kapilavastu, has been doubted.'[25]

Such doubts were not new. On the grounds that the Siamese knew nothing but fables about the Buddha, that they viewed him merely as the renewer of an already existing religion, Loubère doubted 'that there ever was such a man'.[26] The Carmelite Father Paulinus denied the historical existence of the Buddha, maintaining that mankind could never for so long a time have worshipped a man. Buchanan took issue with him in 1799. He drew on the eighteenth-century theory of euhemerism to account for the fact that the Buddha could have been both man and god. For, on the euhemerist account, all the gods were in their origins mere human beings only subsequently elevated to the heavenly realm.[27] Thus, for Buchanan,

the whole difficulty of PAULINUS is removed by the doctrine of GODAMA. His followers are strictly speaking atheists, as they suppose every thing to arise from fate: and their gods are merely men, who by their virtue acquire supreme happiness, and by their wisdom become entitled to impose a law on all living beings ... That the *Egyptian* religion was allegorical, I think, the learned father, with many other writers, have rendered extremely probable; and consequently I think, that the doctrine of the *Brahmens* has in a considerable measure the same source: but I see no reason from thence to suppose that BOUDDHA, RAMA, KISHEN, and other gods of *India* may not have existed as men: for, I have already stated it as probable, when the *Brahmens* arrived in *India*, that they adapted their own religious doctrine to the heroes and fabulous history of the country.[28]

Such euhemerist justifications of the historical existence of the Buddha did not survive the end of the eighteenth century. In the following century, the identity of the Buddha and the gods was more likely to suggest the Buddha's non-historicity. For Ersch and Gruber in 1824 in their *Allgemeine Encyclopaedie*, the identification of the Buddha with numerous divine and historical figures did indicate how developed studies of the Buddha had become; but it also led to the question whether the Buddha existed as a real person at all.[29] Even in 1849, Salisbury was moved to lay to rest the doubts 'whether Buddha is not altogether the creation of a philosophical mythology, and not at all a historical personage who originated the Buddhist system'.[30]

Generally, however, by the end of the 1850s, with the notable exception of Horace Wilson, the historical existence of the Buddha was undisputed. William Knighton maintained in 1854 that 'whether he lived a thousand, or only five hundred years before our Saviour, there can be no doubt that such a man as Gotama Buddha actually did live ...';[31] and Charlotte Speir in her well-received *Life in Ancient India*, although she was dependent on Wilson, yet differed from him on this question: 'as smoke betokens fire, so the floating gaseous wreaths of Buddhist story may be believed to spring from a fact, the existence of a man of individual and decided character who lived between the years 640 and 560 before our era'.[32] Carl Koeppen in 1857 found it quite unthinkable that Buddhism could have arisen without a founder.[33] In the following year, Henry Yule announced that 'There can be no longer a doubt that Gautama was a veritable historical personage ...',[34] while in 1864, William Simpson in his new edition of Moor's *The Hindu Pantheon* asserted that the individual of a speculative turn of mind who, according to Wilson, may have set up a school in opposition to Brahmanism *was* Sakiya, Gotama or Buddha.[35]

Particularly because of the uncertainty about the actual period in which the Buddha may have lived, it was difficult for him to gain a foothold in history. Such uncertainty was commonplace in the Western history of Buddhism. In 1810, for example, Edward Moor sketched the confused scenario in the following way:

ABU'L FAZEL, in the *Ayin Akbery*, 1366 years before CHRIST. – The *Chinese*, when receiving a new religion from *India*, in the first century of our era, made particular inquiries concerning the age of BUDDHA, whom, having no *B* in their alphabet, they call FO, or FO-HI, and they place the birth in the 1036th year before CHRIST: other *Chinese* historians, according to M. de GUIGNES, say he was born about 1027 years before CHRIST, in the kingdom of *Kashmir*. – The *Tibetians*, according to GIORGI, 959; the *Siamese* and *Japanese*, 544; and the *Ceylonese*, 542 years, anterior to the same period. – M. BAILLY, 1031; and *Sir* W. JONES, about 1000.[36]

In the case of the last-mentioned, Sir William Jones, there was a clear desire to bring India within the ambit of a chronology determined by the Mosaic accounts in the Bible. Jones, following the Chinese dating of the Buddha as proposed by Couplet, de Guignes, Giorgi, and Bailly, set the Buddha in the period 1000 B.C. Around this date, he arranged the Puranic kings, and merged the whole with a Biblical chronology which, like many such eighteenth-century chronologies, placed the creation in 4006 B.C.[37] The popularity of such chronologies was fading at this time. But as late as 1816 Faber, challenging Jones's dating of the Buddha, used a Biblical chronology as his framework. Both Buddhism and Brahmanism, he argued, 'appear to me to have existed from the very days of Nimrod; because there is no country upon the face of the earth, in which I do not find distinct traces of one or both of them'.[38] Elsewhere he gave 2308 B.C. as the date of the Tower of Babel, and consequently placed Nimrod around 2325 B.C.[39]

The Chinese dating, if not the Biblical chronology in which Jones had fixed it, was to remain popular until the middle of the nineteenth century. In 1836, for instance, *The British Cyclopaedia of Literature, History, Geography, Law, and Politics*, following Abel-Rémusat, maintained that the Buddha was born in 1029 B.C. and died in 950 B.C.[40] In the same year, *The Penny Cyclopaedia* reported on the 1,877 years' difference between Tibetan datings of 2420 B.C. and the Ceylonese dating of 543 B.C. It concluded, however, that it was possible, since a large proportion of statements concurred in placing the Buddha in the eleventh century, 'that the Tibetan and Mongol account which fixes his birth in either 1022 or 1027, and his death in 942 or 947 before Christ ... may come very near the truth'.[41] *The Penny Cyclopaedia*'s account was repeated verbatim in *The National Cyclopaedia of Useful Knowledge* in 1847.[42] Indeed, the Chinese dating of the Buddha persisted into the 1850s in the works of the writers on China who seemed quite oblivious to other alternatives: in, for example, John Kesson's *The Cross and the Dragon* in 1854, in Michael Culbertson's *Darkness in the Flowery Land* in 1857, and in that same year in Sir John Davis's *China*, a book described at the time as the best work on China in the English language.[43]

The first half of the century saw also many supporters of a much later date for the Buddha, one which corresponded, to a greater or lesser extent, with the date proposed by Ceylonese, Burmese, and Siamese Buddhists. In 1799, Buchanan argued that the latest date was the one most likely to approach the truth and consequently he favoured 538 B.C. as the date of the Buddha's death.[44] Captain Mahony in 1801 followed the Ceylonese dating and set the Buddha's death in 542 B.C.,[45] while in that same year, Joinville opted for 543 B.C.[46] A quarter of a century later, Eugène Burnouf and Christian Lassen in their *Essai sur le Pali*, ignoring the alternative Chinese dating, remarked that the agreement of Joinville, Mahony, and Samuel Davis on the period of the Buddha was 'of a kind to inspire complete confidence',[47] an opinion they still held, albeit on better grounds, in 1844 and 1849 respectively.[48] Brian Hodgson also concurred with the latest date. In 1828, he suggested that profane chronology was a science the Buddhists seemed never to have cultivated but 'the best opinion seems to be that Sákya died about four a half centuries before our era'.[49]

From the beginning of the Victorian period, there began a drift of opinion away from the Chinese dating towards the earlier

Ceylonese dating. This is clearly shown by several consecutive entries in editions of the *Allgemeine Deutsche Real-Encyclopädie*. According to the article on the Buddha in the eighth edition in 1833, 'Sākya Mūni was born towards 1000 B.C. in the north-Indian province of Mâgadha ...'[50] But in the next edition, the 1843 entry on the Buddha was revised to read, Sākya Mūni 'was born in the sixth century B.C.',[51] a claim that remained in the two subsequent editions of 1851 and 1864.[52] So we can see that, in this period, there has been a clear shift of opinion towards the later dating. And it was one that stabilized. By 1858, *The Christian Remembrancer* could report that 'The researches of scholars have now established, beyond any reasonable doubt, that it [Buddhism] originated in India in the sixth century before the Christian era.'[53] The exact years of the Buddha within this broad period still remained a bone of contention at the end of the century. For both the Pali chronicles and the continuing discovery and interpretation of the edicts of Asoka provided grist for the mill.[54] But for our concerns, what is crucial is that the placement of the Buddha in the fifth to sixth centuries B.C. or later brought him within near reach of the beginnings of Indian history in the strict sense, that is to say, close to the reign of Chandragupta Maurya in the late part of the fourth century B.C. In effect, this made quite unviable the earlier tendency to see the Buddha as essentially a divine being located in mythical time, and initiated the quest for an historically viable account of his life.

THE LIFE OF THE BUDDHA

Buddha, 'tis hard for one thus later-born
To sing of thee and tell thy life aright;
So rich the lives wherewith, all misty-bright,
Old legends and quaint tales of Indian lore
Have decked thy deeds till larger than before
They loom like shadows on the Brocken hill,
Thus too thou hast been traced by poet's skill
In dainty pages delicately wrought
With rainbow colours from the skies of thought.
Ours may it be, unwinged for flight so high,
To pierce the mists and there thyself descry,
Living like us a life of deep unrest,
Weak, conquering, conquered, struggling to be blest.[55]

By the beginning of the 1860s, the historical existence of the Buddha was taken as certain. But, as the above verse from Sidney Alexander's poem indicates, the actual details of the life of the Buddha seemed entangled in a web of myth, miracle, and legend. To some, this suggested the impossibility of determining the details in the Buddha's life; to others, the necessity of developing a method by which the original elements could be separated from the later accretions. For Spence Hardy, for example, the element of the miraculous ruled out all possibility of knowledge of the historical Buddha. The deeds and doctrines of the Buddha, he maintained, 'are so much mixed up with the tedious details of things absurd or impossible, that an attempt to separate the trustworthy from the fanciful, would be like the search for a handful of pearls amidst a shell-mound high as the monumental towers erected in various places over the relics of his disciples'.[56]

Most were not as pessimistic as Hardy. They proceeded on the principle that the miraculous and the supernatural were to be excluded and the remainder considered historical. This rationalistic method was in operation as early as 1856. After a brief account of the 'facts' of the Buddha's life, *The Westminster Review* concluded, 'Such appears to be the historic kernel of an immense mass of Buddhist Sutras, concerning the life of Sākya Muni himself. But the legends themselves, from which a credible account of the reformer is to be extracted, are amplified into the most extravagant and tedious productions of Oriental exaggeration.'[57] To Oldenberg also, it was later centuries that had built up a history of Buddha 'with wonders piled on wonders' and had surrounded 'the form of the blessed child with the extravagant creations of a boundless imagination'.[58]

However, a number of commentators found that, in spite of the mass of enveloping legend, the strength of the character of the Buddha still shone through. Jonathan Titcomb, for example, found much to admire and respect beneath what he called the incrustations of the idle legend which 'may appear grotesque and foolish to our own habits of thought'.[59] To the author of 'Buddhism and its Founder' for the *Dublin University Magazine* in 1873, the Buddha transcended the imagery with which his figure had been besmirched:

Sometimes gorgeous, and touched with the spirit of oriental poetry, but often simply puerile and ridiculous, the supernatural machinery which has been invented for the grand epic of the life of Buddha is purely exoteric, has no vital connection with his life story, and when it is thrown into its congenial dust-heap, we have then something of more importance than an eastern demi-god; we have the spectacle of a sincere lover of truth giving up all that men hold dear – power, riches, pleasure, love – that he might attain true wisdom and communicate it to his fellow-men.[60]

Thus, in spite of the scepticism about the Buddha engendered by the legendary character of the biographical sources, a positive assessment of the Buddha remained customary. Richard Armstrong argued, for example, that the character of the Buddha – 'self-sacrificing and fervent, courageous and constant, gentle, humble, and full of universal love' – is not such as Oriental myths create: 'They may add tinsel and gewgaws. But the beautiful original shines brighter than its uncouth trappings.'[61]

In contrast to most, Rhys Davids found that the legends and myths had an intrinsic value, that they were not merely, as he put it, the offspring of folly and fraud, but 'the only embodiment possible, under these conditions, of some of the noblest feelings that have ever moved the world'.[62] But only rarely do we find echoes of his opinion among his contemporaries. Even his appeal to his colleagues not to lose patience with the accounts of the Buddha's life on account of their miraculous elements tended to fall on deaf ears.[63] Not untypical was the reaction of Lord Amberley. In his review of Beal's *A Catena of Buddhist Scriptures*, he argued that the method of determining the life of the Buddha by abstracting the legendary had to fail. The whole, he maintained, is almost entirely fabulous. Although the origin of Buddhism may be attributed to the Buddha, 'no single incident of his life ... is guaranteed by any trustworthy authority ... It is obvious that we are dealing with a myth and not with a history.'[64] Rhys Davids himself was not immune from such criticism. Edgar Ware in *The Fortnightly Review* critized his rationalistic approach. 'The modern system', he wrote,

of rejecting whatever is supernatural, and accepting the residue as historical, gives a very charming and not improbable romance, as may be seen in Mr Rhys David's [*sic*] graceful article in the present edition of the *Encyclopaedia Britannica*. But this account is not a whit more trustworthy than early Roman history as constructed on the principle of Niebuhr or a German or French life of Jesus of Nazareth.[65]

The reference in the passage just quoted to life-of-Jesus research is an interesting one. For there is a very real sense in which, especially as regards its methodology, British research into the life of the Buddha paralleled that of European research into Jesus. The existence of any *direct* influence of the latter on the former is difficult to ascertain. There are, to be sure, very occasional references to J. Ernest Renan or to David Friedrich Strauss in the review literature. But none of the British materials appear consciously to have modelled their approach to the Buddha on that of the Continental *Lebens Jesu Forschung*. Still, it would not be unreasonable to surmise that, indirectly at least, there may have been some influence. For it is clear that in England in the late 1850s and in the 1860s both Renan's *Vie de Jésus* and Strauss's *Leben Jesu* had had a considerable impact. Certainly, the impact made on Christian orthodoxy was a negative one; the methodological principle of excluding the miraculous and the supernatural drew the divided parties of British Christianity together in union against the rationalism and positivism of Strauss and Renan. To John Tulloch, for example, like Strauss's *Leben Jesu*, Renan's *Vie de Jésus* marked

the spring-tide of an advancing wave of thought inimical to Christianity. As the former was the result of Hegelian speculation, and of the crisis reached by rationalistic criticism, the natural consummation of the anti-Christian activity of the German intellect through many years; so the work of M. Renan is the result, and it may be hoped, the consummation, of the course of materialistic thought – known as Positivism – which since then has been active, not only in France, but in England, Germany, and elsewhere, and of an historical criticism divorced from all faith and true reverence.[66]

There were of course lives of Jesus written by British rationalists. And we can discern similarities between the critically constructed figure of the Buddha and the Jesus of, say, Thomas Scott's *The English Life of Jesus*.[67] But on the whole, Jesus continued within the English context to be traditionally conceived and the Gospel story to be literally interpreted. The consequence of this was the contrast between a critically constructed life of the Buddha and an uncritically examined life of Jesus. Samuel Kellogg exemplifies the way in which this contrast could be used when he offered the following grounds for accepting the miraculous element in the life of Jesus and rejecting it in the case of the Buddha:

Were there no other reason whatever, we should still be obliged to reject the stories of miracles recorded of the Buddha, simply because not a single one of these stories can be shown to rest upon the testimony of an eye-witness, or even of a contemporary of the Buddha. But when we have, on the contrary, as Renan assures us, a record – as, *e.g.*, in the case of Matthew's Gospel – proven to have come in substantially its present form from a personal companion and intimate friend of Jesus, then it should be clear as light to any ordinary mind that the case is totally different. And thus, to argue that because one rejects the stories of the miracles of Buddha, he should in consistency reject also the testimony of the apostles to the miracles of Jesus, is only to display one's ignorance and folly.[68]

In the case of D. Z. Sheffield, it was less a matter of historical assessment than of value judgement. In the stories that surround the birth, renunciation, and illumination of the Buddha extravagance and childishness 'contrast with the appropriateness and modest dignity of the stories of the birth, the temptations, the teachings, and works of the Divine Redeemer'.[69] The Reverend Thomas Berry also claimed that there was nothing in the Buddhist canon that corresponded to the Gospels, since legend, extravagant myth, and absurd miracles have dominated actual facts.[70]

Such claims as the above were based, in part at least, on the awareness that the validity of Christianity depended much more crucially on the veracity of the records of *its* founder's life than did the validity of Buddhism on the historicity of its accounts.[71] Added to this was the not unjustified feeling among many Christian writers that the tendency by apologists for Buddhism to emphasize the close analogies between Jesus and the Buddha was the result of an illicit borrowing of titles and assimilating of phrases from Christianity for illuminating Buddhism.[72] Others explained any similarity between the lives of Jesus and the Buddha by supposing that details of the life of Jesus had been borrowed and adapted by followers of the Buddha,[73] a theory that became something of a cottage industry in the latter part of the century.

But there were a number of commentators who were sensitive to the possibility that both Jesus *and* the Buddha were quite simply singular and unique individuals, to be appraised as such. J. Estlin Carpenter, the ecclesiastical historian, in an important account of the possible historical connections between Buddhism and Christianity, found the parallels between Jesus and the Buddha to have resulted from the possibilities inherent in human nature generally. Of the Buddha, he wrote:

That a life of self-devotion thus conceived and fulfilled should remind us almost at every stage of the life which we have hitherto regarded as the highest type of self-sacrifice, is not perhaps after all so remarkable. The needs and cares, the desires and fears of men, do not change from land to land, or from age to age ... And hence it is also less surprising than it might at first sight appear, to find the same principles of human conduct declared, and the same methods of illustration employed to enforce them among the fields and palm-groves of India as among the pastures and the vine-clad hills of Palestine.[74]

A similar point was made by Robert Green at the Literary and Philosophical Society of Liverpool in the late 1880s. According to him, both Jesus and the Buddha 'are men whose lives, stripped of the halo of legend and enthusiasm that has surrounded them, have come down to us unsullied by the suspicion of a single evil deed, and illumined by patience and courage, by fixity of purpose and stern devotion, by the most heroic self-denial and the most perfect charity'.[75] In short, the Buddha was assuming heroic proportions.

THE BUDDHA AS HERO

From the period when the history of the Buddha began to take shape, the success of Buddhism as a religion came more and more to be attributed, not to anything intrinsic to it as a religion but, to the personality and character of its founder. He became clothed in the mantle of Thomas Carlyle's Great Men, one of the heroes whose life had influenced the course of history. To David Armstrong in 1870, for example, the teachings of the Buddha had been distorted into weird or grotesque absurdities. However, what remained indelibly was a personality. 'And that personality', he continued, 'has endured this score of centuries, and is as fresh and beautiful now when displayed to European eyes, as when Siddharta [*sic*] himself breathed his dying breath in the shades of Kusinagara. As in Christianity, so in Buddhism, the personality of the founder has been the only thing unchanged in the whirl and struggle of the ages.'[76] Reginald Copleston, Bishop of Calcutta, writing anonymously for *The Quarterly Review* in 1890, affirmed that it was 'something in the personal gifts of Gautama; his charm, his tact, his tenderness, – the union of the sage with the friend, – not anything in his discovery or in his institutions, which gave him so vast and abiding an influence'.[77] Auguste Barth in his *The Religions of India* maintained that 'We cannot, in fact, ascribe too much in the conquests of Buddhism to the personal character of its founder and to the legend regarding him',[78] a character he went on to describe as one of calm and sweet majesty, of infinite tenderness and compassion, and of perfect moral freedom. Similar opinions are to be found among less erudite authors, such as the extraordinarily prolific W. H. Davenport Adams, a man damned with faint praise by *The Saturday Review* as an example of the average writer who had read a good deal but digested little or nothing.[79] Be that as it may, Adams was certainly reflecting a very popular notion in ascribing the success of Buddhism to the simple ritual enjoined and the pure morality taught by the Buddha, along with 'the spirit of love, tenderness, gentleness, compassion, and toleration which he inspired'.[80]

The status of the Buddha was enhanced enormously by the perception that he had been an opponent of Hinduism, for in this he was aligning himself with the vast majority of Victorians. Of course, Victorian antipathy to Hinduism was not novel. By the beginning of the Victorian age, there had been some three hundred years of European interpretations of Hinduism which had generally been unsympathetic. As Peter Marshall remarks, 'Even if some intellectual curiosity about Hinduism was aroused, the attitude of the great mass of Europeans who came into contact with it was always either ridicule or disgust. Books were filled with accounts of a multiplicity of deities, repellent images and barbarous customs.'[81]

Such attitudes were, if anything, to harden in the nineteenth century. Francis Buchanan, for example, suggested that under the Brahmans, the laws attributed to Manu 'have become the most abominable, and degrading system of oppression, ever invented by the craft of designing men';[82] and Ward in 1817 described the Hindu system as 'the most puerile, impure, and bloody of any system of idolatry that was ever established on earth'.[83] But it was James Mill's extremely critical account of Indian religion and culture in his *The History of British India* that established a norm for Victorian attitudes to Hinduism. In 1818, in his review of Ward's works on the Hindus, he remarked that there was an ambivalence about European accounts of Indian society: by one class 'it is extravagantly praised'; by another, 'it is represented as exciting a deeper disgust, and a greater contempt and abhorrence, than that of any other portion of the race'.[84] *The History of British India* in the previous year had however made it abundantly plain that Mill himself stood with the latter group. Moreover, there is the suggestion that this was the only position that one could reasonably take: 'there is an universal agreement', he exclaimed,

respecting the meanness, the absurdity, the folly, of the endless, childish, degrading, and pernicious ceremonies, in which the practical part of the Hindu religion consists ... Volumes would hardly suffice to depict at large the ritual of the Hindus, which is more tedious, minute, and burthensome; and engrosses a greater portion of human life than any ritual which has been found to fetter and oppress any other portion of the human race.[85]

As early as 1843, Buddhism was being favourably compared with Hinduism. Captain Anderson of the 19th Infantry wrote:

> Where, free to range the temple through,
> No hallow'd shrine withheld from view;
> No gloomy rites that shun the light,
> Involv'd in mystery and night,
> But all is open to the eye
> As the surrounding woods and sky!
> Oh, how unlike in each degree,
> The Hindoo's foul idolatry,
> Whose pond'rous pyramidal pile,
> What strange disgusting rites defile!
> Where crafty Brahmins guard those shrines
> On which no lively sunbeam shines,
> Where never strangers' searching eyes
> Can pierce their horrid mysteries,
> And where in many a dark recess
> Forms that no language can express,
> Vile beastly idols grin around,
> And grisly monstrous gods abound!
> May never such a horrid creed,
> To Buddha's simple faith succeed.[86]

To William Knighton in 1854, it was this depravity of Hinduism that motivated the Buddha to renounce all things:

He saw Brahmanism in active operation around him, and of all creeds, Brahmanism is the most foul and soul-polluting. The frenzied widow, shrieking on the funeral pile of her husband under the scorching influence of the flames ... the devotees crackling beneath the wheels of Juggernaut's car, their dying groans drowned in the horrid music of the Brahmans ...

71

Gotama saw all this, and a thousand times more than European public could be told, or would believe.[87]

The stridency of this attack came to be softened as the century proceeded. Thus, the contrasts between Buddhism and Hinduism appeared less harsh, the continuities more often expressed. In 1877, Rhys Davids argued that Buddhism, far from showing how depraved and oppressive Hinduism was, suggested quite the contrary. For Buddhism was the product of those phases of Indian belief out of which Hinduism itself later arose.[88] Similarly Maurice Bloomfield, writing in the American context in the early 1890s, maintained that the teachings of the Buddha were products of the Brahmanical development evidenced in the Vedic hymns, the Brahmanas, the Upanishads, and so on.[89]

Still, for the most part, it was as a reformer of the evils of the Hindu system that the Buddha was valued. In particular, he was perceived as having attacked the pretensions of a Brahmanical hierarchy, the inequities of the caste system, and as having proclaimed the equality of all men. As early as 1835, it had been suggested that the Buddha had aimed 'at the entire subversion of the edifice of *castes*, and consequently at reforming the social system of the Hindus'.[90] This theme was constantly repeated for the remainder of the century. In 1847, Daniel Gogerly, the influential Pali scholar, regarded the Buddha as a local reformer who steadily opposed the influence of caste.[91] Alexander Cunningham in 1854 looked upon the Buddha as 'a great social reformer who dared to preach the perfect equality of all mankind, and the consequent abolition of caste, in spite of the menaces of the most powerful and arrogant priesthood in the world'.[92] In contrast to a religion that insisted on the absolutely impassable barriers between different classes of men, *The Christian Remembrancer* for 1858 saw Buddhism as having proclaimed the entire equality of all mankind;[93] and Max Müller in *The Times* saw the Buddha as announcing, in spite of castes and creeds, 'the equality of the rich and the poor, the foolish and the wise, the "twice-born" and the outcast'.[94] Linus Brockett in 1861, William Sargant in 1864, *The Intellectual Observer* in 1867, Otto Kistner in 1869, and Richard Armstrong in 1870, all saw Buddhism as a protest against a despotic, tyrannical, oppressive, and corrupt Brahmanical priesthood, and the institution of caste that it supported.[95] As late as 1899, Sir William Rattigan still found it possible to view the Buddha, along with Mohammed and Nanak, in their roles as reformers, as great men. In spite of the limitations that their times placed upon them, 'such men are still entitled to be called "great" for the courage they displayed in championing the cause of reformation, in denouncing the corruptions of the age and society in which they lived, and for the general purity and elevation of the doctrines they preached'.[96]

It was perhaps inevitable that the Buddha, *qua* religious reformer, should be compared with Martin Luther, and that Buddhism should be compared with the Protestant Reformation; inevitable, not only because of Carlyle's vision of Luther as he who broke the idols of Formulism and pagan Popeism, but also because the historical Buddha entered Western history in the 1850s during an especially virulent outbreak of anti-Catholicism in England.

It is interesting to note that the claim that 'Buddhism is the Lutheranism of the Hindoo Church' was rejected by the reviewer of Neumann's *Catechism of the Shamans* in the *Asiatic Journal and Monthly Register* for 1831. The Buddha, he argued, totally demolished the philosophical base of Hinduism whereas, by contrast, Luther maintained the fundamentals rejecting only the outward observances.[97] But when the comparison next emerges, in 1850, no such scruples were evident. 'Gótama was a Protestant against the Religion of his country', declared *The Prospective Review* in 1850.[98] In 1858, *The Christian Remembrancer* suggested that the comparison of Protestantism to Catholicism and Buddhism to Brahmanism held, even down to minute points of resemblance.[99] In the mid-1860s, the *Journal of Sacred Literature* declared:

Gautama did for India what Luther and the Reformers did for Christendom; like Luther, he found religion in the hands of a class of men who claimed a monopoly of it, and doled it out in what manner and in what measure they chose; like Luther, he protested that religion is not the affair of the priest alone, but is the care and concern of every man who has a reasonable soul: both laboured to communicate to all the knowledge which had been exclusively reserved for the privileged class ... And as Europe bestirred herself at the voice of Luther, so India answered heartily to the call of Gautama.[100]

Clearly, the analogy between the Buddha and Luther, between Buddhism and Protestantism served, not only to illuminate Buddhism, but also for anti-Catholic polemic. This is particularly well demonstrated by Unitarian James Freeman Clarke in his 'Buddhism: or, the Protestantism of the East', later reprinted in his enormously popular *Ten Great Religions*. In 1869, he asked, 'Why call Buddhism the Protestantism of the East, when all its external features so much resemble those of the Roman Catholic Church?' His reply? 'Because deeper and more essential relations connect Brahmanism with the Romish Church, and the Buddhist system with Protestantism.' He continued, 'Buddhism in Asia, like Protestantism in Europe, is a revolt of nature against spirit, of humanity against caste, of individual freedom against the despotism of an order, of salvation by faith against salvation by sacraments.'[101] Such polemics were not absent from *The Westminster Review* of 1878 either. There it was observed that the Buddha's reformation bore to Brahmanism the same relation as Protestantism to Roman Catholicism. Buddhism, it went on, was a protest against the sacrificialism and sacerdotalism of the Brahmans: 'it rejected all bloody sacrifice, together with the priesthood and social caste so essentially bound up with them'.[102]

The analogy of the Buddha with Luther served iconoclastic ends, highlighting in a particularly potent way the contrast of Buddhism and Hinduism. But the image of Luther was also sufficiently elastic to allow the originality of the Buddha to be played down. Especially towards the end of the century, the Buddha was viewed as the *reformer*, like Luther, of an already existing tradition rather than as the creator of a new one, as it were, *ex nihilo*. Ernest Eitel, for example, admitted the originality of the Buddha but *as* a great reformer, 'the Martin Luther of a sect which existed perhaps for centuries before him';[103] Hampden Dubose, the Chinese missionary, likewise saw him, not so much as the founder of a new sect but, as 'the Martin Luther among the Brahmans';[104] and George Grant described him as 'the Hindu Luther, in whose voice all previous voices blended, and whose personality fused into living unity forces that had long been gathering ...'[105]

The relationship of Buddhism to Hinduism was sometimes, perhaps surprisingly rarely, seen as analogous to that of Christianity to Judaism. *Chambers's Encyclopaedia* in 1874 declared that Buddhism was to Brahmanism as Christianity to Judaism, for Buddhism was an attempt to make Brahmanism more catholic, 'to throw off its intolerable burden of ceremonies'.[106] But it was the image of Luther and Protestantism that dominated a period more anti-Catholic than anti-Judaic; and it was this image that came under attack from a number of sides during the latter two decades of the century.

At several points in the preceding discussion, I have alluded to the fact that there was a softening of the contrast between Buddhism and Brahmanism; and consequently we find less stress laid on the cruciality of the Buddha for the formation of Buddhism. The scholarly groundwork for this revision of the status of the Buddha was laid by Hermann Oldenberg. 'People are accustomed', he wrote,

to speak of Buddhism as opposed to Brahmanism, somewhat in the way it is allowable to speak of Lutheranism as an opponent of the papacy. But if they mean ... to picture to themselves a kind of Brahmanical Church, which is assailed by Buddha, which opposed its resistance to its operations like the resistance of the party in possession to an upstart, they are mistaken.[107]

From the time of the English translation of Oldenberg's *Buddha* in 1882, the literature is replete with references to his having established that the Buddha was not a social or political reformer, and therefore that, in contrast to his previous image, he was not concerned to break down an iniquitous caste system and promote the liberty and equality of all mankind. How can we explain this quite remarkable change of opinion?

Without denying the strength of Oldenberg's case, there are various clues in the literature which suggest that this revision is to be more socially explained. It was, in effect, the result of an attempt to protect the Victorian Buddha from being perceived as an early proponent of those forms of socialism that were perceived by many as threatening the structure of English society from the beginning of the 1880s especially. It is illuminating to see this process at work at some length in *The Saturday Review*'s account of Oldenberg's volume in 1882:

We are apt to look on Buddha as the personal opponent of the Brahmans; as a democratic reformer who broke up the caste system; as 'the victorious champion of the lower classes against a haughty aristocracy of birth and brain'; and this because the distinction of class has found no place in his system ... On this, as on many other points, Dr Oldenberg has been enabled to set the question in its true light by a searching examination of the early records.[108]

It went on to remark that 'We are wont to look on Buddha as the great communist', but 'Nothing, indeed, seems to have been further from Buddha's aims than the accomplishment of a political or social reformation.'[109] It concluded:

> If we have dwelt somewhat at length on the absence of all socialistic tendency in Buddha's teaching, it is because we believe that this subject has not been adequately brought forward by previous writers on Buddhism. Under Dr Oldenberg's learned treatment, backed by the citation of authorities, there would scarcely seem to be room for further doubt on this point.[110]

This may well be a case of protesting too much; but the rhetoric is significant for a number of reasons. First, we may recall that Oldenberg had denied the image of Buddha as an iconoclastic Luther destroying the idols of Catholicism though not in such strong terms as *The Saturday Review* suggests. But Oldenberg's denial was expressed in *The Saturday Review* in quite different terms – in terms drawn from the realm of political theory. A religious discourse – Protestantism, sacramentalism, sacrificialism, sacerdotalism – has been replaced by a political one – democratic, lower classes, aristocracy, socialist. Second, in a context of anti-Catholicism, a radical social reformer rejecting the pretensions of a priestly ruling class could be embraced. But in a context of anti-Socialism, a radical social reformer rejecting the pretensions of the secular ruling class was unacceptable. The Buddha, too culturally powerful to be simply ignored, was moved to the right wing of the political spectrum.

To be sure, there was the occasional voice that dissented from Oldenberg's position. Andrew Fairbairn, the Congregational divine, maintained in 1885 that Oldenberg laid too much stress on the affinities and too little on the differences between Brahmanism and Buddhism.[111] Dawsonne Strong in 1900 also criticized Oldenberg in noticeably political terms for arguing that Buddhism 'was only suitable for the cultural classes, and not for the ordinary working-man'. On the contrary, he argued, not only the princes, plutocrats, and notorious courtesans, but also the 'much oppressed proletariat of India ... were ripe to receive a gospel which upheld the equality of all men and breathed forth in ever-recurring beauty those solemn truths touching the existence of sorrow, the cause of sorrow, and the cessation of sorrow.'[112] But more typical perhaps was George Bettany's endorsement of Oldenberg that appeared alongside the editorial marginal comment 'Buddha not a socialist'. According to him, Oldenberg strongly combated the notion of the Buddha as a social reformer who broke the chains of caste and raised the poor and humble:

There is no notion in his teaching of upsetting the established order of things and supplanting it by a new one ... It is scarcely even true that Buddha practically presented an equal front to all classes of people. Those who were among his early chosen adherents were almost exclusively drawn from the upper classes, nobles, Brahmans, merchants, educated persons.[113]

ASSESSING THE BUDDHA

Sufficient has perhaps been said during the course of this chapter to indicate the remarkable unanimity that existed during the Victorian period on the personality and character of the Buddha. There were naturally some exceptions. Charles Galton in 1893 suggested that he was either a mad quack or a wicked imposter.[114] But such an evaluation was rare compared with the almost universal acclaim he received. Charlotte Speir, for example, found it almost impossible to dwell upon his career 'without feeling a deep interest and a strong wish to reconcile the contradiction presented by the sublimity of the man and the poverty of his religion';[115] and in the same year, 1856, *The Westminster Review* maintained that, although he was mistaken in his account of the problem of life and its solution, his sincerity, purpose, and self-denial could not be doubted.[116] Twenty years later, Felix Adler observed that if the Buddha was not one of the wisest benefactors of mankind, 'he will ever be counted in the number of those whom the heart of humanity cherishes as its most loving ...'[117]

Without doubt, he was thought of as a figure of enormous historical importance. His career, 'distinguished an epoch in the history of our race',[118] remarked the *London Quarterly Review* in 1858; and in 1886 it maintained that the Buddha was one of the most striking figures in the religious history of the world.[119] Agnes Machar saw his life as one of the most important landmarks in the history of mankind, 'second only in its character and effects to that of ... the founder of Christianity Himself',[120] while Rhys Davids argued that he was 'one of the greatest and most original thinkers on moral and religious questions whom the world has yet seen ...'[121]

In the light of such attitudes to the Buddha, it is fruitful to examine those personal qualities which the Buddha was held to have possessed: fruitful, not only for the insight that it gives us into the Victorian view of the Buddha, but also for the view it affords us of the Victorian image of the ideal man. Richard Armstrong, for instance, extolled the Buddha's rigid truthfulness; rare humility, extreme chastity, unwearying patience, filial devotion, boundless self-sacrifice, and genuine deep and constant 'enthusiasm of humanity'.[122] Fannie Feudge in 1873 pointed to his noble physique, superior mental endowments, purity of life, sanctity of character, integrity of purpose, and patient endurance.[123] John Caird, professor of Divinity at Glasgow University, remarked upon his zeal, serene gentleness and benignity, his wisdom and eloquence as having given force to the doctrines he taught. The overall impression, he declared,

is that of a man who combined with intellectual originality other and not less essential elements of greatness, such as magnanimity and moral elevation of nature, superiority to vulgar passions, an absorption of mind with larger objects, such as rendered him absolutely insensible to personal ambition, also self-reliance and strength of will – the confidence that comes from consciousness of power and resource – the quiet, patient, unflinching resolution which wavers not from its purpose in the face of dangers and difficulties that baffle or wear out men of meaner mould. Along with these, we must ascribe to him other qualities not always or often combined with them, such as sweetness, gentleness, quickness and width of sympathy.[124]

Of all the qualities praised, it is the Buddha's compassion and sympathy that was most often remarked upon. Millions were won by his intense sympathy for suffering, observed Joseph Edkins.[125] According to *The Westminster Review* in 1878, his was 'the example of a life in which the loftiest morality was softened and beautified by unbounded charity and devotion to the good of his fellowmen';[126] and *The Church Quarterly Review* for 1882 viewed him as one 'who, born a prince, sympathized with the sorrows and the moral struggles of the meanest; who ... opened his arms to receive as a brother every one who pursued goodness, truth, unselfishness, as his ideal ...'[127] George Grant remarked in 1895 that, after making all allowances for accretions, the picture remains of an extraordinary man 'the memory of whose unselfish life, thirst for truth, and love for humanity ought to be honoured to the latest generations'.[128] Fittingly, in the last year of the century, William Rattigan drew together the Victorian assessment of the Buddha:

having regard to the intellectual and religious darkness of the period, it is impossible not to accord a high degree of admiration to Gautama for the lofty precepts he enunciated, for the gentleness and sereneness which pervade his utterances, for the deeply sympathetic and profoundly humanitarian spirit which underlie his doctrines, and for the manly endeavour he made to arouse a true feeling of self-reliance amongst a people prone to lean for support upon others.[129]

In fine, the Buddha was an ideal Victorian gentleman, a 'verray parfit gentle knight'.

4

The Victorians and Buddhist doctrine

PESSIMISM

Now this, monks, is the noble truth about Ill:
Birth is Ill, decay is Ill, sickness is Ill, death is Ill: likewise sorrow and grief,
woe, lamentation and despair. To be conjoined with things which we dislike:
to be separated from things which we like, – that also is Ill. Not to get
what one wants, – that also is Ill. In a word, this body, this fivefold mass
which is based on grasping, – that is Ill.

Now this, monks, is the noble truth about the arising of Ill:
It is that craving that leads to birth, along with the love and the lust that
lingers longingly now here, now there: namely the craving for sensual
pleasure, the craving to be born again, the craving for existence to end.
Such, monks, is the noble truth about the arising of Ill.

And this, monks, is the noble truth about the ceasing of Ill:
Verily it is the utter passionless cessation of, the giving up, the forsaking,
the release from, the absence of longing for this craving.

Now this, monks, is the noble truth about the practice that leads to the
ceasing of Ill:
Verily it is this noble eightfold way, to wit: right view, right aim, right
speech, right action, right living, right effort, right mindfulness, right
concentration.[1]

It was the experience of suffering that supplied the motive for
Buddhist thought. The analysis of suffering and the way to release
from it constitute its contents. In the four noble truths that the
Buddha delivered in the Deer Park of Isipatana near Benares, the
nature of suffering and the way to liberation from it form the central

theme. But for most Victorian interpreters of Buddhism, it was the theme of suffering rather than that of the path to release from it that most impressed itself upon them. For the greater part, Buddhism was viewed as, essentially, a system of pessimism; and the Buddha's sermon in the Deer Park was seen in this light. As Hermann Oldenberg put it, 'The four truths give expression to Buddhist pessimism in its characteristic singularity.'[2]

The number of nineteenth-century authors who seized on the negative side of the teaching of the Buddha is quite striking. Barthélemy St Hilaire, for example, saw 'its deep and miserable melancholy' as Buddhism's most characteristic point.[3] Monier-Williams characterized it as a morbid form of pessimism.[4] John Caird found it, of all creeds, the most cheerless and unattractive, the most 'destitute of either real or spurious conditions of success';[5] while *The Church Quarterly Review* for 1891 asserted, 'It was pessimism of the most unmitigated kind, leading ... to a paradoxical negation of all human interests and joys, to the abolition of all social ties, with a view to the ultimate extinction of all individual being.'[6]

A number of suggestions were made to account for the pessimistic nature of the Buddha's teaching: an imperfect digestion, a morbid temperament, the disgust of satiety. For Hermann Oldenberg, it was explained as a natural expression of the Indian character, a result of their world-weariness. 'Of this life', he observed,

which promises to the cheerful sturdiness of an industrious struggling people, thousands of gifts and thousands of good things, the Indian merely scrapes the surface and turns away from it in weariness ... The Buddhist propositions regarding the sorrow of all that is transitory are the sharp and trenchant expression, which these dispositions of the Indian people have framed for themselves, an expression, the commentary to which is written not alone in the sermon at Benares and in the apothegms of the 'Dhammapada', but in indelible characters in the whole of the mournful history of this unhappy people.[7]

Related to this explanation of Buddhist pessimism was, as we saw in Chapter 2, the theme of the effect of the environment on human nature.[8] But Buddhist pessimism was also seen as having its roots in its own peculiar doctrines, or rather perhaps, in the absence of those characteristics taken as definitive of religion:

the absence of belief in a personal God, in heaven, in prayer, in providence and resurrection, in a gracious divine Spirit, in an atoning Saviour. As J. Wesley Johnston put it,

There is no incentive to noble living, no impulse toward vigorous, stalwart character ... When one thinks of these hundreds of millions living under a sky from which no sunlight ever streams, in which the glint of star is never seen, from which the clouds never break or pass away, it is impossible not to feel something of the sadness and hopelessness which have befallen them.[9]

Johnston's climatic mataphor would have probably been more apt had he written of England rather than India. Be that as it may, the point remains that for him, and for a number of others, the doctrinal deficiencies which led to Buddhist pessimism were precisely those not absent from Christianity. The religion of optimism – Christianity – could be effectively contrasted with the philosophy of pessimism – Buddhism. The American Unitarian minister James Bixby contrasted the cheerful Christian view of life (in which Christ proclaimed that he came that men might have life) with a Buddhism that pessimistically proclaimed that life in itself is an evil.[10] William Bryant compared what he called the religion of Pessimism with one which promised an eternal activity 'bringing the deepest, richest, most positive enjoyment';[11] and Frank Ellinwood juxtaposed 'the deep shadows of a brooding and all-embracing pessimism' and 'the glow of hope and joy with which the Sun of Righteousness has flooded the world ...'[12]

There was a small minority of writers who, against the general trend, stressed the more positive aspects of Buddhist theory. Felix Adler, for instance, while remarking on the more gloomy aspects of the Buddha's doctrines, nevertheless found in the promise of the Buddha yet to come 'the hope of a grander destiny' and an 'eternal trust in the higher and better that is yet to be'.[13] Dawsonne Strong found grounds for a Buddhist optimism in precisely those aspects of it that had so daunted his contemporaries: 'In place of dependence on intermediaries, each man was raised to the position of individual responsibility. Henceforward, he was to stand alone. No god, no priest, no mediator could save him. Herein lies the superb optimism of the Buddhist, who believes that man can be his own saviour.'[14] Rhys Davids, a little tendentiously I suspect, pointed out that, in spite of the general belief to the contrary, Christianity was more pessimistic than Buddhism. 'To the majority of average Christians', he wrote, this world is a place of probation, a vale of tears, tho' its tears will be wiped away and its sorrows changed into unutterable joy in a better world beyond. To the Buddhist such hopes seem to be without foundation ... Here and now, according to the Buddhist, we are to seek salvation, and to seek it in 'right views and high aims, kindly speech and upright behaviour, a harmless livelihood, perseverence [*sic*], in well-doing, intellectual activity, and earnest thought'.[15]

How then can we account for the enormous interest in a tradition which, to most of its interpreters, appeared as one of the most uncompromising and unmitigated systems of pessimism ever elaborated:[16] and what explains the fascination for a religion which, on the face of it at least, stood in such contrast to an age in which Utopia was both anticipated and about to be realized? In part, as we have seen, it was stimulated by the life and character of the Buddha himself. In part too, as we will see in the next chapter, it was the result of the morality that he preached. But especially, it was because pessimism itself was the dark side of the general façade of optimism that the nineteenth century had erected. A period of rapid social change, it produced not only hope for the future but also radical uncertainty about it. James Froude, reflecting on the second half of the nineteenth century, remarked:

We have lived through a period of change – a change spiritual, change moral, social, and political. The foundations of our most serious convictions have been broken up; and the disintegration of opinion is so rapid that wise men and foolish are equally ignorant where the close of this waning century will find us. We are embarked in a current which bears us forward independent of our own wills ...[17]

It was this incipiently pessimistic view of the period that produced the highlighting of this aspect of Buddhist theory. To Samuel Kellogg, for example, the pessimism of the late nineteenth century was 'a sore malady of our time'; and those affected by it, he continued, 'listen to the words of the Buddha with a lively sympathy'.[18] The same idea was repeated by Frank Ellinwood. Of those who were, so to say, the victims of a period of social instability, he disdainfully, even insensitively, declared:

The thousands who have made shipwreck of faith, who have become soured at the unequal allotments of Providence, who have learned to note all who are above them and more prosperous than they, are just in the state of mind to take delight in Buddha's sermon at Kapilavastu, as rehearsed by Sir Edwin Arnold.[19]

The *London Quarterly Review* for 1886 also recognized that the admiration of Buddhism amounted to an admiration of its pessimism. But it went on none the less to castigate its Western followers, notably Schopenhauer, for recognizing the evil but ignoring the remedy: 'Pessimism can only be accepted as the result of an utterly one-sided and jaundiced view of the world ... But admit it, and Buddhism at least shows a plausible way of escape.'[20]

KARMA AND REBIRTH

Deed divides beings into lower and higher ones.[21]

Out of the beginningless, monks, comes the wandering of beings in the cycle of rebirths. No first point can be seen from which these beings, caught in ignorance, bound by craving, rove and wander in *samsāra*.[22]

The Victorian reaction to the Buddhist analysis of suffering reflected both the optimism and pessimism of a period of rapid social change and intellectual uncertainty. But, as the Buddhist analysis of existence is intimately linked to the doctrines of karma and rebirth, so too the Victorian interpretation of the Buddhist concept of suffering was permeated by its understanding of karma and rebirth. For the most part, transmigration or rebirth was viewed by the Victorians with something little short of horror. It could be treated facetiously,[23] dismissed as outrageous nonsense,[24] or viewed as fatalism;[25] but Barthélemy St Hilaire's characterization of it as 'a monstrous doctrine' was more typical.[26] Because of the doctrine of rebirth, *The Westminster Review* for 1856 saw Buddhism as founded upon fear.[27] Similarly, Hampden Dubose saw it as the pivot of the Buddhist system: 'this was the sword the Indian prophet wielded with such frightful terror. What a fearful doctrine! ... This is a fort at which Christianity must level its heaviest batteries.'[28] Even the generally sympathetic Rhys Davids described it as a doctrine 'repugnant to us'.[29]

The doctrine of rebirth was one of those aspects of Buddhism that, for various reasons, were unassimilable by the Victorians. It remained, as a result, totally other. Not surprisingly, it was viewed as one aspect of the Oriental mind. For Emanuel Gerhart, no belief was more firmly and deeply 'rooted in the Oriental mind';[30] and Archibald Scott argued that 'Its true habitat and breeding place, like that of the cholera, is among the degraded and broken-down populations of the East.'[31] In contrast to most of his contemporaries, Ernest Eitel suggested that for many Westerners, for whom life is dear and death to be feared, rebirth had a certain attraction. But it is a different matter, he argued, for those for whom life is suffering. The son of the hot climates, the indolent native of India, or the sedentary Chinaman, he argued, counts death a blessing if he may rest afterwards. To suffer, even for millions of years,

is not half as frightful an idea to him as to be forced to act, to labour, to work for aeons, being subject to death, indeed but with no welcome rest after death, being condemned to die only to be immediately reborn again, perhaps as a hard-worked animal or an unclean cur. This is the view that makes the hearts of Oriental nations tremble with terror, and this is the weapon with which eloquent Buddhist priests subdued the stubborn hearts of Eastern Asia.[32]

According to Eitel, one aspect of the fear that the East had about rebirth was the possibility of being reborn in an animal form. Certainly, this is part of the Buddhist notion of rebirth as suffering. But also, and for our purposes more importantly, the possibility of rebirth in a non-human form was a significant component of the very negative Western attitude towards the doctrine. Barthélemy St Hilaire, for example, quoted a Buddhist text in which is detailed the possibility of assuming the form of a tree, leaves, flowers, fruit, rope, broom, vase, and mortar. The text is not identified, and rebirth in a non-animate form is not part of Buddhist tradition. But on the basis of it, he was led to remark, 'Thus the Buddhists have so monstrously exaggerated the idea of transmigration that the human personality is lost sight of and confounded with the lowest things on earth.'[33] Similarly, William Sargant, having read the same text probably in Barthélemy St Hilaire's work, declared 'There is nothing in the heavens, in the waters, on the earth or under the earth, which may not once have been human, and may not once more become human: – a creed scarcely credible to us, but if credible then disgusting and awful.'[34] As early as 1857, Michael Culbertson had found the doctrine degrading. 'The poor Buddhist', he asserted, 'can certainly have no very high conception of the dignity of human nature. Today, indeed, he is a man ... but tomorrow he may be a poor whining dog, or mewing cat.'[35]

This aesthetic distaste for the doctrine of rebirth was grounded in a sense of the qualitative uniqueness of the human species.

It had its theological roots deep in the Judaeo-Christian tradition. According to Spence Hardy, the Buddha did not know 'that man had received within himself, in the beginning, the breath of life; and that in creation he is alone, with an essential difference, and an impassable distance, between himself and the highest of the other creatures in his own world'.[36] Hardy's statement was made some seven years after this notion of man's qualitative uniqueness had been assailed, not from the East but, from another quarter altogether. For it was in 1859 that Charles Darwin's *The Origin of Species* implied that man, far from being unique, was merely another beast of the field. It is interesting to observe that the period during which there occurred the most vehement attacks on the evolutionary account of man corresponded with that of the most savage criticisms of the Buddhist doctrine of rebirth. During the 1860s especially, both Buddhism and evolutionary theory were seen as destructive of the theological and biological uniqueness of the human species, though according to Barthélemy St Hilaire, Buddhism had erred more:

It is true that we possess doctrines that degrade man to the level of a beast, and which refuse to recognize in him anything but a superior kind of animal; but what is this error – serious as it is – beside the one in which Buddhism has lost itself? Man, according to its doctrines, has nothing to distinguish him from ordinary matter.[37]

Anti-evolutionary fervour had subsided among most churchmen by the 1880s. But it was still necessary for Rhys Davids, in apologetic mood in 1881, to stress that rebirth, far from being one of the distinguishing characteristics of Buddhism, was of relatively minor importance.[38] And it was still possible for more conservative Christian writers to express disquiet at both evolution's and Buddhism's dissolution of the distinction between man and animal. James Kellogg, for instance, wrote in 1885, 'In full accord with the antitheistic type of evolution, Buddhism denies any impassable gulf between the irrational animals and man. A pig or a rat may become a man, not indeed in the sense of the Western evolutionist but none the less truly.'[39]

Still, it would be a gross distortion of the Victorian image of the doctrine of rebirth were we to concentrate only on the completely negative assessments of it. To be sure, these were in the majority; but there were a number of more positive appreciations of it throughout the second half of the century. William Knighton, for example, without doubt one of the more open-minded of early commentators on Buddhism, was persuaded by his Buddhist partner in dialogue that he had been too hasty in regarding the doctrine of rebirth as an absurdity beneath the serious belief of enlightened men: 'What Pythagoras, Plato, and Socrates, and more than half the world besides, for ages, have regarded as true cannot be ridiculous unless seen from an erroneous or a prejudiced point of view.'[40] Similarly, J.M.M., the author of the article on Buddhism for the 1865 volume of the *Journal of Sacred Literature*, maintained that a doctrine that had spread so far and been held by so many must be, if not true then, at least plausible.[41] The argument that the plausibility of a doctrine is proportionate to the number of people that have held it is not a particularly cogent one. Still, both Knighton and J.M.M. do demonstrate a sensitivity to those who believe the doctrine of rebirth, and indicate that not all Victorians saw it as an Oriental mental aberration. Indeed, for J.M.M., it was the result of an attempt rationally to come to terms with the problem of death: 'The indignant protest of the soul within them forbad [*sic*] them to believe that it was annihilated when the body returned to dust, and the changes of the seasons, of matter, and of all the visible things about them, seemed to countenance the thought that the spirit passes from body to body.'[42] For a number of commentators, the doctrine of rebirth was part of an intellectual attempt to explain the problem of human suffering. Thomas Huxley saw it as a plausible vindication of the ways of the cosmos to man, which none but the hastiest thinkers would reject on the grounds of its inherent absurdity. 'Like the doctrine of evolution itself,' he suggested, 'that of transmigration has its roots in the world of reality ...'[43] And similarly, George Cobbold maintained that the Buddha saw it as affording a convenient solution to the problem of the unequal distribution of happiness in this life, and the absence of any satisfactory exercise of justice, of rewards and punishments.[44]

Both Huxley and Cobbold saw the doctrine of rebirth, quite rightly, as crucially connected to the notion of karma, and, in the light of this connexion, as a quite rational belief. As with the doctrine of rebirth, so also with that of karma, we find diverse and opposing evaluations of it. These different evaluations were the result of judgements as to whether karma was conducive or inimical to the practice of a moral life. Lord Amberley was one of those who viewed it as congenial to morality. Buddhism, he declared, has the credit of placing morality far above everything else as a means of obtaining the blessing promised to believers ... Whatever objections may be made to the doctrine of 'Karma' there can hardly be a question that it is strictly in accordance with the highest conception of morality ... It is our Karma that determines the character of our successive existences ... The balance, either on the credit or debit side of our account must always be paid – to us or by us, as the case may be.[45]

Others were much less sympathetic. Rhys Davids called it 'this wonderful hypothesis, this airy nothing, this imaginary cause beyond the reach of reason'.[46] Eitel argued that it converted morality 'into a vast scheme of profit and loss'.[47] As a method of retribution, Spence Hardy saw it as imperfect and altogether unsatisfactory.[48] As early as 1854, Knighton commented on the fact that almost every European writer on the subject notices 'the inadequacy of the motives it presents on the one side for a moral and religious life, and of the dissuasives it holds out from a bad one on the other'.[49] The harshest criticism, however, was to come almost forty years later from the pen of Alfred Benn while reviewing Copleston's *Buddhism*. According to this,

If Gotama, or anyone else, ever seriously put forward this fantastic fiction as a true theory of life, one can only say that his notions of evidence were, if anything, rather below those of primitive man, and that the persons who import this sort of rubbish into Europe as the last word of human wisdom ought to be sent to an intellectual reformatory for seven years. If, on the other hand, as seems more probable, it was intended ... as an incentive to good conduct in the minds of the ignorant and credulous multitude, one can only describe it as a receipt for catching 'the storm birds of passion' by putting salt on their tails.[50]

Although the doctrines of karma and rebirth were shared by both Hinduism and Buddhism, the issues were further complicated in the latter's case by its insistence on the denial of any permanent entity at the base of the individual. The denial of a soul or self had been a problem within Buddhism itself since its inception. The Victorians were quick to perceive the same problem: in the absence of a soul or self which survives death and enters a new body, what could be reborn? As Henry Alabaster expressed it, 'The Buddhist tells me there is no soul, but that there is continuation of individual existence without it. I cannot explain his statement, for I fail thoroughly to understand it, or to appreciate the subtlety of his theory.'[51]

For some commentators, the doctrine of rebirth remained the essential one and, consequently, they were inclined to reject the theory of non-self. James Clarke, for example, asserted:

The fundamental doctrine and central idea of Buddhism is personal salvation, or *the salvation of the soul by* personal acts of faith and obedience. This we maintain, notwithstanding the opinion that some schools of Buddhists teach that the soul itself is not a constant element or a special substance, but the mere result of past merit or demerit. For if there be no soul, there can be no transmigration. Now it is certain that the doctrine of transmigration is the very basis of Buddhism ... Without a soul to migrate, there can be no migration. Moreover, the whole ethics of the system would fall with its metaphysics, on this theory; for why urge man to right conduct, in order to attain happiness, or Nirvana, hereafter, if they are not to exist hereafter. No, the soul's immortality is a radical doctrine in Buddhism, and this doctrine is one of its points of contact with Christianity.[52]

Others took the opposite tack and maintained that, in the light of the theory of non-self, the doctrine of rebirth ought to have been abandoned. Thomas Berry argued that the retention of it involved difficulties which led some Buddhists to affirm the existence of souls, and others to complicated systems of metaphysics in order to avoid their opponents' charges of inconsistency.[53] Frank Ellinwood maintained that the Buddha was forced to bridge an illogical chasm as best he could. Nevertheless, he declared, 'Kharma without a soul to cling to is something in the air. It alights like some winged seed upon a new-born set of Skandas [that together compose the empirical person] with its luckless boon of ill desert, and it involves the fatal inconsistency of investing with permanent character that which is itself impermanent.'[54]

The link between the series of existences in the absence of a soul was explained in Buddhism by *paticcasamuppāda* – the doctrine of 'conditioned origination'. Without putting too fine a point on it, in its various forms within the Pali Scriptures, this doctrine is now generally thought, in line with classical Buddhist exegesis, to express the relationship between an individual's past, present, and future existences. As Hans Schumann remarks,

Since there is no immortal Self which runs through the various lives like a silk thread through a string of pearls, it cannot be the same person who reaps the fruit of kammic seeds of past existences in rebirth. On the other hand the reborn person is not completely different, for each form of existence is caused by, and proceeds from, its previous existence like a flame which is lit by another one. The truth lies in between identity and isolation: In conditional dependence.[55]

The recognition in the modern period that the doctrine elucidates the connections between a sequence of lives has enabled modern writers to come to a clearer understanding of the doctrine than their Victorian predecessors. They, for their part, were able without exception to make little sense of it. From a very early time, it was recognized to be of great importance in Buddhist theory. *The Westminster Review* in 1856 saw it as the key to the Buddha's philosophy. But it went on to suggest that it was hardly coherent; and it warned its readers that 'in the employment of the word Cause, we must not expect that precision or unity of application which we should demand in an European philosophical discussion'.[56] Spence Hardy saw it as proposing a theory of causation 'to which we cannot assent'.[57] At the best, to Bishop Bigandet for instance, it was 'very abstruse and almost above the comprehension of those uninitiated to the metaphisics [*sic*] of Budhists', though he went on to admit that the Buddhist, unlike the European 'can pass from the abstract to the concrete, from the ideal to the real, with the greatest ease'.[58] More typically, Victorian writers pressed the doctrine in directions it was not perhaps intended to go; and they unhesitatingly denounced it as confused, without a connected meaning, obscure, inconclusive, unintelligible, and more or less self-contradictory.[59]

COSMOLOGY

In the last section, we saw that for a number of Victorian writers on Buddhism, the doctrine of rebirth appeared to have a compatibility with an evolutionary view of the world. Buddhism and biology presented, on the face of it, a united front against a biblically inspired view of man as qualitatively unique. In the 1860s, especially – the period during which Christianity was still in process of adapting itself to the discoveries of Darwin – the compatibility of rebirth and evolutionary theory, and the incompatibility of both with biblical anthropology could not but have appeared threatening to all but the most liberal of churchmen.

The case was, however, quite otherwise with the relationship between Christianity, Buddhism, and science on the questions of the nature of the universe and the physical geography of the earth. Christianity had had some few hundred years to come to terms with a scientific view of the universe not in accord with the Biblical picture; and Protestant Christianity had, in the main, done so. By the middle of the nineteenth century, Copernicus was commonplace, and the discordance between the Genesis description of the cosmos and the scientific one was no longer theologically problematic. In 1860, in *Essays and Reviews*, Charles Goodwin gave the following account of this process. To the minds of the seventeenth century, he wrote:

The mobility of the earth was a proposition startling not only to faith but to the senses. The difficulty involved in this belief having been successfully got over, other discrepancies dwindled in importance. The brilliant progress of astronomical science subdued the minds of men; the controversy between faith and knowledge gradually fell to slumber; the story of Galileo and the Inquisition became a school commonplace, the doctrine of the earth's mobility found its way into children's catechisms, and the limited views of the nature of the universe indicated in the Old Testament ceased to be felt as religious difficulties.[60]

On this issue therefore, it was possible for some Christian authors, even those antipathetic to biological and geological science, to align themselves with scientific cosmology against Buddhist cosmology. Scientific cosmology could function within Christian apologetics.

This apologetic use of science is well exemplified in Spence Hardy. For example, he argued that Galileo's telescope 'upset all the old notions about an earth at rest and a revolving sky'. But, far from seeing this as in any way a threat to the Biblical account, he sees it as 'an agent of destruction to the supremacy of Buddha ...'[61] Indeed, he went as far as to assert that all of the geography and astronomy of the Buddhists was proved false and unreal by the demonstrations of science.[62] Hardy's evangelistic intentions were never far from the surface in his writings. For, he argued that if the Buddhist texts were incorrect on a matter of natural science, then they were not to be trusted on issues religious.[63] And he maintained that if the Buddha's cosmology was wrong, then his religious views also were untrustworthy: 'The whole of his cosmogony, and of his astronomical revelations is erroneous; and there are statements in nearly every deliverance attributed to him upon these subjects which prove that his mind was beclouded by like ignorances with other men; consequently, he cannot be, as he is designated by his disciples, "a sure guide to the city of peace".'[64]

A number of other writers were directly influenced by Hardy. They viewed the adoption by Buddhists of Western views of the nature of the universe as a necessary preliminary to acceptance of Christianity. *The Intellectual Observer* in its review of Hardy's *Legends* in 1867 found that Buddhist astronomy, physical geography, and natural history offered 'an easy victory to real science wherever members of the Buddhist faith can be induced to study it ...'[65] After referring to Hardy's *Manual of Buddhism*, *The Christian Remembrancer* suggested that there would be no great difficulty in breaking down the absurd mass of physical facts to which Buddhism was committed. Thus, it concluded, 'an advance in secular knowledge may ... be an indispensable preliminary to their reception of divine truth ...'[66] James Alwis saw the Mission Schools in Ceylon as an essential part of this process. He was convinced that

with the growth of intelligence, and the increase of scientific knowledge, the Singhalese will, ere long, perceive the errors of Buddhism; and that the detection of one error will lead to the discovery of another, and another, until at last the people will not only be constrained, but prepared in all soberness, to adopt the religion of the Bible.[67]

There is something of a delightful naïvety in the view that science will, as it were, make the path smooth for the progress of the Christian faith. This is not merely because generally science and Christianity have often been uncomfortable bedfellows, but also because it could be argued that both Buddhism and Hinduism present cosmologies more compatible with a scientific view of the universe than the geocentric one of the Bible. Buddhism and Hinduism depict a vast array of world systems of which ours is but one, and their cosmologies are just as likely to evoke Pascal's despair at infinite spaces as is modern Western cosmology. Interestingly, though, we can surmise from several of the works of Joseph Edkins that there were Easterners during the nineteenth century who were quite aware of the connections that could be made between their cosmological views and those of the West. Indeed, the arguments of such people seem to have necessitated the following attempt by Edkins to stress their incompatibility:

The inventors of the cosmogony of the Northern Buddhists were meta-physicians who denied the existence of matter, and when they spoke of immense assemblages of worlds in various parts of space, only intended them to be the imaginary abodes of imaginary Buddhas, partaking in no way of reality ... The Chinese reader of their works ... will, as in this case, mistake their object, and see in these ideal creations of the subtle Hindoo intellect proofs of a sagacity that he thinks can bear comparison with ... the genius of such men, for example, as Copernicus and Newton.[68]

Not all Victorian authors were as quick to dismiss Buddhism on the grounds of an alleged non-scientific view of the universe as were Hardy and Alwis, nor to use this as part of an anti-Buddhist apologetic. On the contrary, some were at pains to emphasize that its cosmology was tangential to the question of its value as a religious system, an argument prompted no doubt from the developing awareness that the value of the Christian tradition was not dependent on the truth of *its* cosmology. Bishop Bigandet, for example, saw Buddhist cosmology as an inessential part of a system primarily intended to be the vehicle, not of Hindu geography and cosmology but, of moral doctrines.[69] Ernest Eitel declared that the Buddhist Scriptures 'have not observed the wise reticence with regard to natural science, by which our Christian bible is marked', a remark cited by Hampden Dubose some years later, albeit incorrectly and without acknowledgement.[70] However, Eitel did go on to reflect on the relation of natural science to Buddhism in a way much like that in which more liberal Christian thinkers of the same time were relating natural science to Christianity:

Those crude, childish and absurd notions concerning the universe and physical science do not constitute Buddhism ... They are merely accidental, unimportant outworks, which may fall by the advance of knowledge, which may be rased [*sic*] to the ground by the progress of civilisation, and yet the Buddhist fortress may remain as strong, as impregnable as before. A Buddhist may adopt all the results of modern science, he may become a follower of Newton, a disciple of Darwin, and yet remain a Buddhist.[71]

RELIGION OR PHILOSOPHY?

During the course of the nineteenth century, we can discern a clear shift in emphasis in Western descriptions of Buddhism. In the earlier part of the century, there was a characteristic tendency to see cosmology as central to Buddhism,[72] a tendency that reached its zenith in the earliest works of Spence Hardy in the middle of the century. By the end of the century, there is an inclination to see it as tangential as above, or to ignore it altogether.[73] Even Monier-Williams, in a brief account of it in 1889, refrained from any negative evaluations of it.[74] This was one result of the fact that religion and science had come to be seen as entities that were not mutually exclusive. And it was the result too of the fact that an increased knowledge of Buddhism, together with its textual reification in the second half of the century, had made it possible to classify Buddhism taxonomically as a religion like Christianity, or at least as a philosophy like Comtism, but not primarily as a scientific theory about the nature of the universe.

The question whether Buddhism was a religion or a philosophy was one much debated towards the end of the century. It was of course one that had been raised before. In 1847, from his experience of Ceylonese Buddhism, Daniel Gogerly had claimed that Buddhism was not so much a religion as a school of philosophy.[75] Samuel Beal, drawing on his knowledge of the tradition in China, saw it otherwise. In 1871, after a discussion of the issue, he concluded that 'on no ground can we accept the assertion that Buddhism is not a Religion, but a school of philosophy'.[76] Beal continued to argue his case into the 1880s,[77] but the weight of opinion was by this time significantly against him, if not yet decisively. Max Müller, Monier Monier-Williams, Bishop Piers Claughton, Joseph Edkins, and Thomas Berry all maintained that Buddhism was essentially a philosophy.[78]

There were a number of grounds upon which this claim was made. Prime among these was the alleged atheism of Buddhism. By definition, no system which professed atheism could qualify as a religion. As Max Müller expressed it, 'If religion is meant to be a bridge between the visible and the invisible, between the temporal and the eternal, between the human and the divine, true Buddhism would be no religion at all; for it knows nothing invisible, nothing eternal; it knows no God, in our sense of the word.'[79] Buddhism would have to wait some twenty more years before Natham Söderblom's and Rudolf Otto's definitions of religion in terms of 'holiness' and 'the Holy' would make possible the inclusion of an atheistic tradition under the category of religion.[80]

We must shortly return to the issue of Buddhist atheism. But before doing so, we need to examine another distinction that gained prominence in the literature from the 1870s, for it bears not only on the claim that Buddhism was a philosophy and not a religion, but also on the question of its atheism. This is the distinction between Northern and Southern, or Mahayana and Hinayana Buddhism. Without doubt, in a variety of ways, Mahayana Buddhism – the Buddhism of Tibet, Mongolia, China, and Japan, has a more theistic ambience than its Hinayana counterpart – the Buddhism of the Pali canon, of Ceylon, and South-East Asia. Why was it then, that for many mid and late Victorian writers, Buddhism was almost unquestionably assumed to be *essentially* an atheistic system? Ignorance of the Mahayana tradition cannot account completely for this assumption. To be sure, between 1850 and 1880, virtually no important Sanskrit Buddhist text, except for the *Lalitavistara*, had been published. But by the 1870s Victorian writers on Buddhism were aware of the more theistic flavour of Mahayana Buddhism. Both the assumption of the *essentially atheistic* nature of Buddhism, and perhaps also the apparent lack of interest in Sanskritic Buddhism, were the result of the combination of two factors.

The first of these was that of the assumption by the mid-1870s of the chronological priority of the Pali texts, and hence that of the priority of Pali or Hinayana Buddhism. Second, and crucially, there was the obsession throughout the middle and latter part of the nineteenth century with the quest for origins – biologically, geologically, and historically. Underlying the historical quest for origins was the assumption that the original was the essential. Thus, Pali Buddhism, its priority having been established, came to be seen as containing the essence of Buddhism.

Corresponding to the historiographical assumption of the essentiality of the earlier Buddhism was that of the degeneracy of later Mahayana Buddhism. A discourse of 'pure' versus 'corrupt' Buddhism was developed on the foundation of the historical priority of Pali Buddhism and the posteriority of Mahayana Buddhism. Rhys Davids, for example, referred to earlier Buddhism as 'pure Buddhism', to Tibetan Buddhism as 'corrupt Buddhism', and to Tantric Buddhism as loathsome and nauseous.[81] Monier-Williams wrote of 'true Buddhism – that is, the Buddhism of the Piṭakas or Pāli texts', and contrasted it with the 'corrupt phase' of Buddhism in Tibet, Mongolia, and other Northern countries.[82] Marcus Dods concluded that it was difficult 'to detect any close relationship between the superstitious and idolatrous religion of the Northern

Buddhists and the original system of Buddha';[83] while Eitel saw the Mahayana as having replaced plain practical morality with listless quietism, abstract nihilism, and fanciful degrees of contemplation and ecstatic meditation.[84] For some writers, it was the more theistic character of Mahayana that suggested its degradation for it had led to polytheism and idolatry. According to Charles de Harlez:

The Buddhism of the South has, in general, remained faithful to primitive teachings and simplicity. The Buddhism of the North, on the contrary, has estranged itself more and more in proportion as it withdrew itself from the common cradle. How strange it is that the Mahāyāna which reigns in the North, after having commenced by nihilism and the most complete atheism, arrived at last beyond the Himalays at monotheism, the worship of men more or less deified, and even so far as the extravagance of polytheism and idolatry ... Buddhism displays there [in Tartary and China] the outside appearance of a religion which its founder would certainly have reproved as fundamentally and totally erroneous, if not culpable; and of a nature that would entice those who practised it far away from deliverance and into new and miserable births.[85]

ATHEISM

The vision of a Buddhism that was essentially philosophical and atheistic was grounded in the historiographical assumption of the purity of the historically prior. This image was blurred by the clearly religious and more theistic tradition of Mahayana Buddhism, but it remained nevertheless the predominant idea from the mid-1870s onwards.

Prior to the establishment of the chronological priority of Pali Buddhism, there was much less certainty on the question of the atheism of Buddhism. To be sure, from a very early period, claims that Buddhism was atheistic were plentiful, particularly among those who had come into contact only with the cultural expressions of the Pali tradition. Loubère, for example, remarked in 1693 that in the doctrine of the Siamese, he found no idea of a divinity.[86] This judgement recurred in the early part of the nineteenth century. William Ward found the atheism of Buddhism abhorrent, albeit somewhat mitigated by the notion of *dharma*.[87] In 1824, Ersch and Gruber quoted the Baptist missionary to Burma Adoniram Judson to the effect that 'one can declare the Buddhists atheists to some extent'.[88] Both Joseph Edkins and Horace Wilson in 1856 agreed that belief in a Creator and ruler of the world was not part of Buddhism, the latter seeing it as unquestionably 'a modern graft upon the unqualified atheism of Sákya Muni ...'[89] In 1858, in its review of, amongst others, Turnour's *The Mahawanso*, Burnouf's *Introduction*, Tennent's *Christianity in Ceylon*, and Hardy's *Eastern Monachism* and *Manual of Buddhism*, the *London Quarterly Review* felt able to assert that Buddhism was essentially atheistic.[90] In the same year, *The Christian Remembrancer*, while recognizing that the question was a disputed one, maintained that 'whatever the system may have been speculatively, we cannot be wrong in regarding it as practically of atheistic tendency'.[91]

In contrast to these assertions of its essentially atheistic character, claims that it was theistic in nature were also plentiful. The *London Encyclopaedia* in 1829 argued that Burmese Buddhism taught belief in a supreme deity.[92] In 1833, the *Allgemeine Deutsche Real-Encyclopädie* declared that it was a central doctrine of Buddhism that an invisible, non-sensuous supreme Being ruled the world, a claim it repeated in subsequent editions in 1843, 1851, and 1864.[93] To a large extent, the claim that Buddhism was theistic was connected to belief in the chronological priority of Mahayana Buddhism. *The Penny Cyclopaedia*, for example, maintained that the Buddhists of Nepal had preserved ancient Buddhism with the greatest purity, and went on to observe that all schools of Nepalese Buddhism 'concur in admitting the primeval existence of the Deity, who was when nothing else was, and who is thence called Adi-Buddha or "the First Buddha"'.[94] For Frederick D. Maurice, relying on *The Penny Cyclopaedia*, an original theism was only later transmuted into atheism.[95] *The Calcutta Review* in 1845 cited Francklin, Joinville, Mahony, and Ward as accepting the atheistic view, but nevertheless adopted the opinions of Hodgson, Upham, and Erskine that it acknowledged the existence of a god.[96] Even as late as 1864, to William Simpson, following Alexander Cunningham, Buddhism 'began with the belief in a celestial, self-existent BEING termed *A'di Buddha* or *Iswara*'.[97] After the mid-1870s, that period during which it became generally accepted that Pali Buddhism was historically prior, claims that Buddhism was originally theistic disappear. Only in the writings of Arthur Lillie do we find it argued that early Buddhism accepted belief in a supreme God. In marked contrast to the generally accepted opinion, Lillie argued in 1883 in his reply to Rhys Davids's *Lectures* that atheistic and soulless Buddhism was drawn from Mahayana Buddhism whereas the original tradition as presented in the edicts of Asoka was theistic. But in spite of the occasional sympathetic review, Lillie's arguments were received coolly and critically, and they played no significant role in subsequent scholarship.[98]

For the last thirty-five years of the nineteenth century, then, the image of a godless Buddhism predominated; and this, in spite of the recognition of a theistic Mahayana. As Daniel Gogerly observed, 'There are many who are called Buddhists who acknowledge the existence of a Creator, but they do this from ignorance of the teaching of Buddha. The Buddhist system does not acknowledge the possibility of such a being existing.'[99] In 1869, James Freeman Clarke took an unacknowledged leaf from Voltaire's book when he argued that the Buddhist, like a child, 'is neither deist nor atheist: he has *no* theology'.[100] Less subtly, most writers simply declared Buddhism to be, in Titcomb's colourful language, 'darkened by the dull fog of Atheism'.[101]

Buddhist atheism was perceived as having parallels in the modern West. Ernest Eitel, for instance, drew an analogy between atheistic Buddhism and atheistic Darwinianism. Both acknowledged, he argued, a pre-existing spontaneous tendency to variation as the real cause of the origin of species; and both, he concluded, stopped short of 'pointing out Him, who originated the first commencement of that so-called spontaneous tendency, and who laid into nature the law which regulates the whole process of natural selection, God, the creator and sustainer of the universe'.[102] In his response to the first edition of Eitel's *Buddhism*, Thomas Watters reminded Eitel that Darwin had ended *The Origin of Species* affirming the activity of a Creator.[103] But, in spite of this, Eitel was not deterred from repeating his claim in all the subsequent editions of his book. Indeed, he went as far as to suggest that most atheistic philosophy of the nineteenth century was the immediate result of Buddhist endeavours in the West. Feuerbach, Schopenhauer, von Hartmann, Comte, Emerson, and hosts of others, he declared, 'have all imbibed more or less of this sweet poison and taken as kindly as any Asiatic to this Buddhist opiate'.[104] Again, his words were incorrectly cited without acknowledgement by Hampden Dubose;[105] and again, Watters went to some pains to point out the differences between the positions of these philosophers and Eitel's opiate of the Eastern masses.[106]

Even so, Eitel was not without supporters. 'There was no more of God in primitive Buddhism than there is in Comtism, there was less in Spencerism', observed the *London Quarterly Review*.[107] And Archibald Scott remarked that Mr Alabaster's 'modern Buddhist' found 'a co-religionist not only in the disciples of Feuerbach and von Hartmann, but in every "fervent atheist" who ... has been compelled to daily humanity'.[108] Some writers found Thomas Huxley's term 'agnosticism' to be a more fitting description of the Buddhist attitude to the existence of a deity. Coined by Huxley around 1869,[109] the term was first used in the Buddhist context by Rhys Davids in 1880. The Buddha, he wrote,

was an Agnostic ... A European – I had almost said a Christian – Agnostic – says with respect to all the arguments and statements of theologians concerning the nature and attributes, the power and action of God, 'We do not know.' Gautama's attitude, in the face of the discussions and statements of the Indian Pantheists regarding their Great Spirit and First Cause, was the same.[110]

In the following year, Davids was to repudiate his own argument by stating that the Buddha, far from being an Agnostic, was in the fullest possible sense a Gnostic.[111] But others were to take up Huxley's term. Samuel Kellogg, for instance, remarked that it was as an agnostic rather than an atheistic system that Buddhism found sympathizers among the agnostic atheists of Christendom.[112] Robert Green maintained that the Buddha's disbelief in God did not amount to a denial but was nevertheless 'the most hopeless Agnosticism',[113] and Archibald Scott concluded that modern Buddhism was almost 'identical with modern Agnosticism'.[114]

The discussion of Buddhist atheism during the Victorian period was also permeated by two interrelated motifs that had played an important role in European thought at least from the middle of the sixteenth century.[115] These were, first, the notion of the innate religiousness of mankind; and, connected closely with this, the impossibility of the existence of nations of atheists. In spite of the asseverations of Pierre Bayle, John Locke, and David Hume to the contrary, these motifs remained potent throughout the eighteenth and into the nineteenth century.

On the face of it, the existence of Buddhism as an atheistic philosophy sounded the death knell for the notion of the impossibility of atheistic nations. Certainly a number of nineteenth-century commentators drew this conclusion. In 1870, Richard Armstrong wrote:

When the question of natural religion engaged the shrewd and sparking intellects of the France of the last century, it was not wonderful that Theism should be conceived as an axiom of mankind. It was urged that no state or community of atheists ever existed; and so far as men then knew, no such society ever had existed. But the last forty years have given us the materials for a knowledge of Buddhism ... And this Buddhism exhibits to us not one, but unnumerable communities born, bred, dying without thought or desire of God ... Therefore, to insist that God is naturally revealed to all men, however dimly, is to ignore the largest fact in all history, and to hug a conclusion which is destitute of premises. It may be quite true that *we* have intuitive sense of Deity, but there are 300,000,000 of human beings in whom that sense is not to be detected.[116]

It was possible to sustain this kind of argument only on the assumptions that *all* Buddhist nations were atheists and/or that *all* Buddhists were atheists. Both of these assumptions were to come under attack from numerous apologists for the innateness of religion and the innateness of the idea of God.

The assumption that all Buddhists were atheists was questioned by a number of writers. This was frequently effected by the distinguishing between an atheistic philosophical Buddhism for the elite and a theistic Buddhism for the masses. To Joseph Edkins in 1859, Buddhist atheism was suitable only for subtle logicians and not for common men: 'The feeling natural to man that there is a Divine Power present in the universe must express itself ... The powers attributed to the Buddhas and Bodhisattwas are supposed to be exercised in answer to the prayers of men, and they take the place of God in the minds of common believers in that religion.'[117] *The Saturday Review* in 1883 explained the combination of idolatry and atheism in Buddhism by referring the latter to a learned few, and the former to the 'unlearned multitude, who have the common craving of mankind for supernatural aids ...';[118] and Marcus Dods maintained that the atheism of the Buddha was too abstract and impersonal for popular acceptance so that 'the religious instincts of the masses introduced various forms of quasi-divine worship'.[119] Bishop Bigandet also adverted implicitly to the assumption of the innate religiousness of man. He explained the Burmese worship of *Nats* in terms of man's natural proclivity to believe in some great Being.[120] And Samuel Beal saw the Buddhist worship of trees, *stupas*, and images as the result of the strong impulse in the mind to worship something.[121]

The assumption that all Buddhists were atheists was also assailed from another direction. To those who accepted the temporal priority of Pali to Mahayana Buddhism, the more theistic ambience of later Buddhism was an exemplary vindication of the innate religiousness of man. In a letter to *The Times* in 1857, Max Müller showed his commitment to this assumption:

The ineradicable feeling of dependence on something else, which is the life-spring of all religion, was completely numbed in the early Buddhist metaphysicians, and it was only after several generations had passed away, and after Buddhism had become the creed of millions, that this feeling returned with increased warmth ... deifying the very Buddha who had denied the existence of a Deity.[122]

Henry Yule pointed out in the following year that, in spite of the atheism of Buddhism, the conscience or religious instinct of its followers led them to speak in a way consistent only with their recognition of an eternal God;[123] and fifteen years later, Bishop Claughton, while assessing the Buddhist system as one that excluded worship, nevertheless declared, 'but *men will* worship, and if they are taught there is no God, they will still "feel after Him, if haply they might find Him?" It is man's *nature* – and in the higher and truer sense of the word – to *believe in God* ...'[124] The same point was made by Eitel. According to him, 'the consciousness of God, this divine legacy inherited by every human soul, recoiled from the godless Atheism of the metaphysician ...'[125]

The historiographical assumption of the purity of the chronologically prior Pali Buddhism led, as we have seen, to the perception of Buddhism as essentially atheistic; and this entailed that the more theistic Mahayana was a decadent and corrupt form of Buddhism. In contrast to this, the assumptions of the innateness of the idea of God and the innate religiousness of humanity cast a different light on the Buddhism of a later period and the Buddhism of the masses. To be sure, they verged on the polytheistic and the idolatrous and supported the rhetoric of a corrupt and decadent Buddhism. But simultaneously, they were evidence, not so much of a corrupt and decadent Buddhism, as of a Buddhism which had sufficiently freed itself from the shackles of a repressive scholasticism to allow man's natural instincts to worship a deity to emerge. A discourse of early 'pure' versus late 'corrupt' was combined with or juxtaposed to a discourse of innate religiousness and natural theism. These quite different discourses, entailing quite different evaluations of the development of Buddhism, and reflecting Victorian cultural assumptions which, when applied to Buddhism, were not compatible with each other, did not allow for easy resolution. As we will see, similarly incompatible cultural assumptions were at the foundation of the Victorian discussion of the nature of the Buddhist *summum bonum*, Nirvana.

NIRVANA

Of all the aspects of Buddhist doctrine with which the Victorians dealt, the question of the nature of Nirvana aroused the most interest and the most controversy. In part, this was because quite different kinds of questions were asked about it – ontological *and* soteriological ones. In part too, because it involved distinctions between philosophical and popular Buddhism, Mahayana and Pali Buddhism, the Buddha's agnosticism and Buddhist gnosticism, the attainment of Nirvana in this life and its fulfilment after death. And the question of its nature was influenced by received opinions on other central aspects of Buddhism: the nature of the Buddha, the soul, the human constitution; the questions of rebirth, karma, and morality; and, of course, atheism.

Ontologically, the central issue in this hotly disputed question concerned what the attainment of Nirvana meant for the existence of the previously suffering individual. The majority opinion throughout the nineteenth century was that Nirvana, *essentially*, entailed the annihilation of the individual. As early as 1795, the annihilationist view was proposed to English readers of Abbé Grosier's *A General Description of China*. To obtain happiness as a Buddhist, he wrote,

we must endeavour by continual meditation, and frequent victories over ourselves, to acquire a likeness to this principle [viz. of nothingness]; and to obtain that end, we must accustom ourselves to do nothing, will nothing, feel nothing, desire nothing ... The whole of holiness consists in ceasing to exist, in being confounded with nothing; the nearer man approaches to the nature of a stone or log, the nearer he is to perfection ...[126]

Grosier's statement of the meaning of Nirvana was both cited and endorsed by the *Encyclopaedia Britannica* in 1810 in its article on

'China'. The Buddha, it remarked, had declared that all things had proceeded from a vacuum and from nothing and would return to the same. 'This doctrine', it went on, 'produced a corresponding mode of action, or rather of inaction, in those who believed it: for thus the great happiness of man was made to consist in absolute annihilation; and therefore the nearer he could bring himself to this state during life, the happier he was supposed to be.'[127]

The annihilationist account of Nirvana appeared frequently from this time onward, as much in writers on Mahayana as on Pali Buddhism, as much in the accounts of diplomats as in missionaries. Ann Judson, wife of the Baptist missionary to Burma Adoniram Judson, described Nirvana or *Nigban* as 'the *state* in which there is no existence'.[128] Walter Medhurst, probably relying more on Grosier than on his own experiences in China, declared that 'One of the most favourite doctrines of Buddha is, that all things originated in nothing, and will revert to nothing again. Hence, annihilation is the summit of bliss; and *nirupan*, *nirvana*, or nonentity, the grand and ultimate anticipation of all.'[129]

There was also much scholarly opinion in favour of the annihilationist explanation. In 1876, in his article on Buddhism for the ninth edition of *The Encyclopaedia Britannica*, Rhys Davids argued that there could no longer be any doubt that Nirvana meant annihilation:

Spence Hardy and Bigandet find in the modern Sinhalese and Burmese books the same opinion as Alvis [*sic*] and Gogerly and especially Childers have found in the more ancient authorities; and though the modern books of the Northern Buddhists are doubtful, Eugène Burnouf has clearly proved that their older texts contain only the same doctrine as that held in the South. Buddhism does not acknowledge the existence of a soul as a thing distinct from the parts and powers of man which are dissolved at death, and the Nirvana of Buddhism is simply Extinction.[130]

To the names of Burnouf, Hardy, and Bigandet, Barthélemy St Hilaire, himself an ardent and, needless to say, vocal supporter of the annihilationist interpretation, added the names of the Wesleyan Missionary to Ceylon Benjamin Clough, of the Ceylonese administrator George Turnour, and the European scholars Isaak Schmidt and Philippe Foucaux.[131] Horace Wilson was, in sum, speaking for many of his contemporaries when he remarked, 'Utter extinction, as the great end and object of life is also a fundamental, and in some respects a peculiar, feature of Buddhism. Nirvana is literally a blowing-out, as if of a candle, – annihilation ...'[132]

The scholarly weight of opinion on the side of the annihilationist account was to be found also at the more popular level. In the first edition of his *Christ and Other Masters* in 1855, Charles Hardwick observed, 'It was formerly disputed whether more is meant by the expression *nirvāna* than "eternal quietude", "unbroken sleep", "impenetrable apathy": but the oldest literature of Buddhism will scarcely suffer us to doubt that Gautama intended by it nothing short of absolute "annihilation" ...'[133] The annihilationist view was utilized by those anxious to reject the Buddha of Sir Edwin Arnold who had proclaimed, 'If any teach NIRVĀNA is to cease, / Say unto such they lie.'[134] Samuel Kellogg declared that annihilation was 'the final issue of that great salvation, over the Buddha's supposed discovery of which the poet apologist for heathenism [viz. Arnold] waxes so enthusiastic';[135] and William Wilkinson, in a savage and vitriolic attack on Arnold, responded to the latter's view of Nirvana by asserting that 'The true antithesis to existence is non-existence, and non-existence, pure annihilation, beyond doubt, the Buddhist Nirvana is.'[136]

Kellogg's and Wilkinson's stress on the annihilation of the individual as the aim of Buddhism was intended to shock their readers. Undoubtedly, in a large number of cases, they would have produced the desired effect. The *nature* of life after death was an issue of considerable controversy in the Victorian period.[137] But the fact of it, or at the very least, the assumption that all persons innately desired it, was axiomatic. It was as a result of this widely held assumption that so many recoiled from the apparent annihilationism of Buddhism. As early as 1821, John Davy described the idea of annihilation as a final reward as monstrous in relation to sound reason, though he went on to admit that it was compatible with a system that saw existence itself as essentially one of pain and misery.[138] The same sentiments were voiced some fifty years later by Unitarian Richard Armstrong. He too described the quest for annihilation as appalling even though he was quite familiar with it close to home: 'It is the opinion of one', he declared, 'who for a score of years has laboured amid the poorest of London poor, that that great population ignores God altogether, and looks to death with longing, not as a better birth, but the end, deliverance, annihilation. These are our English Buddhists. *Their* hope, too, is Nirvana.'[139] Barthélemy St Hilaire described it as 'a monstrous conception, repugnant to all the instincts of human nature, revolting to reason, and implying atheism'.[140] The deep-seated, almost intuitive, inability to come to terms with a system that strove for annihilation as its goal was most powerfully expressed by Bishop Bigandet: 'Indeed', he exclaimed,

it is impossible not to seet [*sic*] in the meaning of this world [*sic* - word, viz. Nirvana] the horrifying idea of absolute annihilation. The writer frankly avows that he has been, during many years, unwilling to adopt a conclusion, which the obvious meaning of the words pointed out in a clear manner. He hoped that a deeper insight into the system of Budhism would lead him to a conclusion more consonant with reason. But he has been completely disappointed in his expectations. By what process of arguing has the founder of Budhism arrived to such a despairing terminus? How has he been led into that horrible abyss? How has he contrived to silence the voice of conscience, and set aside the clearest innate notions of human mind?[141]

Not all adhered to the annihilationist account of Nirvana. During the first half of the century, before Buddhism had become a religion defined primarily in terms of its own textuality, the *summum bonum* of Buddhism was often assimilated to that of Hinduism. Consequently, Nirvana was spoken of in terms of absorption, even though there was often uncertainty about what such absorption amounted to. In 1817, for example, Ward remarked that the highest state of glory for the Buddhist was absorption. But he did explain in a footnote that, since the Buddhists reject the doctrine of a separate Supreme Spirit, 'it is difficult to say what are their ideas of absorption'.[142] The *Asiatic Journal and Monthly Register* for 1831 recognized that Buddhism rejected the idea of a god but nevertheless saw the ultimate aim of Buddhism to be that of dissolution or absorption of the spirit into the absolute or the non-entity from which it sprang.[143] The *Allgemeine Deutsche Real-Encyclopädie* in 1833 declared that the Buddha had attained 'union with the highest Being' after his death, a claim it continued to make in a number of subsequent editions.[144] The *Penny Cyclopaedia* in 1836 virtually identified the aspirations of Buddhists with those of Hindus. The Hindu notion of the liberation of the soul from rebirth and its return to a lasting union with the Divine Being, it claimed, 'developed in a peculiar manner, forms likewise the basis of the Bauddha creed'.[145] The *Prospective Review* for 1850 suspected that the Buddha meant by Nirvana 'no more than what Wordsworth sings – "Man who is from God sent forth, Must yet again to God return"'; [146] while the Prinsepses and Cunningham saw it as 'absorption into the Divine Spirit'. [147] To Francis Barham in 1857, Nirvana was 'deification, apotheosis, absorption of the soul into God, but not its annihilation ...', [148] though his argument was probably influenced by the doctrines of the religion of 'Alism' of which he had the dubious distinction of being the founder.

This view, that Nirvana meant absorption, was to appear very occasionally until the end of the century. [149] But often, it was suggested that absorption in Buddhism meant, to all intents and purposes, annihilation. As Michael Culbertson put it, 'The highest state of happiness, according to the Buddhist theory, consists in absorption into the deity ... This is a state of absolute abstraction from all outward objects – a state of utter uncon-sciousness. It is, in fact, annihilation.' [150] The virtual demise of the absorptionist view from the 1860s onwards was of course related to the belief generally accepted during this same period that Buddhism denied the existence of any absolutes, whether underlying the universe or the individual. Buddhist atheism and the Buddhist theory of non-self were incompatible with the interpretation of Nirvana as absorption into some Ultimate. 'I would only, with all due deference,' inquired the Countess of Jersey, 'ask the opponents of the annihilation theory two questions, i.e. What remained to be absorbed? and, Into what was it absorbed?' [151]

The annihilationist interpretation of the doctrine of Nirvana came to determine the overall picture of Buddhism. But alternative interpretations of the doctrine were proposed by those who tended to see Buddhism more as a theory of salvation than as a piece of abstruse metaphysics. Soteriologically interpreted, the doctrine of Nirvana took on a more positive flavour than it had done when interpreted ontologically in terms of annihilation. In 1857, Max Müller had seen Nirvana as suggesting annihilation although he was aware that for the millions who embraced Buddhism, Nirvana came to take on 'the bright colours of a paradise ...' [152] But by 1869, he had come to view the annihilationist account of Nirvana as a deviation which Buddhism owed to its philosophers, a deviation from the much more positive view of its founder. After examining a number of passages, Müller was led to observe:

On considering such sayings ... one recognizes in them a conception of Nirvāna, altogether irreconcilable with the Nihilism of the third part of the Buddhist Canon ... If these sayings have maintained themselves, in spite of their contradiction to orthodox metaphysics, the only explanation, in my opinion, is, that they were too firmly fixed in the tradition which went back to Buddha and his disciples. It represented the entrance of the soul into rest, a subduing of all wishes and desires, indifference to joy and pain, to good and evil, an absorption of the soul in itself, and a freedom from the circle of existences from birth to death, and from death to a new birth. This is still the meaning which educated people attach to it, whilst, to the minds of the larger masses, Nirvāna suggests rather the idea of a Mohammedan paradise or of blissful Elysian fields.[153]

Few were to follow explicitly Müller's differentiation of the theory of Nirvana into three different phases. Indeed it was criticized by Childers in his *Dictionary* only one year later.[154] But his view of Nirvana as a state of rest was not without its supporters. In 1871, Samuel Beal quoted Müller as his authority to reinforce his claim that 'there is a general agreement respecting the Nirvāna of the Buddhists, in their own works, viz., that it signifies a condition of Rest and of Peace'.[155] The *Dublin University Magazine* for 1873 argued, following Müller, that the Buddha taught that Nirvana was a place of rest, not unlike the Christian idea of heaven: 'Shall we not rather think, then,' it somewhat rhetorically asked, 'that the Master offered to the faithful servant ... that repose which is the contrast to the turmoil of the present life. Would he not lead the weary one through the green fields, and by the pleasant streams, and let him see the glories of the asphodel vallies beyond the dark river of death?'[156] And *The Westminster Review*, in a review of a number of Beal's works, continued the tradition established by Müller. 'Some people', it observed 'not in harmony with the mind of Buddha, have spoken of Nirvāna as though it meant annihilation. But there is no thought of annihilation in the mind of the Founder who said, "I devote myself wholly to moral culture, so as to arrive at the highest condition of moral rest, Nirvana."'[157]

Hermann Oldenberg is also to be classed amongst those who, against the annihilationist interpretation, stressed the soteriological aspect of the doctrine. According to Oldenberg, to describe Buddhism as a religion of annihilation is to succeed in missing the main drift of early Buddhism.[158] Although, like Bigandet, he saw the logic of Nirvana as suggesting annihilation, he viewed the craving for eternal life, for sanctification, as an essential part of human existence. The Buddhist doctrine of Nirvana is, consequently, a compromise between the cravings of the thirsty for immortality, and the logic of non-being:

Does the path lead into a new existence? Does it lead into the Nothing? The Buddhist creed rests in delicate equipoise between the two. The longing of the heart that craves the eternal has not nothing, and yet the thought has not a something, which it might firmly grasp. Farther off the idea of the endless, the eternal could not withdraw itself from belief than it has done here, where, like a gentle flutter on the point of merging in the Nothing, it threatens to evade the gaze.[159]

Oldenberg's position was an influential one. It was reflected in Jonathan Titcomb's suggestion that 'there lies concealed the idea of cessation from consciousness in Nirvana, only in relation to time and matter; while it may still have some inexplicable survival without any relation either to time or matter'.[160] In 1890, on the authority of Oldenberg, Colinet absolved the Buddha, if not his disciples, from the charge of nihilism, as did Archibald Scott in the same year, and John Beames some years later.[161]

Oldenberg's attempt to place the doctrine of Nirvana between the extremes of existence and non-existence was paralleled by those who interpreted Nirvana negatively as the absence of those characteristics which comprise phenomenal existence. Such accounts had had a long history. In 1799 for example, Francis Buchanan described Nirvana in the following way:

when a person is no longer subject to any of the following miseries, namely, to weight, old age, disease and death, then he is said to have obtained *Nieban* [.] No thing, no place, can give us an adequate idea of *Nieban*: we can only say, that to be free from the four above mentioned miseries, and to obtain salvation, is *Nieban*.[162]

Sangermano in 1833 drew attention to a treatise on religion written in 1763 by a celebrated Burmese monk. He had understood Nirvana as 'a state exempt from the four following evils: conception, old age, sickness, and death ... the exemption from the above-mentioned evils, and the possession of perfect safety, are the only things in which it consists'.[163]

Soteriological definitions of this sort, couched in negative terms, were to appear throughout the second half of the nineteenth century.

From his experiences in Ava in 1855, Henry Yule was able to inform his readers:

Anitya, Dukha, Anatta, Transience, Pain, and Unreality (so the devout Buddhist mutters as he tells his beads), these are the characters of all existence, and the only true good is exemption from these in the attainment of nirwāna; whether that be, as in the view of the Brahmin or the theistic Buddhist, absorption into the supreme essence; or whether it be, as many have thought, absolute nothingness ...[164]

James Clarke in 1869 interpreted the Buddhist statement that Nirvana is nothing as meaning that it is *no thing*, 'that it is nothing to our present conceptions; that it is the opposite of all we know, the contradiction of what we call life now, a state so sublime, so wholly different from anything we know or can know now, that it is the same thing as nothing to us'.[165] To the poet William Davies, as well as to Samuel Beal, Bishop Copleston, George Grant, and Richard Collins, the state of Nirvana was 'purely negative, and one of which Buddhism does not attempt to give any account or description. It is simply the destruction of all we know of mundane life when its consequences as fruits or results have been neutralized, and the effects of all action exhausted.'[166]

We saw earlier that the horror expressed at the idea that Nirvana could mean annihilation of the individual was motivated by the axiom that the desire for personal immortality was innate in human nature. For some, this was so inalienably a feature of humanity that there was no possibility of any human being ever having taught the post-mortem annihilation of the individual.[167] For most, the innate human quest for immortality had found expression in Buddhism, despite the apparent intention of the system to offer its followers, at the worst, annihilation, at the best, the eternal absence of those characteristics that compose the empirical person. This was facilitated by utilizing a distinction that operated in the Victorian analysis of Buddhist atheism, that of the distinction between a Buddhism of a philosophical elite and a Buddhism of the masses. The innate impulse for personal immortality, repressed in the former, inexorably and necessarily found expression in the latter. *The Christian Remembrancer* in 1858 observed that, far from accepting a negative view of Nirvana, the popular mind naturally aspired to the reward of Paradise.[168] Joseph Edkins described the idea of the 'Paradise in the West' as 'something more gratifying to common human feelings'.[169] W.H. Davenport Adams argued that the Buddha preached annihilation and that this was apparently accepted by his millions of followers. But, he went on to ask, 'did they really accept it as he preached it? No; the truth is, they read into it, as it were, their own innate unconquerable belief in a hereafter, and converted his Nirvāna into a Paradise ...'[170] Of the notion of a Pure Land in the West, Ernest Eitel was moved to remark,

this whole dogma, beautiful as it is in its conception, and a true response to the natural yearnings of the human heart for an eternal Sabbath in heaven, is a flat contradiction to all the leading doctrines of Buddhism, granting as it does such an easy egress out of the Sansara [sic] and substituting personal immortality for the utter annihilation of the Nirvāna theory.[171]

We began this chapter with a discussion of the Victorian view of Buddhism as pessimistic. It is perhaps not inappropriate to have ended it on the more optimistic note of Paradise and immortality. For this contrast is just one of many that have come to our attention throughout the course of this chapter. The Victorian period demonstrated a remarkable diversity in the analyses it made, and the attitudes it adopted, to the central doctrines of Buddhism. Although there is no unity to be perceived in the answers to the questions it saw Buddhism as raising, the Victorian age was none the less united by its concern for the issues that Buddhism brought into focus. Buddhism in theory spoke eloquently to a period united by the questions of creation and cosmology, of the Bible and biology, of theism and atheism, of annihilation and immortality, of human nature and its apparent exceptions. Buddhism provided diverse answers, but the questions asked of it were pointedly Victorian ones.

5

Victorian precepts and Buddhist practice

MORALITY

Many persons regard everything which tends to discredit theology with disapprobation, because they think that all such speculations must endanger morality as well. Others assert that morality has a basis of its own in human nature, and that, even if all theological belief were exploded, morality would remain unaffected ... it seems to me extravagant to say that the one does not influence the other. The difference between living in a country where the established theory is that existence is an evil, and annihilation the highest good, and living in a country where the established theory is that the earth is the Lord's and the fulness thereof, the round world and they that dwell therein, has surely a good deal to do with the other differences which distinguish Englishmen from Buddhists.[1]

In 1877, *The Nineteenth Century* published a symposium entitled 'The Influence upon Morality of a Decline in Religious Belief'. Sir James Stephen began the discussion with the words quoted above. His contribution reflected, as did the symposium as a whole, the deep-seated Victorian sense of the intimacy of the connexion between morality and religion. Of the general effect of the symposium, Owen Chadwick has remarked that, from ultramontane to positivist, there was agreement that 'religion was powerful in morality and that a decline of religion would mean a decline in standards of behaviour; and that while this truth did not invariably apply in individuals, it applied in society'.[2] As we can see in the passage by Stephen, as early as 1877 Buddhism was playing a part as counterpoint in this quite characteristic Victorian dilemma. The Victorian stress on the moral sense as a key element in religious consciousness was a central theme in the nineteenth-century analysis of Buddhism. As a consequence, the Victorian image of Buddhist morality demonstrates in a remarkably clear way that polarity of assimilation and rejection which, as we have seen, typified the Victorian view of the Buddhist tradition.

From the early part of the Victorian age, Buddhism had often been seen as primarily an ethical system. The *Encyclopaedia Britannica* in 1842 pointed out that 'The doctrine and law of Gautama consist chiefly in observing five commandments, and abstaining from ten sins.'[3] To Eduard Roer in 1845, it was the moral element that prevailed in Buddhism: 'it is essentially a religion, in which the highest object is Dharmma, the realization of the moral law by a finite being, as the only means of receiving true liberation ...'[4] Even as late as 1880, Edgar Ware maintained that the Buddha's teaching 'seems to have been purely ethical, and not to have touched on either theology or philosophy'.[5] At the very least, its morality was seen as a key factor in its success. John Caird declared that there could be no doubt 'that the comparatively pure and elevated morality which Buddha taught and exemplified is one of the causes to which we must ascribe the marvellous success he achieved in his own day, and the deep hold which his system has taken of the religious consciousness of the East through succeeding ages'.[6] And Thomas Huxley suggested that it was to its ethical qualities that 'Buddhism owes its marvellous success'.[7]

Among the religions of the world, Buddhist ethics was seen as superior to all, Christianity alone excepted. This was an item in discourse about Buddhism that established itself early among its interpreters. Francis Buchanan, for example, found that the moral system of the Burmese was 'perhaps as good, as that held forth by any of the religious doctrines prevailing among mankind'.[8] Its singularly individualistic character and its closeness to the moral injunctions of the Jewish Decalogue were to appeal to the Victorians. Even among those most critical of Buddhist doctrine, there was an almost unanimous appreciation of its morality. James Tennent, for instance, asserted that 'the injunctions of Buddhu prescribe a *code of morality* second only to Christianity itself, and superior to every heathen system that the world has ever seen, nor excepting that of Zoroaster'.[9] Henry Sirr believed 'Buddhaical doctrines and precepts to be the best pagan religion known',[10] and *The Westminster Review* for 1856 saw Buddhist morality as the 'one bright spot in the darkness of Buddhism ...'[11]

Such views were to reappear repeatedly for the remainder of the century. Ernest Eitel declared that only Christianity 'teaches a morality loftier, stronger, holier than that of Buddhism ...'[12] John Caird, James Alwis, and Samuel Kellogg agreed that Buddhism was pre-eminent among the non-Christian religions on account of its morality.[13] It was by virtue of its analogies to Christian morality, or rather to the Victorian understanding of it, that Buddhist morality was capable of assimilation by the Victorians. *The Church Quarterly Review* for 1882 shows clearly the way in which Buddhist ethics was refracted through a prism of Victorian virtues:

We can admit, without fear of misunderstanding, that in regard even to points of duty which in the common opinion have been satisfactorily treated by Christianity alone, the Buddhist ideas do not fall one whit short of the Christian. The Buddhist precepts with regard to patience under injuries, the cultivation of unselfishness and of sympathy, the duty of endeavouring to relieve the distresses of others, the temperance, soberness, and chastity, of resignation, of bridling the tongue and the temper, of almsgiving and the practice of works of mercy, of the avoidance of any ostentation of goodness, even of repentance and acknowledgement of sin, are, when regarded on the human side alone, unsurpassed by those of Christianity; for in truth, with minor differences of detail, both teach the same thing.[14]

But unreservedly positive evaluations of Buddhist morality were rare. Almost universally, grounds for the rejection of Buddhist ethics gathered alongside laudatory accounts of it. The reader of the literature cannot but be struck by the seeming inexorability with which the Victorian interpreter, however sympathetic to Buddhist morality, was moved to declare it vitiated either by its connection to unassimilable Buddhist doctrines, or by the failure of Buddhist societies to put it into practice.

Overall, Buddhist theory was seen as providing insufficient motives or sanctions for the moral life. The doctrines of karma and rebirth, for example, were considered detrimental to the practice of morality for a variety of sometimes conflicting reasons. Daniel Gogerly argued that retribution for sins committed was effectively excluded in Buddhism since, in spite of the view that sinful conduct in this life entails suffering in a future one, the Buddhist idea of individuality effectively means that it will be a different individual who will bear the merited misery.[15] While for Gogerly the links between one life and the next were insufficiently strong to bear the weight of the demands of morality, for Ernest Eitel the connection of morality with a karmic system of rewards and punishment vitiated its validity as a *moral* system. Morality, he argued, is converted 'into a vast scheme of profit and loss'.[16] The Bishop of Colombo argued that the incentive to virtuous conduct in this life is ruined by the conviction that it is 'but a trifling unit in an immense series, incapable of resisting in any degree the consequences of the actions of past lives, and entailing consequence on a future existence which has only a very shadowy continuity with the present',[17] an argument he repeated several years later in his anonymous review of Monier-Williams's *Buddhism*.[18]

The doctrine of Nirvana also played a role in the evaluation of Buddhist morality. For those who, like Samuel Beal, saw Nirvana as a condition of rest and peace, it provided a sufficient motive for correct and virtuous conduct.[19] But it was quite otherwise for those who adopted the annihilationist interpretation of Nirvana. Felix Adler, for example, claimed that the doctrine of Nirvana 'neutralized the active principle that inspires and invigorates Buddhist ethics',[20] and *The Saturday Review* in 1883 saw the defects in the ethical teaching of Buddhism as arising from its aim of sinking into apathy.[21] The Buddhist, Marcus Dods averred,

reaches the highest development, not to become serviceable to the world at large, but to pass away into nothingness. 'He that hateth his life in this world, shall keep it unto life eternal' – that is the well-balanced, far-seeing, quiet enunciation of the real law of existence; but the Buddhist Nirvana is a travestie [*sic*] of this, and magnificent as is the conception of man's highest moral state, it is stultified by the end for which it is to be attained.[22]

But the evaluation of Buddhist morality was influenced not only by the axiomatic belief in immortality, but also by the Victorian debate on the necessity of belief in God to the practice of morality. Many criticized Buddhist ethics for its failure to have founded its morality on the existence of God. Bishop Claughton, in his address to the Victoria Institute, maintained that the morality of Buddhists was 'impossible because baseless, and without an object to whom their responsibility can be referred ...'[23] The *London Quarterly Review* expressed this vividly. The omission of God in Buddhism, it asserted, 'makes the same difference in the moral world, which the destruction of the sun would make in the physical universe'.[24] And Charles Galton drew on the metaphor of the physically handicapped body: even when viewed as a human moral system, the absence of God 'cripples it to total lameness'.[25]

The stridency of the claims about the insufficiency of an atheistic Buddhist morality reflected something of the unique position which Buddhism held in any debate on the connection of theism and morality. For Buddhism provided a striking verification of the claim that theism was not absolutely essential to the cultivation of a moral and virtuous life. Samuel Kellogg listed this as one of the major reasons for the interest of many of his contemporaries in Buddhism. The Buddhist system of morals, he observed 'is thought by some to settle at least this, that a high standard of morals, and its actual attainment in life, is not inseparable from a belief in God, since here we have a moral code of a high order recognised where there is no belief in God at all'. The Buddha, he went on to say, 'affords a living argument [to some] to show that not only theoretical but practical morality of a high type may be realised without faith in the existence of God'.[26] Henry Chandler, Wayneflete Professor of moral and metaphysical philosophy, was one of these. In his response to Bishop Claughton, he wrote:

If Buddhism does teach that there may be – must be right and wrong, even though there be no God – then I no longer wonder at its influence. It is a strong thing to say, but it is, I believe, true, that we are all of us far more certain that there is a binding right, a repellent wrong, than we are that there is a God, and that, had man no distinct sense of right and wrong to begin with, he would never have dreamed of a God, or would have soon awoke from it.[27]

The positivist Frederic Harrison thought likewise: 'The morality of Confucius and of Sakya Mouni, of Socrates and of Marcus Aurelius, of Vauvenagues, Turgot, Condorcet, Hume, was entirely independent of any theology.'[28]

By far the most common criticism levelled at Buddhist morality was that of its selfishness. Barthélemy St Hilaire, for example, praised Buddhist ethics, especially that of Asoka. But he nevertheless maintained, 'In vain does Buddhism profess self-renunciation and self-sacrifice, it is in reality narrow and self-interested.'[29] Such sentiments were often to be heard. To Linus Brockett, it was a religion of intense selfishness: 'The good of our fellow-men, the feeling of gratitude, or of disinterested love, finds no place in it.'[30] In 1869, James Clarke saw Buddhist morality as resting on pure

individualism – 'each man's object is to save his own soul';[31] and
Spence Hardy described it as 'a principle of selfishness'.[32] For both
Titcomb and Eitel, in the absence of belief in God, the motive for
morality could only be a selfish one.[33]

This polarity of assimilation and rejection is constantly evident.
The *London Quarterly Review* for 1886 described Buddhist ethics as
noble but defective, for 'In its highest form virtue is a means in order
to a personal end.'[34] Marcus Dods called the framework of the
Buddhist ethic beautiful and all but perfect; but, as if impelled, he
added, 'the moving spirit of it is radically selfish'.[35] Archibald Scott
declared that its ethical system was its strength and glory, and the
secret of its attractiveness and long continuance.[36] However, he
still found it to be 'a religion of every man for himself' and even
lacking in the altruism of Positivism.[37] Thomas Berry was struck
by the beauty and insight of the moral precepts of Buddhism but
he too found the whole system to be grounded in the question 'Will
this be to my advantage?'[38]

Still, it needs to be remarked that some voices are to be heard
protesting against the dismissal of Buddhism as 'the religion of
glorified Selfishness'.[39] Richard Armstrong, for example, argued
against Barthélemy St Hilaire that the Buddha inculcated aspirations
'almost as remote from sordid self-interest as the sublime sacrifices
of the New Testament'.[40] Henry Alabaster, one of the most sympathetic apologists, pointed out that the key to the liberation of the
self in Buddhism was the quest to ameliorate the suffering of all;
and consequently, he argued, 'Selfishness producing unselfishness
cannot be very seriously condemned.'[41] Edgar Ware maintained
that the Buddhist renunciation of self was for the sake of others. It
looked, he wrote, 'for no other reward than its own fulfilment,
partially in this life, by the conquest of desire, and completely
hereafter, in Nirvana, which is the cessation of existence'.[42]

Without doubt though, such views as these were in the minority.
Assimilation was generally juxtaposed to rejection, the yes to the
no. A number of reasons may be suggested for the predominance
of this polarity. First, in part, the criticism of Buddhist ethics as selfish
was motivated by the desire to assert the final superiority of Christianity. As Eugene Dunlap explained it, 'The two worlds which
characterize Christianity and Buddhism are as unlike as light and
darkness. Christianity – love, Buddhism – selfishness.'[43] But
more crucially, I think, it was determined by the cultural hegemony

of the West over the East. This necessitated the view that, however ideal in precept Buddhist ethics might be, in practice it could not but be unconducive to the maintenance of society. James Dennis, one of the most imperialist of all missionary writers, described Buddhism as a system of spiritual monasticism which aimed at a withdrawal from social responsibility: 'Its social creed is the isolation or withdrawal of self for the benefit of self. It is a policy of scuttling, and leaving society to sink beneath the waves.'[44] J. Dyer Ball saw it as destructive of that most Victorian of all institutions – the family: 'it was in some of its aspects a disintegrating force, as far as the family was concerned – monkery and monasteries, nuns and convents bear testimony to the abrogation of the divine command, and the throwing down of the family altar, set up under the aegis of the Creator himself at the beginning of human life on this world ...'[45]

The polarity of assimilation and rejection of Buddhist ethics among Victorian writers is therefore suggestive of the desire of the West ideologically to suppress the autonomy of the East, and thus to control it. Buddhist ethical precepts could be and were assimilated. But the idea that Buddhist societies failed to put them into practice made possible the rejection of the cultural viability of these societies, and validated the cultural hegemony of the West.

This contrast of moral precept and moral practice was a common theme in much writing of the period. As early as 1821, John Davy in his account of Ceylon regretted that the moral system of Buddhism was not more strictly adhered to and followed.[46] In 1850, James Tennent declared that, at both an individual and social level, Ceylonese Buddhism was virtually effete: 'Neither hopes nor apprehensions', he wrote, 'have proved a sufficient restraint on the habitual violation of all those precepts of charity and honesty, of purity and truth, which form the very essence of their doctrine ...'[47] Knighton was sufficiently aware of the beam in his own eye to allow Marandhan, his Buddhist partner in dialogue, to remind his readers that Christian morality did not appear to be practised in England.[48] But his was very much a voice crying in the wilderness. Bishop Claughton's claims were much more likely to be heard. Asked by the Reverend J. Sinclair to compare the amount of immorality in England with that of Ceylon, he replied:

Do not suppose I do not know that there is a vast amount of evil of that kind [*viz.* dishonesty, want of purity in thought, word, and deed] in

England; but on these points, I must confess, the amount of evil in Ceylon is terrible. In our own country, no sensible parents will allow their children to be too much with their servants, it is not desirable; but there it is not simply a matter of caution but a matter of absolute necessity, for otherwise the most improper things are placed before them ... But the greatest comparison that I would make is this: here there are bad men and good men, and sometimes what are called good men are tempted to evil and lapse in to badness. There, if a man who is naturally a good, kind-hearted man, and not at all cruel, happen to have the besetting sin of covetousness – which is common enough among all these races, not the Bhuddists [sic] in particular – and somebody interferes with his interests, he thinks no more of putting the man out of life than you would think of killing a noxious animal ... It is not that they are worse than we as natural men, but things that would horrify us, with all our faults they are not surprised at ... I do not like to stand forth as their accuser, but if you ask me honestly, there is no comparison at all between them and our own people, with all our faults and badness.[49]

Similar judgements were made of the practice of Buddhist morality in other countries besides Ceylon. In 1845, for example, the *Encyclopaedia Metropolitana* quoted Buchanan to the effect that, in spite of the powerful motives to morality presented by alluring rewards and horrible and protracted punishments, 'the practice of morality among the Barmans [sic] ... is by no means correct. In particular, almost total want of veracity, and a most insatiable cruelty in their wars and punishments, are observable among them ...'[50] Henry Yule suggested that in no other country than in Burma 'has human life been more recklessly and cruelly sacrificed, whether in punishment of crime, or in judicial and private murder'.[51] Charles Gutzlaff claimed not to have found one honest man among the Siamese.[52] The indefatigable missionary – adventurer James Gilmour complained that Buddhist good works in Mongolia often did more harm than good. Indiscriminate almsgiving becomes, he observed, 'a blast and a curse to the land and the people'.[53] Reginald Copleston was speaking for most Victorian interpreters of Buddhism when he remarked in 1890 that the ineffectiveness of Buddhist motives and sanctions 'is too amply borne out by the facts observed in Buddhist countries, in which a varnish of good humour and good temper covers too often extreme untruthfulness, a shocking indifference to purity, and great spitefulness and cruelty'.[54]

BUDDHIST MONASTICISM

This image of morally bankrupt Buddhist societies was further reinforced, in Victorian eyes, by the presence in Buddhism of the monastic ideal. With few exceptions, Buddhist monasticism met with strident criticism. In part, we may put this down to an anti-Catholic bias in Victorian society. But in particular, it had its roots in the Victorian gospel of work. Walter Houghton comments, 'parents and preachers, writers and lecturers, proclaimed as with a single voice that man was created to work, that everyone had his appointed calling in which he was to labour for God and man, that idleness was a moral and social sin'.[55] Small wonder then that Buddhist monasticism was seen as pre-eminently selfish and anti-social. William Sargant, for example, declared that the monasteries were 'filled with persons whom we Protestants have learned to regard as the drones of the human hive'.[56] Eitel declared monasticism to be productive of evil tendencies and a selfish seclusion,[57] and Titcomb observed that the monks took 'little or no interest in the general good of, or in affectionate care for the morals of the people'.[58]

Although the Victorian view of the sacred nature of work was to bring to its critique of Buddhist monasticism its own particular flavour, criticisms of the monastic life were not absent from earlier periods. David Hume, for example, had placed 'Celibacy, fasting, penance, mortification, self-denial, humility, silence, solitude, and the whole train of monkish virtues' in the catalogue of vices.[59] Nor were criticisms of Buddhist monasticism absent from Jesuit descriptions of China. Abbé Grosier, for instance, had described the Chinese Buddhist 'bonzes' as 'generally men without character, brought up, from their infancy, in effeminacy, luxury and idleness, and who, having an aversion to labour, for the most part, devoted themselves to that kind of life, merely for the sake of a subsistence'.[60] More important for the English interpretation of Chinese Buddhist monasticism was the Jesuit Louis le Com[p]te's *Memoirs and Observations*, the English translation of which went through three editions between 1697 and 1699 with new versions in 1737 and 1739.[61] His evaluation of the Chinese monks was to appear continually for the first thirty years of the nineteenth century in a variety of encyclopaedia entries under 'Bonzes'. The *Encyclopaedia Britannica* began the tradition. 'The Chinese bonzes,' it declared in 1797, 'according to F. le Compte, are no better than a gang of dissolute idle fellows.'[62]

119

The same description of bonzes, with the reference to le Compte was often repeated: in *The English Encyclopaedia* in 1802, the *Encyclopaedia Perthensis* in around 1807, the *Pantologia* in 1813, Platts's *Manners and Customs of All Nations* in 1827, and in *The London Encyclopaedia* for 1829.[63]

The rhetoric of an indolent and decadent Chinese monasticism occurred in a variety of forms throughout the Victorian period. Gutzlaff described the Chinese priests as 'a stupid and indolent class of men' who 'are naturally very gross in their appetites, and from want or habit are knaves'.[64] Philosinensis in 1834 declared that the morals of the priests of Buddha 'are notoriously bad, and pinching poverty has made them servile and cringing ... I have been in the *chen-tangs* or halls of contemplation, and have found them the haunts of every vice. How can it be otherwise, if the mind is unoccupied and the hands not employed with any good work.'[65] Clearly, it was these words of Philosinensis that John Kesson had in mind some twenty years later when he wrote, 'Their morals are bad, their conduct mean, their bearing cringing. They are unskilled and, with few exceptions, very stupid ... and their *chentang*, or halls of contemplation, have been found the haunts of every vice.'[66] Sir John Davis spoke of their 'swinish laziness and stupidity', and Michael Culbertson found them to be not only idle and useless but also often immoral and wicked.[67]

This imaginative vision of the Chinese Buddhist monks as indolent and degenerate was supplemented by the claim that they verged on imbecility. Of a monk who had spent three years in seclusion, Culbertson declared, 'His idiotic look indicates that he has succeeded in debasing his intellect, so as to reduce himself well nigh to a level with the brutes ...'[68] Similarly, Davis observed, 'They have, nearly all of them, an expression approaching to idiotcy [*sic*], which is probably acquired by that dreamy state in which one of their most famous professors is said to have passed nine years with his eyes fixed upon a wall!'[69] Edward Neale viewed the external formalism of Buddhism as affecting its intellectual character, and went on to report that 'modern observers describe the priests in its monasteries as seeming in many cases to be in a state not far removed from idiotcy [*sic*]'.[70] D. M. Balfour declared that monastic Buddhism was sharing the fate that attended all religions that encouraged a professional class of monks 'who lead unnatural lives, cumbered with dogmas and absurdities, the result of warped, fantastic and prurient minds'; and he blamed the monastic system for initiating a system of meditation which, 'in lieu of expanding the mind, tends to contract it almost to idiocy'.[71]

To be sure, there were some who protested against these criticisms of Buddhist monasticism in Mahayana societies. As early as 1804, John Barrow claimed that there was, among the monks, 'a decency of behaviour, a sort of pride and dignity'. He, like *The Encyclopaedia Britannica* in 1842, blamed the Roman Catholic missionaries, mortified by the resemblances of Buddhism to their own faith, for unjustly circulating calumnies against them.[72] Ninety years later, George Cobbold observed that the Japanese monks whom he had encountered, 'With countenances often indicating close spiritual application [!] ... appeared to perform their sacred duties with reverence and attention ...'[73]

Still, in spite of these scattered alternative readings of the Buddhist monks' mien, the image of a decadent Mahayana monasticism was dominant. So pervasive was this image that it resulted in the unfavourable comparison of Mahayana Buddhist monasticism with its Ceylonese counterpart. Henry Sirr, for example, found the Buddhist priesthood in Ceylon moral and inoffensive, 'thus presenting a pleasing contrast to their brethren in the Celestial Empire, who generally are the most depraved and ignorant set imaginable'.[74] William Knighton found some priests of Ceylon lamentably ignorant but nevertheless generally distinguished by affability, kindliness of manner, and unbounded hospitality. But he too reflects the dominant image of Chinese monasticism: 'In China, the Budhistic priesthood seems to have fallen into greater disrepute than elsewhere ...'[75]

There was, however, no dearth of criticisms of monasticism in Ceylon. *The Prospective Review* in 1850 made the claim that 'travellers usually report that the Priests are in an extreme degree dull and stupid ...', though it did admit that, from the manners of the priesthood, 'a gentleman may find hints on etiquette, not altogether useless to our Democratic populations, which imagine falsely that rude manners are the signs of honest hearts'.[76] And the *London Quarterly Review*, adopting the classical theory that false religions are framed for the benefit of the priesthood, declared that the monks of Ceylon 'are not surpassed in grasping covetousness, sensuality, lying, deceitfulness, and the indulgence of almost every passion that disfigures the human soul, by any body of men on the face of the earth'.[77]

Burmese monasticism was perhaps a little more fortunate in having had Francis Buchanan as an early commentator. According to him, the monks were 'very decent in their lives, remarkably kind and hospitable to strangers, the best informed men in the country, and very highly respected by the inhabitants'.[78] And this view was cited by, for instance, both *The London Encyclopaedia* in 1829, and *The Edinburgh Encyclopaedia* in 1830 in their entries on 'Burmhand Empire' and 'Birman Empire' respectively.[79] But Bigandet's analysis was to be the influential one. In spite of his disclaimer that he never entertained the slightest intention of casting a malignant contempt or a sneering ridicule upon the Burmese monks,[80] this was undoubtedly the general effect of such passages as the following:

Ignorance prevails to an extent, scarcely to be imagined, among the generality of the Phongyies [monks] ... Their mind is of the narrowest compass ... They have no ardour for study ... There is no vigor in their intellect, no comprehensiveness in their mind, no order or connection in their ideas ... the notions stored up in their memory, are at once incoherent, imperfect, and, too often, very limited. They are cold, reserved, speaking with affected conciseness: their language is sententious, seasoned with an uncommon dose of pretension ... Vanity and selfishness, latent in their hearts ...[81]

This quite negative view of Buddhist monasticism was further reinforced by the inability of Victorian interpreters to assimilate the Buddhist practice of contemplation. The use of words like 'indolence' and 'idiocy' signals the failure of the Victorian writer to come to terms with a passive element in religion that contrasted so much with their more active, 'muscular' vision of the Christian life. There are, as a result, remarkably few references to, or accounts of, this very central aspect of the practice of Buddhism. Even where they do occur, the difficulties that the Victorians found in finding analogies to it within their world-view are apparent. Max Müller was probably reflecting the opinion of most of his contemporaries when he observed that few people 'will take the trouble of reasoning out such hallucinations' as the states attained by the Buddha prior to his death.[82] Daniel Gogerly suggested that the Buddha's meditative state was 'something similar to that which is called the mesmeric trance ...'[83] *The Christian Remembrancer* for 1858 supposed that its account of the stages in the Buddhist path of meditation would seem 'to our readers, as it does to ourselves, a monstrous tissue of absurdity ...'[84] And

Graham Sandberg remarked somewhat sarcastically of the attainment of meditative states, 'he who is able to plunge himself into mental vacuity, and, we might fairly add, idiocy, merely by his own effort ... will soon be endowed with ... the supernatural powers of a saint'.[85] Samuel Beal, Jonathan Titcomb, Henry Alabaster, and Monier Monier-Williams recognize the importance of it to the Buddhist system, but devote little space to any detailed analysis of it.[86] Only in a few instances was it compared with the mystical strand in Christianity, either overtly or implicitly.[87]

BUDDHISM AND CATHOLICISM

The Victorian antipathy to Buddhist monasticism was influenced too by the closeness of many of its aspects to the practice of Catholicism. Already by the beginning of the Victorian period, the similarity of Mahayana Buddhism to Catholicism had become a familiar item in English accounts of China and Tibet. In 1777, for example, John Stewart in a letter to Sir John Pringle wrote of the Tibetan lamas:

their celibacy, their living in communities, their cloysters, their service in the choirs, their strings of beads, their fasts, and their penances, give them so much the air of Christian monks, that it is not surprizing an illiterate capuchin should be ready to hail them as brothers, and think he can trace the features of St Francis in everything about them.[88]

In the journal of his embassy in China from 1793 to 1794, Lord Macartney said of the grand Pagoda at Potala:

The paraphernalia of religion displayed here – the altars, images, tabernacles, censers, lamps, candles and candlesticks – with the sanctimonious deportment of the priests and the solemnity used in the celebration of their mysteries, have no small resemblance to the holy mummeries of the Romish Church ...[89]

And John Barrow, one of Macartney's secretaries, was clearly drawing on Macartney's account when he wrote that

The paraphernalia and almost all the mummeries of the Romish church, the bells, the beads, the altars, the images, the candles, the dress, and the sanctimonious deportment of the priests in the hours of devotion, their chanting and their incense, were already made familiar to the people [of China] in every temple of Fo.[90]

This comparison between Buddhism and Catholicism appeared also in some of the Encyclopaedia literature. *The Encyclopaedia Edinensis*, for instance, in 1827 compared the institutions of the bonzes to the monastic establishments of the Church of Rome.[91] Platts's *Manners and Customs* observed that 'there is so strong a likeness between the apparent worship of many of the priests of Fo, and that which is exhibited in churches of the Roman faith, that a Chinese conveyed into one of the latter might imagine the votaries he saw there were adoring the deities of their own country', and this passage appeared in virtually identical form in *The London Encyclopaedia* in 1829.[92]

Much of the information about the parallels between Catholicism and Chinese Buddhism especially was mediated to Victorian writers through the works of the Catholic Missionaries. As Walter Medhurst summarized it in 1838,

The celibacy, tonsure, professed poverty, secluded abodes, and peculiar dress of the priests: the use of the rosary, candles, incense, holy water, bells, images and relics, in their worship; their belief in purgatory, with the possibility of praying souls out of its fires [and so on] ... are all such striking coincidences, that the catholic missionaries were greatly stumbled at the resemblance between the Chinese worship and their own ... and some of them thought, that the author of evil had induced these pagans to imitate the manners of holy mother church, in order to expose her ceremonies to shame.[93]

The Catholic view that the Buddhist resemblances to Catholicism were satanically inspired was often cited. Both James Clarke in 1869 and *The Westminster Review* in 1878 quoted the Portuguese missionary to China, Father Bury, to the effect that 'There is not a piece of dress, not a sacerdotal function, not a ceremony of the court of Rome, which the Devil has not copied in this country';[94] and John Davis in 1857 cited Père Prémare's conclusion that the devil had practised a trick to perplex his friends the Jesuits.[95] Michael Culbertson, Rhys Davids, and Robert Green all refer to the satanic-inspiration account of the Catholic missionaries.[96] In Davis, Culbertson, and Davids there is too the muted suggestion that those aspects of Buddhism which the missionaries found to be satanically inspired are, for them, equally objectionable parts of Catholicism. Others were less subtle. The *Westminster Review* in 1856 declared that, if it were shown that Catholicism had influenced the development of Buddhism, the former would have nothing on which to pride itself.[97] Henry Alabaster explained the failure of the Catholic priests to see the differences between Christianity and Buddhism as the consequence of their addiction to the same mummeries.[98] Hampden Dubose simply concluded, 'Romanism is Buddhism prepared for a foreign market – Buddhism adapted to a Western civilization.'[99] Robert Anderson spoke of Christianity and Buddhism 'having developed errors and superstitions so precisely similar that the *apparatus* of the one cult could easily be adapted to the other'.[100]

The question of Buddhist idolatry played a role, albeit a minor one, in the discussion of the relationship between Buddhism and Catholicism. Many interpreters of Buddhism were aware that Buddhists rejected the charge of idolatry and argued that the physical representations that abounded in the tradition were not, in spite of appearances, worshipped; and they accepted that this was, in principle, the Buddhist position. But they argued nevertheless that, in practice, idolatry abounded. James Clarke, for instance, remarked that the Buddha would have been the first to condemn this idolatry, but (with a probable glance in the direction of Rome) 'fetich [*sic*] worship lingers in the purest religions'.[101] Samuel Kellogg pointed out that Buddhism, no less than Christianity, 'according to its theory, stamps idolatry as folly'; yet, for all that, 'In all Buddhist countries the images of the Buddha himself are venerated ...'[102] James Gilmour argued that, in spite of its theory, 'it is impossible to overlook the fact, that the great mass of the people worship the lumps of brass, wood, or mud before which they bow'.[103] Bishop Claughton, surprisingly perhaps, accepted the Buddhist denial of idolatry as a sincere one, but warned of the dangers of physical representations to both Buddhists and (presumably) Catholics:

What I do think is that the sort of devotion or frame of mind which such external objects excite is one of the dangers of all corruptions of true worship, which Buddhism has not escaped, just as in Christianity itself, without imputing idolatry to our brethren, we cannot fail to observe an idolatrous tendency as the result of encouraging the use of external objects to excite reverence, or to assist worship by producing a frame of mind consonant with worship.[104]

Jonathan Titcomb was far less tactful. On the claim that the Buddha is revered not worshipped, he declared, 'This is a very similar defence of Image worship to that offered by the Roman Catholic Church;

and which, if not capable of being called actual Idolatry, comes so near to it that it is very hard to distinguish between the name and the thing.'[105]

BUDDHISM AND CHRISTIANITY

In an age of developing historical consciousness, the similarities between Mahayana Buddhism and Catholicism, between Christian and Buddhist ethics, between the lives of Jesus and the Buddha cried out for explanation. To the Victorians in general, the Catholic missionary theory of satanically inspired imitation was not acceptable. But, as Max Müller asked, 'if the similarities between Buddhism and Christianity must not be explained by the wiles of the Tempter, what remains?'[106] There were, he decided, only two possibilities: 'Either, one of these two religions borrowed from the other, or the similarities between them must be traced back to that common foundation which underlies all religions.'[107] Both of these possibilities were to have numerous supporters throughout the Victorian period.

From the middle of the 1830s, there had been suggestions that the similarities between the traditions were due to the influence of Nestorian Christians on Buddhism. *The Penny Cyclopaedia* in 1836, for example, reminded its readers that at the time Buddhism was introduced into Tibet, Nestorian Christians had ecclesiastical settlements in Tartary; and it pointed out that both French and Italian missionaries had penetrated the Far East.[108] Ernest Eitel suggested that the parallels between the lives of Jesus and the Buddha were to be explained by Buddhism's familiarity with Nestorian Christianity;[109] and his position was cited and endorsed by Agnes Machar.[110] Samuel Kellogg devoted some eighty-three pages to the issue before concluding that, if anything, the parallels were the result of a Syrian church in India and the Nestorians.[111]

The claim that Christianity had influenced Buddhism was not without interest for the Victorians. But it was not a controversial claim. In contrast to this, the alternative claim – that Buddhism had significantly influenced Christianity – was a matter not only of historical interest but of theological importance. To be sure, no-one was especially outraged by the Prinsepses' claim that from India 'Christianity derived its monastic institutions, its forms of ritual, and of church service, its councils or convocations to settle schisms on points of faith, its worship of relics, and working of miracles through them, and much of the discipline, and of the dress of the clergy, even to the shaven heads of the monks and friars.'[112] After all, this was mainly grist for an anti-Catholic mill; and only the Catholic Bishop Bigandet felt moved to argue against such claims.[113] But claims that Buddhism had played an important role in the *origins* of Christianity were a different matter altogether.

As can be seen from the writings of both Bigandet and Charlotte Speir, the view that Christianity had been in part *formed* by Buddhism was a familiar one in the 1850s and 1860s; and they were both concerned to argue against it.[114] But it came into special prominence in the 1880s as a result of the writings of Arthur Lillie and Ernest de Bunsen. Not without good reason, Arthur Lillie was to find little support for his eccentric arguments in support of his claim that Christianity was substantially in debt to Buddhism. In its review of Lillie's *Buddha and Buddhism*, *Literature* made its opinion of Lillie abundantly clear:

> Mr Lillie's fantastic notions about Buddhism have been so often detailed that they would suffer from excessive mustiness but for their vivacity. Some one said of this lively writer many years ago that he possesses 'a suicidal gift of imagination which he lets loose upon every department of learning with a recklessness almost as amusing as it is astounding'. We have not forgotten his 'Early Buddhism' of 1881, and the present little book has all the wild eccentricity, the want of logic, the irrelevance of the former work. We know exactly when to expect the gnostics on the scene, and how Asoka's inscriptions will be treated, and when it is time to bring out the Essenes … The general object of the book, as far as finite minds can grasp it, seems to be to prove that Buddhism (meaning thereby only the northern variety) is the source of Christianity 'at least the Alexandrian portion of it' – of Roman Catholic ritual, of Norwegian cults, and Mexican rites; in short of everything that has the smallest resemblance to it, real or imaginary. In a chapter of coincidence he cites parallels between what he takes to be early Buddhism and the apocryphal gospels, as if these proved anything to the point. At every moment he rushes off on some tangential wild-goose chase, and his master principle is *post hoc ergo propter hoc*. Mr Lillie is a monumental example of wide reading and quick intellect led astray by a lurid fancy. The book is not only useless; it is misleading.[115]

Ernest de Bunsen's *The Angel-Messiah of Buddhists, Essenes, and Christians* was less historically quixotic. But his argument that the doctrine of the Angel-Messiah in Buddhism was transmitted to the

Essenes, and then to Christianity, fared little better.[116] Rhys Davids, not I think guilty of being disingenuous, admitted that de Bunsen was a writer of thoroughly earnest and unbiased mind. But, Davids asserted, 'I will only say that I have carefully considered it throughout with a mind quite open to conviction, and that I can find no evidence whatever of any actual and direct communication of any of these ideas from the East to the West.'[117]

Davids himself, like Müller, was committed to the second of the latter's options, that the similarities between Buddhism and Christianity were to be explained by their shared status as *religions*. Thus, the parallels in ethics are to be explained in terms of the general similarity in the prior intellectual conditions out of which the traditions respectively arose. The issue of parallels between the founders' lives was seen by Davids as being more complex. The legends of the Buddha, he maintained, were formed from the union of the two Indian ideals of the Seer and the King of the Golden Age (the '*Cakkavartin*'), those of Jesus from the concepts of the Messiah and the Logos. There is, consequently, both similarity and difference:

The ideas were in many respects quite different. But in both cases the two overlap one another, run into one another, supplement one another. In both cases the ideas cover the same ground only as far as the different foundations of the two religions will allow ... In each case it seemed perfectly natural and proper that the revered teacher should resemble what they held, and no doubt rightly held, to be noblest and best.[118]

In an era to become increasingly interested in the study of religion without theological premises and progressively more methodologically sophisticated, it was this sort of account that was to carry over into the twentieth century.

A CIVILIZING INFLUENCE?

There was one feature of Buddhism which, in the eyes of many, marked it out as superior to Christianity. This was its tolerance of other religions, and its non-violent methods of evangelization. We need not be surprised that Francis Buchanan, heir to the Enlightenment attitude to toleration in matters religious, should have seen Buddhist toleration as one of its great virtues.[119] But the Victorian endorsement of toleration does deserve emphasis in the light of the fact that we are often inclined to see the nineteenth-century view of other religions exemplified in Bishop Heber's 'The heathen in his blindness / Bows down to wood and stone.' In fact, we can find a quite significant number of positive evaluations of the missionary policy of Buddhism. 'We must not suppose', *The Prospective Review* for 1850 pointed out, 'that the spread of Buddhism was accompanied with such wars as those of Mahomet, or the bloody persecutions of the Christians'.[120] The same theme reappeared regularly for the remainder of the century. Edward Neale, for example, observed in 1860 that the annals of Buddhism were marked by a singular spirit of toleration.[121] The *Journal of Sacred Literature* for 1865 declared Buddhism illogical and erroneous in many of its doctrines, but, it declared, 'it has at least not disgraced itself by resorting to the machinery of inquisitorial torture to put down other forms of worship, or to establish its own'.[122] James Freeman Clarke agreed that, in this respect, Buddhism could teach Christianity a lesson: 'The Buddhists have founded no Inquisition; they have combined the zeal which converted kingdoms with a toleration almost inexplicable to our Western experience.'[123] And the *Dublin University Review* for 1873 maintained that it was the most tolerant of all religions: 'Its doctrines have never been enforced by persecution; its records have no Torquemada; it has never lighted Smithfield fires for heretics, nor filled dungeons with its opponents. Its disciples ... have never condemned to everlasting torment those who refused to receive it.'[124]

But if the fact of Buddhist tolerance seemed undeniable, other less eirenic interpretations could be placed upon it. Philosinensis, for instance, in 1834 condemned its tolerance as mere opportunism.[125] James Tennent in 1850 saw Buddhist tolerance arising from 'the strength of its self-righteousness';[126] while, by contrast, Archibald Scott described it as the result of Buddhism's lack of certainty.[127] John Kesson and Samuel Kellogg saw tolerance as indicative of indifference to religious truth, and this was perhaps the most popular of all criticisms of Buddhist tolerance. To Samuel Kellogg, for instance, Buddhist tolerance was 'the tolerance of that indifference to truth which comes to him who has become convinced that life itself is a falsehood and a mockery ...'[128] Moreover, the equation of tolerance and indifference allowed some authors to create a theological virtue out of historical necessity. William Bryant saw Christianity's intolerance as enlightened: 'Christianity is, beyond question, an intolerant faith, and most of all is it intolerant as against the ferocity of mere blind intolerance; just as, in its character of the religion of Reason, it must even repudiate the equally blind tolerance which, through mere complaisance, permits all opinions alike to pass unchallenged.'[129]

The question of Buddhist toleration was also connected to the broader issue of the effects of Buddhism in general upon those who adopted it. As early as 1830, John Crawfurd had argued that among Asiatic nations, those which professed Buddhism were of secondary rank only, not one of them having ever attained the first rank in arts or arms. Indeed, he went on to argue, the abhorrence of shedding blood in Buddhism 'has had no influence whatever in elevating and humanizing the character of its votaries: for the history of the Singalese, the Burmans, the Peguans, and Siamese abounds in acts of the utmost cruelty and ferocity ...'[130] But Crawfurd's was a minority view. Most were inclined rather to credit Buddhism with having had a significant civilizing influence. Edward Upham, for example, saw Buddhism as the cause of 'the rapid and remarkable progress of the Singhalese in every branch of national improvement'.[131] Eduard Roer, in 1845, maintained that it was undeniable that 'a great part of mankind were humanized by it, and that for the civilization of central and western Asia it has done the same as Christianity has for the barbarians of Europe'.[132] William Knighton and James Alwis saw it as having had a humanizing and civilizing influence throughout Asia.[133] Even Charles Hardwick, albeit with a hint of muscular Christianity, could maintain that, much as the Buddhist virtues of meekness, resignation, equanimity under suffering, and forgiveness of injuries 'are found to differ from the corresponding virtues of the Christian, and symptomatic as they often are of womanly, instead of manly and heroic qualities, they could scarcely fail to benefit a multitude of savage tribes to which they were propounded'.[134] And both Barthélemy St Hilaire and Samuel Kellogg saw Buddhism as an improvement on what had preceded it – from them, high praise indeed![135]

During the couse of this chapter, we have seen that there was, in the Victorian interpretation of Buddhism in practice, a polarity of assimilation and rejection that was determined by various aspects of Victorian culture. Predominant amongst these was that most characteristic aspect of Victorian religion – its emphasis on activity. As Owen Chadwick has pointed out, the Victorians were 'servants of God, under his eye, and their hands found plenty to do in his cause …'[136] Consequently, it was the active side of Buddhism, its ethics especially, that the Victorians were particularly interested in, were most easily able to assimilate, and in general to endorse. But conversely, those parts of Buddhism redolent of the passive contemplative religious life and not apparently conducive to a benevolent activism were rejected. Monasticism, and its accompaniments, found little support. Moreover, wariness about anything analogous to Catholicism militated against assimilation of much Buddhist practice. The relationship between Buddhist doctrine and Buddhist morality also caused problems for the Victorians. For Buddhist morality was tainted for many because of its intimate connection to unassimilable Buddhist doctrines. The image of moral precept versus moral practice also influenced the Victorian polarity of assimilation and rejection. In spite of the general opinion that Buddhism had been a benevolent influence in the East, the ideology of the West's superiority over the East, and the necessity of maintaining its cultural hegemony, often resulted in assertions of the Buddhist East's inability to put into practice that which its founder had so eloquently preached.

6

'The heathen in his blindness'?

CHRISTIAN TRUTH VERSUS BUDDHIST FALSEHOOD

Throughout the course of this study we have seen Victorian interpretations of Buddhism evidencing a polarity of assimilation and rejection: assimilating Buddhism in so far as it correlates with normative Victorian ideas and values; rejecting Buddhism in so far as it is incommensurable with these. To this extent, the analysis of the Victorian view of Buddhism simply *is* an analysis of the broad range of evaluations of it. Be that as it may, it is fruitful to concentrate briefly on the specific understandings which Victorians had of the truth and value of Buddhism and, in particular, how they measured it against what was to them in general the final criterion of religious truth and value – that is, their own understanding of the Christian tradition.

As is to be expected from what we have seen thus far, there are a variety of evaluations of Buddhism ranging from complete rejection of its religious truth and value to virtual acceptance of it as a necessary Eastern preliminary to the Christian tradition.

Certainly there is throughout the Victorian period no unified evaluation of it. Indeed, ambivalent and various evaluations of it had accumulated by the middle of the century. In 1854, for example, John Kesson observed that, 'By many it has been praised as a most enlightened form of idolatry, and superior in its religious spirit to either Confucianism or Taoism. Others have decried Buddhism as the very doctrine of devils.'[1] In part, of course, this was the result of the fact that, in the nineteenth century as in most other centuries since Christ, there was a range of Christian attitudes to other religions. In part, too, at least in the middle of the nineteenth century, this diversity of opinion was the consequence of uncertainty about the main features of Buddhism. As *The Christian Remembrancer* for 1858 remarked, readers of works on Buddhism would find themselves puzzled by the extraordinary difference of opinion about its teaching. For, it went on to point out, 'Mr Turnour considers it in the light of a revelation; Mr Hodgson speaks of it as a deification of human reason; Lassen finds no clear intimation of a Deity in the primitive Sutras, and ... M. Cousin has described it as *un nihilisme absolu.*'[2]

Still, one constantly reiterated theme in the evaluation of Buddhism was that of the irredeemably false nature of Buddhism in contrast to Christian truth. This was an assessment that occurred among those least informed about it, such as Charles Gutzlaff and Edward Upham. But it was present too among those most informed, such as Spence Hardy and Monier-Williams. It occurred not only among those with acquaintance with Chinese Buddhism but also among those familiar with Pali Buddhism. Edward Upham, for example, declared that every point in the moral and religious code of Buddhism demonstrates 'the paramount duty we owe to the Supreme Being, to endeavour to become the humble instruments of spreading his sacred word, and diffusing the light of his truth in substitution for the dreams and delusions of such a system'.[3] Philosinensis, with evangelical fervour, inquired in 1834, 'When, O when will the darkness which for so many centuries has enveloped China, be penetrated by the light of divine truth, and the only and true God be adored!'[4] Gutzlaff simply dismissed it as nonsense and absurdities.[5] And Kesson maintained that Gutzlaff and other writers had confirmed that the greater part of the Buddhist texts 'contain nothing but absolute absurdities and reveries, unintelligible to the most learned of its votaries'.[6] Even Gogerly felt obliged, in 1838, to apologize for his interest in it by claiming that his intent in unveiling the secret doctrines of Buddhism was 'to shew concerning its author and supporters "that they were vain in their imaginations, that their foolish hearts were darkened, and that professing themselves to be wise they became fools"'.[7]

The harsh attitude of the Protestant missionaries to Ceylon was, of course, influenced by what they perceived as the totally inappropriate support of the British Government for Buddhism, as well as by their own sense of the exclusive truth of Christianity. The *London Quarterly Review* for 1854 – 5 was eloquent testimony, not only to the natural sense which many held of the absolute truth of Christianity, but also to the necessary connexion which many felt to exist between Britain's colonial interests and the spread of the Christian faith. The British flag *was* a *Christian* emblem:

How many glorious associations are suggested by the British flag! It is the flag under which a Wellington conquered, and a Nelson died ... It tells us of Europe delivered, of America founded, of India subdued. It speaks of freedom for the sons of Africa; and its appearance has often kindled hope in the despairing heart of the manacled Negro, borne in his floating prison across the Atlantic's waves; ... Pity it is, that it should ever mingle thoughts of sadness with thrills of joy, – that it should ever call upon the British Christian to weep, whilst it makes the British patriot rejoice. Yet, as it is displayed over the mountain capital of Ceylon, it tells us of principle sacrificed, of religion dishonoured, of atheism perpetuated, of idolatry countenanced, and of a false and wide-spread superstition protected and maintained.[8]

Undoubtedly, the works of Spence Hardy were influential in propagating the view, not only that it was 'the bounden duty of the government of the country, from its possession of the Truth, to discountenance the system [Buddhism] by every legitimate means',[9] but also that Christianity and Buddhism were involved in a conflict the only victor in which could be the former:

There can be no doubt as to the result of the contest now carried on; for although it may be prolonged and severe, it must end in the total discomfiture of those who have arisen against the Lord and his Christ, and in the renunciation of the atheist creed that now mars the happiness, and stays the enlightenment, of so many of the dwellers in Lanká ...[10]

Spence Hardy's words found a sympathetic response in the writings of Monier-Williams. Of all the scholarly interpretations of Buddhism, his were the most scathing in their rejection of Buddhism's claims to religious truth and value. To be sure, he did admit that, at one time, he was attracted by the view that non-Christian religions were a part of the evolution of man's religious instincts and aspirations, and that Christianity was the fulfilment of them all. But he came, none the less, to reject such a view:

I contend ... that a limp, flabby jelly-fish kind of tolerance is utterly incompatible with the nerve, fibre, and backbone that ought to characterise a manly Christian. I maintain that a Christian's character ought to be exactly what the Christian's Bible intends it to be ... Vigour and manhood breathe in every page. It is downright and straightforward, bold and fearless, rigid and uncompromising. It tells you and me to be either hot or cold ... Only one Name is given among men whereby we may be saved. No other name, no other Saviour, more suited to India, to Persia, to China, to Arabia, is ever mentioned – is ever hinted at.[11]

DIVINE TRUTH AND HUMAN TRUTH

Monier-Williams was not without his supporters. In its review of his *Buddhism, The Church Quarterly Review*, for example, declared that Christianity is bound up with a body of definite truth, and consequently, 'it is at war with that which contravenes this truth'.[12] But the view that it was a matter of Christian truth versus Buddhist falsehood was, just as often, rejected. James Freeman Clarke argued that it was inappropriate to class Buddhism with debasing superstitions because the strength of conviction which inspired its teachers 'must have come from the sight of truth, not the belief in error'.[13] *Chambers's Encyclopaedia* made a plea for the empathetic study of Buddhism in contrast to caricatures of it that gave prominence to the extravagances and inconceivable puerilities and absurdities with which, it claimed, the system had been overloaded: 'It is only too common for Christian writers to treat of heathen religions in such fashion. The only fair – the only *true* account of any religion, is that which enables the reader to conceive how human beings may have come to believe it and live by it.'[14] And George Cobbold gave theological reasons for the rejection of the claim that only Christians were saved:

That men, women, and little children, who are distinguished by so many good qualities, and who – with, as we believe, such immeasurably inferior opportunities – present, in many points, so favourable a contrast to ourselves, should be condemned to a future of hopeless and unending misery, for not believing that of which, it may be, they have not even heard, or heard only in crude, distorted statement – can any man *really* think this, who recognizes the providence of a Father of Love; nay, I will dare to say, of a Deity of bare justice? And yet language thus fearfully misrepresenting the Faith of Christ is still used by some who are called by His name; and that it is used is known by the people of Japan.[15]

Many interpreters felt compelled to admit an admiration of Buddhism in spite of their inclinations to the contrary. It generally fared best of all the non-Christian religions. William Knighton saw

Buddhism as approaching as near to Christianity as was possible for a merely human system to come. It lacked the impress of divinity, but 'in its ethics it is an embodiment of the spirit of Christianity'.[16] And Archibald Scott declared that no other non-Christian religion could compare with it 'in respect of its ethical code, its spirit of toleration and gentleness, and its beneficent influence upon many wild populations that have embraced it'.[17] To be sure, as we have seen, Knighton and Scott were sympathetic to it. But even those most critical admitted its superiority to other non-Christian religions. Michael Culbertson, for example, admitted that, 'this system of idolatry contains less that is revolting, and in its morality departs less from the truth, than any other of the false religions that have prevailed among the heathen'.[18] Even Bishop Claughton was of the opinion that there was 'nothing out of Christianity equal to it, still less *superior*';[19] and Jonathan Titcomb considered Buddhism the finest system of heathenism ever devised by man, although not to be placed on a level with the Christian gospel.[20]

There was, then, the conviction that, as a religion created by man, if not by God, Buddhism was supreme. If there was no divine revelation within it, there was none the less much of human truth and value. *The Westminster Review* for 1858 observed that Buddhists, in spite of their atheism, have 'instinctively acknowledged virtue, and in honouring that which is good and beneficent, have, without knowing it, honoured him who is its author: though they have worshipped no Creator and adored no Providence, they have confessed the Infinite God and its manifestation in the human heart'.[21] And it was certain that Buddhists would be among the saved.[22] Of a Tibetan summary of Buddhism, the Prinsepses remarked, 'What is this but Christianity, wanting only the name of Christ as its preacher, and the Mosaic faith for its antecedent?'[23] To *The Westminster Review* of 1878, the Buddha, like many other virtuous pagans, was to be considered an anonymous Christian:

In all times and in all places men have lived pure and holy lives, and have shown themselves Christians even 'before Christ came in the flesh'. Buddha, whose teaching approaches nearer than does that of any other founder of a religion to the teaching of Christ, has won, by the attractive beauty of his character, the unconscious homage of Christendom. He has been placed in the golden roll of Christian saints [i.e. St Josaphat] ... Worthily does he stand among 'the sons of God who were righteous in their lives'.[24]

136

From a number of writers on Buddhism, one sometimes gets the clear impression that it was their implicit recognition that Buddhism was, of all religions, the one most comparable with Christianity that necessitated a more strident rejection of it. *The Church Quarterly Review* for 1882, for instance, maintained that, although the Christian ought to recognize with the fullest sympathy whatever is of excellence in other religions, 'he should at the same time stoutly assert that true Christianity alone sums up all the truths spiritual or moral that exist dispersedly elsewhere, that it alone presents them in fitting mutual proportion, and knows the secret of reconciling the most exalted spiritual aspirations and conceptions with the most energetic practical life'.[25] Samuel Kellogg admitted that truth may be found in Buddhism as in all religions, that all religions had a role in the divine purpose. But he strenuously denied their divine origin: 'we deny that this involves the affirmation of *supernatural* revelation in each case. We deny that these facts give us the slightest right to speak of all as if they were, in the same sense as Christianity, all alike revelations from God!'[26]

BUDDHISM AS 'PRAEPARATIO EVANGELICA'

Others were to have much less difficulty than Samuel Kellogg in finding in Buddhism a divine revelation. As early as 1850, *The Prospective Review* suggested that it was not affection for Christianity but jealousy of other religions that provoked the belief in the exclusive truth of Christianity. It argued, on the contrary, that because there is a light which lights every man that comes into the world, it is 'No wonder then it shines in various quarters of the world.'[27] To Frederick Maurice, it was animated by an Eternal Verity;[28] while to George Grant, through the inspiration of the Divine Spirit, the Buddha had often an insight into the truth.[29] According to Thomas Berry, although God revealed himself fully in Christ, 'He did not prove Himself forgetful of the nations that had strayed away from truth and knowledge.'[30] Although Bishop Copleston's *Buddhism* was rightly criticized by Joseph Carpenter as having an air of patronage about it 'which painfully suggests the apron and the lawn sleeves',[31] Copleston was none the less sensitive to the revelatory ambience of the Buddhist tradition:

Even in the defects and errors which distress him, the Christian sees the traces of longings and instincts, exaggerated here or misdirected, yet implanted by that Heavenly Father, from Whom His children have been so far estranged; while in many a noble aspiration or passage of beauty and truth he thankfully adores the teaching of that Divine Word, who has ever been everywhere the light of the world, and of that Holy Spirit who has never ceased to move, with life-giving influence, over the chords of human thought.[32]

It was but a short step from conceiving of Buddhism as revelatory to conceiving of it as part of God's plan of salvation, more specifically, as a divinely ordained preparation for the Christian gospel. Samuel Beal, for example, saw both Buddhism and Confucianism as preparing the peoples of India and China for the reception of a higher truth.[33] Similarly, William Martin saw the theory and practice of Buddhism as preparing the Chinese for Christianity as Greek philosophy had provided a more perfect vehicle for the Christian fulfilment of Judaism.[34] J. Dyer Ball waxed prophetic:

In the inscrutable wisdom of God the Chinese were to pass through an evolutionary stage, to test the lower and using it as a stepping stone to higher, to better things, discard the dead past for a living present, or happy future, the first streaks of the early dawn of which our eyes are now privileged to see.[35]

In fine, whether rejected or assimilated, as a preparation for the Christian fullness of revelation, Buddhism considered as a totality was weighed in the scales of Christianity. It was the standard against which all the religions were measured. And it is hardly surprising that, weighed against what was considered to be God's last word, the other religions were found wanting. On principle, they could not but fall short. But if the scales of judgement were tipped against all the religions, to a greater or lesser extent, they were tipped least against Buddhism. For however it was evaluated, whether as false, or as containing human truth and value, or as the bearer of divine revelation, for the Victorians it was the religion most likely to approximate to the Christian standard.

138

Conclusion

The varying Victorian evaluations of Buddhism which I examined in the previous chapter are of particular interest, and for at least two reasons. In the first place, they give us a much richer picture of the development during the nineteenth century of a secularist and pluralist understanding of religion, and in particular of Christianity as one religious tradition among many. Broadly speaking, during the Victorian period, there developed the assumption that human nature is essentially secular, and therefore, that religions – Christianity, Buddhism, Islam, Hinduism – are essentially opposing addenda, the value and truth of each of which merit analysis and argument.

But, in the second place, that there were such varying evaluations of Buddhism is of interest in the light of the fact that, as I have tried to suggest, at the beginning of the nineteenth century the Buddhist tradition did not exist as an object of discourse in the West. In the Western imagination, Buddhism is the most recent of the major world religions, its construction and interpretation reaching back a mere century and a half.

Above all, as I have argued, Buddhism was reified as a textual object. By the middle of the Victorian period, Buddhism was seen as essentially constituted by its textuality, and it was the Buddhism thus constructed and thus interpreted that was the criterion against which its manifestations in the 'Orient' were measured, and generally, as we have seen, found wanting. A crucial product of this process of the textualization of Buddhism was the emergence of the historical Buddha. By the middle of the Victorian period, the Buddha had emerged from the wings of myth and entered the historical stage.

No longer identified with the ancient gods, distinct from the Hindu account of him, and his mythical predecessors, the Buddha was a human figure – one to be compared not with the gods but with other historical personalities, and one to be interpreted in the light of the Victorian ideal of humanity.

Clearly, there were enormously diverse judgements on the historical Buddha, just as there were various judgements on the truth and value of Buddhist precept and practice. But there is a unity in the Victorian interpretation of Buddhism which may be discerned beneath the often conflicting intellectual judgements and attitudes. The unifying feature is the sublime certainty with which the Victorians dealt with the material at their disposal. What strikes the reader of Victorian accounts of Buddhism is the sense of sovereign confidence with which – however they assimilated or rejected it – they discussed, summarized, analysed, and evaluated it. However ideologically uncertain they were at the level of conscious reflection, they saw themselves as possessing the criteria upon which the judgement of the religious, social, and cultural value, not only of Buddhism but, of the East as a whole could be made.

It was the Victorians who developed the discourse within which Buddhism was circumscribed, who deemed it a worthy focus of Western attention; it was they who brought forth the network of texts within which Buddhism was located. And it was they who determined the framework in which Buddhism was imaginatively constructed, not only for themselves, but also in the final analysis for the East itself.

In part, at least, this was an aspect of the Western creation of two qualitatively different modes of being human, the oriental and the occidental, the latter of which was essentially other, and which was in most instances perceived as inferior. This fundamental mode of organizing the East provided as we have seen, a conceptual filter through which acceptable aspects of Buddhism could be endorsed, unacceptable ones rejected.

But Buddhism was not only constructed and interpreted through Western images of the Oriental Mind. Its interpretation was influenced by many concerns of the Victorian age, and it too played a role in the shaping of nineteenth-century ideals. Discourse about Buddhism reflected and influenced Victorian discussions of creation and cosmology, of the Bible and biology, of theism and atheism, of annihilation and immortality, and of the essence of human nature. It brought into sharper focus the relation of morality and its deserts, of Christian precept and Christian practice, of monastic quietism and worldly activism, of Catholicism and Protestantism, and of religion and culture. The Victorian world in all its diversity, confident of its cultural hegemony, was incorporated, and crucially so, in its interpretation of Buddhism.

Notes

INTRODUCTION

1. *Trübner's Record*, p.90.
2. Clausen, 'Victorian Buddhism', pp.13–14. See also Wright, *Interpreter of Buddhism*. After the death of Tennyson, Queen Victoria proposed Arnold for the Laureate. Opposed by Gladstone, the decision was postponed. It was later awarded to Alfred Austin.
3. Humphreys, *The Development of Buddhism*, p.10.
4. Cobbold, *Religion in Japan*, p.32. For the American response, see Kellogg, *The Light of Asia*; and Wilkinson, *Edwin Arnold*.
5. Collins, 'Buddhism, and "The Light of Asia"', p.154.
6. Ibid., p.177.
7. Ibid., pp.178–9. For other criticisms of Arnold, see Bryant, 'Buddhism and Christianity', pp.374–5; Martin, 'Is Buddhism a Preparation', p.195; Sandberg, 'Philosophical Buddhism', pp.270–1; *The Quarterly Review*, 1890, p.330; Berry, *Christianity and Buddhism*, p.29.
8. Müller, 'Lecture on Buddhist Nihilism', p.132.
9. *The Quarterly Review*, 1890, p.318. The author was in fact Reginald S. Copleston, from 1875 bishop of Colombo. See *Wellesley Index*, I:771.
10. *London Quarterly Review*, 1888–9, pp.343–4.
11. Monier-Williams, 'Literary Admirers of Buddhism', p.215. For other accounts of the Western admiration for Buddhism, see, for example, *The Saturday Review*, 1884, p.248; Colinet, 'Recent Works on Primitive Buddhism', p.121; Sandberg, 'Philosophical Buddhism', pp.256–7; Strong, 'The Revival of Buddhism', p.272; Ellinwood, *Oriental Religions and Christianity*, pp.153–8.
12. Apart from Clausen, 'Victorian Buddhism', Brear, 'Early Assumptions', and parts of Welbon, *The Buddhist Nirvāna*, there is virtually no recent work on Victorian Buddhism. I am indebted to all the above for much early stimulation. Even in the history of Western scholarship

on Buddhism, there are remarkably few studies. See de Jong, 'A Brief History of Buddhist Studies', pp. 55–6.

13. Said, *Orientalism*, pp. 21–2.

1 THE DISCOVERY OF BUDDHISM

1. The French equivalent of the term 'Buddhism' did not appear in the French literature until the 1820s.
2. See especially, de Lubac, *La Rencontre du Bouddhisme*, Chs. 1 and 2.
3. De la Loubère, *A New Historical Relation*, p. 10.
4. Ibid., p. 134.
5. Chambers, 'Some Account of the Sculptures and Ruins', pp. 161–2.
6. Joinville, 'On the Religion and Manners', p. 415.
7. Mahony, 'On *Singhala*, or *Ceylon*', p. 38.
8. *The English Encyclopaedia*, 1802, II:146.
9. *Encyclopaedia Perthensis*, 1807, IV:462; *Encyclopaedia Britannica*, 1810, IV:778; and 1817, IV:778; *Pantologia*, 1813, II:n.p. *The London Encyclopaedia*, 1829:644.
10. Gutzlaff, 'Journal of a Residence', p. 274. The reactions to Gutzlaff were mixed. Paul Carus, *Buddhism and its Christian Critics*, p. 271, characterized him as an illiterate man, and described his *China Opened* as 'full of the grossest errors'. See also Hibbert, *The Dragon Wakes*, p. 375, n. 26. In contrast, the *Scottish Pilot* called him 'a wonderful man, a heroic Christian, and a zealous philanthropist'. See Allibone, *A Critical Dictionary*, p. 751.
11. Le Comte, *Memoirs*, pp. 320–1.
12. Grosier, *A General Description of China*, II:217. 'Talapoin' is in fact of Ceylonese, and 'Bonze' of Portuguese derivation.
13. Symes, *An Account*, II:34.
14. Sangermano, *A Description of the Burmese Empire*, p. 110.
15. See, for example, *The Edinburgh Review*, 1803, p. 27; and 1807, p. 97; Moor, *The Hindu Pantheon*, p. 240; *The Edinburgh Review*, 1813–14, p. 406.
16. Ward, *History, Literature, and Religion of the Hindoos*, II:206–7.
17. Mill, *The History of British India*, 1817, I:223.
18. Davy, *An Account of the Interior of Ceylon*, p. 172. See also Ersch and Gruber, 'Buddha, Buddhaismus,' p. 330; Erskine, 'Observations on the Remains', p. 495.
19. Francklin, *Researches*, p. 8.
20. Crawfurd, *Journal of an Embassy*, II:92.
21. *The Penny Cyclopaedia*, 1836, p. 526.
22. *New Englander*, 1845, pp. 182–3.
23. Edkins, 'Notices of Buddhism in China'.
24. Buchanan, 'On the Religion', p. 163.

25. Monier-Williams, *Buddhism*, p. 15.
26. Stewart, 'An Account of the Kingdom of Thibet', pp. 476–7.
27. Percival, *An Account of the Island of Ceylon*, p. 141.
28. Ibid.
29. Chambers, 'Some Account of the Scriptures and Ruins', p. 164.
30. Crawfurd, *History of the Indian Archipelago*, II:222.
31. Quoted by *Monthly Review*, 1829, pp. 590–1. George Turnour was highly critical. After pointing out a number of errors in Upham's work, he concluded, 'It is scarcely possible for a person, not familiar with the subject, to conceive the extent of the absurdities involved in these, and other similar passages. It is no burlesque to say, that they would be received, by a Ceylonese buddhist, with feelings akin to those with which an Englishman would read a work, written by an Indian, professedly for the purpose of illustrating the history of Christianity to his countrymen, which stated, – that England was the scene of the birth of our Saviour; that his ascension took place from Derby peak, and that Salisbury cathedral stood on Westminster abbey.' *The Mahawanso*, p. xx.
32. Turnour, *The Mahawanso*, p. xxii.
33. Wilford, 'An Essay on the Sacred Isles', p. 265.
34. See ibid., pp. 247–65.
35. *New Englander*, 1845, pp. 244–5. See also Faber, *The Origin of Pagan Idolatry*, I:392–401.
36. Davy, *An Account of the Interior of Ceylon*, p. 170.
37. Kennedy, *Researches*, p. 249.
38. Erskine, 'Observations on the Remains', p. 503.
39. Symes, *An Account*, II:33. See also *The Encyclopaedia Edinensis*, 1827, I:636.
40. *Oriental Herald*, 1829, p. 94.
41. *Encyclopaedia Britannica*, 1842, V:636.
42. *The Encyclopaedia Britannica*, 1854, IV:723.
43. *Encyclopaedia Britannica*, 1842, V:637. See also *The Encyclopaedia Britannica*, 1854, IV:724.
44. Bird, *Historical Researches*, pp. 66–7.
45. Jones, 'On the Chronology of the Hindus', p. 123.
46. Creuzer, *Symbolik und Mythologie*, pp. 190–1.
47. Faber, *The Origin of Pagan Idolatry*, II:328–9.
48. Erskine, 'Observations on the Remains', pp. 528–9.
49. Quoted by *The Calcutta Review*, 1845, p. 247.
50. Ibid., p. 248.
51. Crawfurd, *Journal of an Embassy*, II:81–2.
52. Kennedy, *Researches*, p. 260.
53. Forbes, 'Notes on the Buddhas', p. 328.

54. Turnour, *The Mahawanso*, pp. li–lii.
55. Knighton, *The History of Ceylon*, p. 66.
56. Sirr, *Ceylon and the Cingalese*, pp. 42–3.
57. Ibid., p. 61.
58. Low, 'General Observations', p. 111.
59. Ibid., pp. 117–18.
60. Cunningham, *The Bhilsa Topes*, p. x.
61. Jones, 'A Supplement to the Essay', p. 401.
62. See Marshall, *The British Discovery of Hinduism*, p. 257.
63. Percival, *An Account of the Island of Ceylon*, p. 145.
64. Moor, *The Hindu Pantheon*, p. 231.
65. Ibid., p. 237.
66. Abel-Rémusat, 'Note sur quelques Epithètes', pp. 625–33.
67. Davy, *An Account of the Interior of Ceylon*, p. 171.
68. Ibid., p. 171. See also Ward, *History, Literature, and Religion of the Hindoos*, II:216.
69. Crawfurd, *History of the Indian Archipelago*, II:209.
70. Cox, *Journal of a Residence*, pp. 415–16.
71. Francklin, *Researches*, p. 72. See also *Asiatic Journal and Monthly Register*, 1827, p. 252, for a similar view.
72. Philosinensis, 'Remarks on Buddhism', p. 221.
73. Gutzlaff, 'Remarks on the Present State of Buddhism', p. 79. But cf. *Allgemeine Deutsche Real-Encyclopädie*, 1833, II:297–8; and *The National Cyclopaedia*, 1847, III:903.
74. *Oriental Herald*, 1829, p. 94. See also Marshall, *The British Discovery of Hinduism*, p. 16.
75. *The Calcutta Review*, 1845, p. 252.
76. Low, 'General Observations', p. 95.
77. Ibid., p. 118.
78. Bird, *Historical Researches*, p. iii.
79. Salisbury, 'Memoir', p. 82.
80. See Tennent, *Christianity in Ceylon*, pp. 197–8.
81. Kaempfer, *The History of Japan*, II:56.
82. These were: a Burmese cosmography extracted from a book by a 'Zarado' or master of the Emperor; the 'maharazaven', or great history of the kings; and the 'Kiam', the classical writings of the Burmese; see Cardinal Wiseman, Preface to Sangermano, *A Description of the Burmese Empire*.
83. Buchanan, 'On the Religion', pp. 233–4.
84. Davy, *An Account of the Interior of Ceylon*, p. 172. See also Ersch and Gruber, 'Buddha, Buddhaismus', p. 333.
85. Hodgson, 'Quotations from Original Sanskrit Authorities', I:66–7.
86. Burnouf, *Introduction*, p. 9.

87. *The Penny Cyclopaedia*, 1836, p. 526. The same passage appeared eleven years later in *The National Cyclopaedia*, 1847, III:903. See also *Allgemeine Deutsche Real-Encyclopädie*, 1843, III:8; *Chambers's Encyclopaedia*, 1861, II:403.
88. *Chambers's Encyclopaedia*, 1874, II:403. See also Müller, 'The Meaning of Nirvana', p. 281.
89. Roer, review of Burnouf, *Introduction*, p. 784.
90. Davids, 'Buddhism', IV:424 – 5, 439; see de Jong, 'A Brief History of Buddhist Studies', for the most comprehensive account of the editing and publishing of Buddhist sources during the nineteenth century.
91. Quoted by de Jong, 'A Brief History of Buddhist Studies', I:71.
92. See ibid.
93. Burnouf and Lassen, *Essai sur le Pali*, p. 146.
94. *Allgemeine Deutsche Real-Encyclopädie*, 1833, II:297; 1843, III:8; 1851, III:405; and 1864, III:830.
95. *The Penny Cyclopaedia*, 1836, p. 530.
96. Turnour, *The Mahawanso*, p. cix.
97. Bird, *Historical Researches*, p. 38.
98. Salisbury, 'M. Burnouf', p. 291. See also *The National Cyclopaedia*, 1847, III:907.
99. Knighton, *Forest Life in Ceylon*, II:25.
100. Wilson, 'On Buddha and Buddhism', p. 241.
101. Childers, *A Dictionary of the Pali Language*, pp. xi – xii. See also p. xi, n. 3. This was an issue that was to become increasingly complex with the increase of text-critical studies in the 1880s, and one not capable of a simple resolution.
102. Joinville, 'On the Religion and Manners', p. 400.
103. Ibid., p. 402.
104. Ibid., p. 404.
105. *The Edinburgh Review*, 1807, pp. 302 – 3.
106. See Faber, *The Origin of Pagan Idolatry*, I:86 – 7; II:234, 330.
107. Coleman, *The Mythology of the Hindus*, pp. 188 – 9.
108. *The Penny Cyclopaedia*, 1836, p. 527.
109. *The Calcutta Review*, 1845, p. 249.
110. Ibid., p. 250.
111. Ibid., p. 249.
112. Ibid., p. 250.
113. Tennent, *Christianity in Ceylon*, p. 197.
114. Knighton, *The History of Ceylon*, p. 337.
115. Roer, review of Burnouf, *Introduction*, p. 786.
116. Ibid., p. 785.
117. Low, 'General Observations', p. 89.
118. *The Christian Remembrancer*, 1858, p. 119.

2 BUDDHISM AND THE 'ORIENTAL MIND'

1. Heyck, *The Transformation of Intellectual Life*, p. 28. See also Altick, *The English Common Reader*, Ch. 13.
2. Oldenberg, *Buddha: His Life, His Doctrine, His Order*.
3. Barthélemy St Hilaire, *The Buddha and His Religion*.
4. Heyck, *The Transformation of Intellectual Life*, p. 33.
5. Quoted in Houghton, *The Victorian Frame of Mind*, p. 105.
6. Ibid., p. 6.
7. See Altick, *The English Common Reader*, Ch. 5; Scott, 'The Business of Belief', pp. 213 – 24; Best, *Mid-Victorian Britain*, p. 226. Although there was a steady decline in the amount of religious publishing throughout the century, even at its end, it still formed a significant percentage of all books published.
8. *The Times*, 12 April 1886, p. 12.
9. Houghton, *The Victorian Frame of Mind*, p. 128.
10. On the Theosophical movement, see Campbell, *Ancient Wisdom Revived*. For a lively account of Spiritualism, see Brandon, *The Spiritualists*. The first British Buddhist to become a monk was Charles Bennett (Ananda Metteyya). Decisively influenced by Arnold's *The Light of Asia*, which he first read in 1890, he was ordained as a monk in Burma in 1902. See Malalasekera, *Encyclopaedia of Buddhism*, I: 539 – 42. I have not dealt with the Esoteric Buddhism of Madame Blavatsky and her English disciple, Alfred Sinnett. Esoteric, it may have been. Buddhism, it certainly was not, at least in the eyes of most late nineteenth-century interpreters of Buddhism.
11. See Humphreys, *The Development of Buddhism*, p. 18. Perhaps the most renowned British Buddhist of this century, Humphreys had a background in Blavatsky's Theosophy. As late as 1968, he wrote, 'I am yet unshaken in my view that the Theosophy of H. P. Blavatsky is an exposition of an Ancient Wisdom-Religion which antedates all known religions and that Buddhism is the noblest and least-defiled of the many branches of the undying parent tree.' *Sixty Years of Buddhism*, p. 18.
12. Edkins, 'Notices of Buddhism in China'.
13. Cunningham, *The Bhilsa Topes*, p. 2.
14. Feudge, 'The Mammouth Religion', p. 354.
15. Beal, *Buddhism in China*, p. 228.
16. Scott, *Buddhism and Christianity*, p. 338. See also p. 335.
17. *The Christian Remembrancer*, 1858, p. 122.
18. Titcomb, *Short Chapters on Buddhism*, p. 182. See also p. 26.
19. *London Quarterly Review*, 1888 – 9, p. 336.
20. *Journal of Sacred Literature*, 1865, p. 293.
21. Bigandet, *The Life, or Legend of Gaudama*, p. 298.

22. Jersey, 'Buddhism and Christianity', p.588.
23. Collins, 'Buddhism, and "The Light of Asia"', p.181. See also Frazer, *A Literary History of India*, pp.133 – 4.
24. Grant, *The Religions of the World*, pp.147 – 8.
25. Quoted by Hardy, *The British Government and the Idolatry of Ceylon*, pp.33 – 4.
26. *London Quarterly Review*, 1888 – 9, p.345. See also *British Quarterly Review*, 1884, p.175.
27. Scott, *Buddhism and Christianity*, pp.336 – 7.
28. Crawfurd, *Journal of an Embassy*, II:97.
29. Barthélemy St Hilaire, *The Buddha and his Religion*, p.152.
30. Hardy, *The British Government and the Idolatry of Ceylon*, pp.45 – 6.
31. Ibid., p.6.
32. *London Quarterly Review*, 1854 – 5, p.437.
33. Baker, *Eight Years in Ceylon*, p.313.
34. Loubère, *A New Historical Relation*, p.64.
35. Ibid., p.64.
36. Ibid., p.90.
37. See especially Glacken, *Traces on the Rhodian Shore*, Pts. 3 and 4.
38. Davy, *An Account of the Interior of Ceylon*, p.218. See also p.141.
39. Barthélemy St Hilaire, *The Buddha and His Religion*, pp.13 – 14.
40. Copleston, *Buddhism*, p.248.
41. Griffin, 'The Burman', p.661.
42. Bryant, 'Buddhism and Christianity', p.258.
43. Ibid., p.258.
44. Oldenberg, *Buddha: His Life, His Doctrine, His Order*, pp.12 – 13.
45. Feudge, 'The Mammoth Religion', p.342. But cf. Candlin, 'What should be our Attitude', p.101.
46. MacDonald, 'Buddha and Buddhism', p.131.
47. Knighton, *Forest Life in Ceylon*, II:7.
48. Colinet, 'Recent Works on Primitive Buddhism', p.137.
49. Machar, 'Buddha and Buddhism', p.39. The article is signed 'Fidelis'. *Poole's Index* ascribes it to A.M. Machar.
50. Kellogg, *The Light of Asia*, p.60.
51. *The Westminster Review*, 1856, p.302.
52. Barthélemy St Hilaire, *The Buddha and His Religion*, p.67.
53. Davids, *Lectures*, p.197.
54. Davids, *Buddhism*, p.188.
55. Berry, *Christianity and Buddhism*, p.41.
56. Sandberg, 'Philosophical Buddhism', p.257.
57. Monier-Williams, *Buddhism*, p.508.
58. Ibid., p.7.
59. *The Christian Remembrancer*, 1858, p.99.

60. Eitel, *Buddhism*, p. 61.
61. Ibid.
62. Medhurst, *China*, p. 215.
63. Barthélemy St Hilaire, *The Buddha and His Religion*, p. 176.
64. Alwis, 'Buddhism', p. 14.
65. Ball, *Is Buddism a Preparation*, p. 21.
66. *Scottish Review*, 1899, p. 288.
67. Ibid., p. 300.
68. Sandberg, 'Philosophical Buddhism', p. 262.
69. Bettany, *The Great Indian Religions*, p. 125.
70. Loubère, *A New Historical Relation*, p. 60.
71. Sangermano, *A Description of the Burmese Empire*, p. 153.
72. Tennent, *Christianity in Ceylon*, p. 205.
73. *The Prospective Review*, 1850, p. 485. See also p. 475.
74. Monier-Williams, *Buddhism*, p. 4.
75. Feudge, 'The Mammoth Religion', p. 344.
76. Sandberg, 'Philosophical Buddhism', p. 263.
77. *The Christian Remembrancer*, 1858, pp. 94–5. See also p. 104.
78. Machar, 'Buddha and Buddhism', p. 37.
79. Grant, *The Religions of the World*, p. 131.
80. Oldenberg, *Buddha: His Life, His Doctrine, His Order*, p. 220.
81. *Chambers's Encyclopaedia*, 1874, II:406.
82. Armstrong, 'Buddhism and Christianity', p. 178.
83. Eitel, *Buddhism*, p. 76. But cf. Salisbury, 'Memoir', pp. 81–2.
84. Ferguson, *Essay on the History of Civil Society*, quoted by Marshall and Williams, *The Great Map of Mankind*, p. 133.
85. Quoted by ibid., p. 133. See also Marshall, *The British Discovery of Hinduism*, p. 3.
86. Tennent, *Christianity in Ceylon*, p. 205.
87. *The Calcutta Review*, 1845, p. 281.
88. Bird, *Historical Researches*, pp. iv–v.
89. *The Intellectual Observer*, 1867, pp. 427–8.
90. Edkins, 'Notices of Buddhism in China'. And see also Bigandet, *The Life, or Legend of Gaudama*, p. 335.

3 THE BUDDHA – FROM MYTH TO HISTORY

1. Philips, *The Story of Gautama Buddha*, pp. 209–10.
2. Barthélemy St Hilaire, *The Buddha and His Religion*, p. 14.
3. Davids, 'Buddhism', IV:425.
4. Loubère, *A New Historical Relation*, p. 139.
5. Chambers, 'Some Account of the Sculptures and Ruins', pp. 162–3.
6. Jones, 'Dissertation 111', p. 80.
7. Faber, *The Origin of Pagan Idolatry*, II:355.

8. Cunningham, *The Bhilsa Topes*, p. x.
9. Buchanan, 'On the Religion', p. 259.
10. Faber, *The Origin of Pagan Idolatry*, II:42.
11. Francklin, *Researches*, p. 146.
12. Ibid., p. 81.
13. Ibid., pp. 177–8.
14. Mill, *The History of British India*, 1817, I:223.
15. Mill, *The History of British India*, 1840, I:361, n. 1.
16. Mill, *The History of British India*, 1858, I:251.
17. Symes, *An Account*, II:37.
18. Faber, *The Origin of Pagan Idolatry*, II:355.
19. Davy, *An Account of the Interior of Ceylon*, p. 173.
20. Ibid., p. 174. See also Ersch and Gruber, 'Buddha, Buddhaismus', pp. 335–6.
21. See, e.g., Fergusson, *Tree and Serpent Worship*, pp. 22–3.
22. *Encyclopaedia Metropolitana*, 1845, XVI:54.
23. *The Calcutta Review*, 1845, p. 250.
24. Wilson, 'On Buddha and Buddhism', p. 247.
25. Müller, 'Buddhist Pilgrims', p. 235.
26. Loubère, *A New Historical Relation*, p. 138.
27. See Manuel, *The Eighteenth Century*, Ch. 3.
28. Buchanan, 'On the Religion', pp. 257–8.
29. Ersch and Gruber, 'Buddha, Buddhaismus', XIII:330.
30. Salisbury, 'Memoir', p. 87. But cf. *Encyclopaedia Metropolitana*, 1845, XVI:54.
31. Knighton, *Forest Life in Ceylon*, II:3.
32. Speir, *Life in Ancient India*, pp. 267–8.
33. Koeppen, *Die Religion des Buddha*, I:73.
34. Yule, *A Narrative*, p. 234.
35. Simpson, *The Hindu Pantheon*, p. 159.
36. Moor, *The Hindu Pantheon*, p. 233. See also Kaempfer, *The History of Japan*, II:57.
37. Jones, 'On the Chronology of the Hindus', pp. 125, 147. See also Marshall, *The British Discovery of Hinduism*, pp. 35–6. On eighteenth-century chronologies, see Manuel, *Isaac Newton Historian*.
38. Faber, *The Origin of Pagan Idolatry*, I:89.
39. Ibid., III:670.
40. *The British Cyclopaedia*, 1836, I:323.
41. *The Penny Cyclopaedia*, 1836, p. 527.
42. *The National Cyclopaedia*, 1847, III:905.
43. Kesson, *The Cross and the Dragon*, p. 178; Culbertson, *Darkness*, pp. 69–70; and Davis, *China*, II:38.
44. Buchanan, 'On the Religion', p. 266.

45. Mahony, 'On *Singhala*, or *Ceylon'*, p. 34. See also Percival, *An Account of the Island of Ceylon*, p. 142.
46. Joinville, 'On the Religion and Manners', p. 434.
47. Burnouf and Lassen, *Essai sur le Pali*, pp. 49 – 50.
48. See Burnouf, *Introduction*, p. iii; and Lassen, *Indische Alterthumskunde*, II:60.
49. Hodgson, 'Notices', I:11.
50. *Allgemeine Deutsche Real-Encyclopädie*, 1833 – 7, II:296.
51. Ibid., 1843 – 8, III:7.
52. Ibid., 1851 – 5, III:405; and 1864 – 73, III:830.
53. *The Christian Remembrancer*, 1858, p. 90.
54. See Müller, *The Dhammapada*, pp. xliii – liii for a useful summary of the position at the end of the century. See also Filliozat, *Studies in Asokan Inscriptions*, pp. 9 – 19.
55. Alexander, *Sakya-Muni*, pp. 7 – 8.
56. Hardy, *Christianity and Buddhism Compared*, p. 2.
57. *The Westminster Review*, 1856, p. 302. See also Barthélemy St Hilaire, *The Buddha and His Religion*, p. 94.
58. Oldenberg, *Buddha: His Life, His Doctrine, His Order*, p. 82.
59. Titcomb, *Short Chapters on Buddhism*, p. 18.
60. *Dublin University Magazine*, 1873, p. 206.
61. Armstrong, 'Buddhism and Christianity', p. 184.
62. Davids, 'Buddhism and Christianity', p. 13.
63. Davids, *Buddhism*, p. 16.
64. Amberley, 'Recent Publications on Buddhism', pp. 306 – 7.
65. Ware, 'The Development of Buddhism', p. 801.
66. Tulloch, *The Christ of the Gospels and the Christ of Modern Criticism*, London: MacMillan, 1864, pp. 3 – 4. Quoted by Pals, *The Victorian 'Lives' of Jesus*, pp. 34 – 5.
67. See Pals, *The Victorian 'Lives' of Jesus*, pp. 72 – 7.
68. Kellogg, *The Light of Asia*, pp. 54 – 5. The reference to Renan is puzzling, but the point of the argument remains clear. See also p. 373.
69. Sheffield, 'Dr. Kellogg's "Light of Asia",' p. 30.
70. Berry, *Christianity and Buddhism*, p. 29. See also p. 46.
71. See, e.g., Cobbold, *Religion in Japan*, p. 36.
72. See, e.g., Copleston, *Buddhism*, pp. 133 – 4 on Rhys Davids.
73. See, e.g., Brockett, 'Buddhism', pp. 220 – 1; and Gmeiner, 'The Light of Asia', p. 7. See also Ch. 5.
74. Carpenter, 'The Obligations of the New Testament', p. 977.
75. Green, 'Christianity and Buddhism', p. 302. See also Jersey, 'Buddhism and Christianity', p. 580.
76. Armstrong, 'Buddhism and Christianity', p. 199.
77. *The Quarterly Review*, 1890, p. 327.

78. Barth, *The Religions of India*, p. 117. See also Dods, *Mohammed, Buddha, and Christ*, pp. 148–9; and *The Saturday Review*, 1883, p. 695.
79. See Allibone, *A Critical Dictionary*, I:13–14.
80. Adams, *Curiosities of Superstition*, p. 25.
81. Marshall, *The British Discovery of Hinduism*, p. 20.
82. Buchanan, 'On the Religion', p. 166.
83. Ward, *History, Literature, and Religion of the Hindoos*, I:ciii.
84. Mill, 'Religion and Character', p. 377.
85. Mill, *The History of British India*, 1817, I:245.
86. Bennett, *Ceylon*, p. 272.
87. Knighton, *Forest Life in Ceylon*, II:10. See also Tennent, *Christianity in Ceylon*, p. 226; Davis, *China*, II:42; *The Intellectual Observer*, 1867, p. 423; and Beal, *A Catena of Buddhist Scriptures*, pp. 144–5.
88. Davids, *Buddhism*, p. 85.
89. Bloomfield, 'The Essentials of Buddhist Doctrine', p. 313. See also Gerhart, 'Original Buddhism', p. 292.
90. Neumann, 'Buddhism and Shamanism', p. 124.
91. Gogerly, *Ceylon Buddhism*, p. 9.
92. Cunningham, *The Bhilsa Topes*, p. 33.
93. *The Christian Remembrancer*, 1858, p. 104.
94. Müller, 'Buddhist Pilgrims', p. 236.
95. Brockett, 'Buddhism', p. 219; Sargant, *Buddha*, p. 22; *The Intellectual Observer*, 1867, p. 424; Kistner, *Buddha and His Doctrine*, p. 1; and Armstrong, 'Buddhism and Christianity', pp. 176–8.
96. Rattigan, 'Three Great Asiatic Reformers', p. 293.
97. *Asiatic Journal and Monthly Register*, 1831, p. 262.
98. *The Prospective Review*, 1850, p. 480.
99. *The Christian Remembrancer*, 1858, pp. 92–3.
100. *Journal of Sacred Literature*, 1865, p. 287.
101. Clarke, 'Buddhism', p. 715.
102. *The Westminster Review*, 1878, p. 331.
103. Eitel, *Buddhism*, p. 6.
104. Dubose, *The Dragon, Image and Demon*, p. 163.
105. Grant, *The Religions of the World*, p. 125.
106. *Chambers's Encyclopaedia*, 1874, II:409. See also Johnston, 'Christ and Buddha', p. 37; and Dods, *Mohammed, Buddha, and Christ*, p. 136.
107. Oldenberg, *Buddha: His Life, His Doctrine, His Order*, p. 170.
108. *The Saturday Review*, 1882, p. 765.
109. Ibid., p. 765.
110. Ibid., p. 766. See also Everett, 'Recent Studies', p. 431.
111. Fairbairn, 'History of Religions', p. 439.
112. Strong, 'The Revival of Buddhism', p. 273.

113. Bettany, *The Great Indian Religions*, p. 129. See also *The Quarterly Review*, 1890, p. 324; and Cobbold, *Religion in Japan*, p. 41.
114. Galton, 'The Founder of Buddhism', p. 154.
115. Speir, *Life in Ancient India*, p. 288.
116. *The Westminster Review*, 1856, pp. 328–9; See also Neale, 'Buddha and Buddhism', p. 442.
117. Adler, 'A Prophet of the People', p. 689. See also Ware, 'The Development of Buddhism', pp. 820–1.
118. *London Quarterly Review*, 1858, p. 517.
119. *London Quarterly Review*, 1886, p. 283.
120. Machar, 'Buddha and Buddhism', p. 35.
121. Davids, 'Buddha's First Sermon', p. 901.
122. Armstrong, 'Buddhism and Christianity', pp. 186–8.
123. Feudge, 'The Mammoth Religion', p. 345.
124. Caird, *Buddhism*, p. 14. See also Bloomfield, 'The Essentials of Buddhist Doctrine', pp. 320–1; Copleston, *Buddhism*, p. 60; Davids, 'Buddhism', IV:428–9; and *The Quarterly Review*, 1890, p. 340.
125. Edkins, review of Beal, *The Romantic Legend*, p. 376.
126. *The Westminster Review*, 1878, p. 330.
127. *The Church Quarterly Review*, 1882, p. 100.
128. Grant, *The Religions of the World*, p. 130.
129. Rattigan, 'Three Great Asiatic Reformers', p. 296. See also Berry, *Christianity and Buddhism*, pp. 49–50; and Huxley, *Evolution and Ethics*, p. 103, n. 10.

4 THE VICTORIANS AND BUDDHIST DOCTRINE

1. *Samyuttanikāya*, V:422.
2. Oldenberg, *Buddha: His Life, His Doctrine, His Order*, p. 212.
3. Barthélemy St Hilaire, *The Buddha and His Religion*, p. 158.
4. Monier-Williams, *Buddhism*, p. 36. See also Titcomb, *Short Chapters on Buddhism*, p. 54.
5. Caird, *Buddhism*, p. 6.
6. *The Church Quarterly Review*, 1891, p. 74. See also *London Quarterly Review*, 1858, p. 522; Clarke, 'Buddhism', p. 728; Hardy, *Christianity and Buddhism Compared*, pp. 74–5; *The Church Quarterly Review*, 1882, p. 95; Eitel, *Buddhism*, pp. 80, 95–6; Scott, *Buddhism and Christianity*, pp. 18–19.
7. Oldenberg, *Buddha: His Life, His Doctrine, His Order*, pp. 220–1.
8. See Armstrong, 'Buddhism and Christianity', p. 178. See also Davids, *Lectures*, pp. 21–2.
9. Johnston, 'Christ and Buddha', p. 39.
10. Bixby, 'Buddhism', p. 556.
11. Bryant, 'Buddhism and Christianity', p. 267.

12. Ellinwood, *Oriental Religions and Christianity*, p. 157. See also Alwis, 'Buddhism', p. 29.
13. Adler, 'A Prophet of the People', p. 689.
14. Strong, 'The Revival of Buddhism', p. 273.
15. Davids, 'Buddha's First Sermon', pp. 890–9. See also Davids, *Lectures*, pp. 214–15.
16. See Kellogg, *The Light of Asia*, pp. 265–6.
17. Froude, *Short Studies*, IV:v–vi.
18. Kellogg, *The Light of Asia*, p. 11.
19. Ellinwood, *Oriental Religions and Christianity*, p. 156.
20. *London Quarterly Review*, 1886, p. 292.
21. *Majjhimanikāya*, III:203.
22. *Samyuttanikāya*, II:179.
23. See Holbrook, *Sketches*, p. 273.
24. See Gutzlaff, *China Opened*, II:224–5.
25. See Monier-Williams, *Buddhism*, p. 116; Torrens, *Travels*, p. 120.
26. Barthélemy St Hilaire, *The Buddha and His Religion*, p. 131.
27. *The Westminster Review*, 1856, p. 312.
28. Dubose, *The Dragon, Image and Demon*, p. 227.
29. Davids, *Buddhism*, p. 49.
30. Gerhart, 'Original Buddhism', p. 292.
31. Scott, *Buddhism and Christianity*, p. 92.
32. Eitel, *Buddhism*, p. 76.
33. Barthélemy St Hilaire, *The Buddha and His Religion*, pp. 133–4.
34. Sargant, *Buddha*, p. 11.
35. Culbertson, *Darkness*, p. 86. See also Knighton, *Forest Life in Ceylon*, II:390, 396–9.
36. Hardy, *Legends*, p. xlv.
37. Barthélemy St Hilaire, *The Buddha and His Religion*, p. 162.
38. Davids, *Lectures*, p. 108.
39. Kellogg, *The Light of Asia*, p. 7. See also Ellinwood, *Oriental Religions and Christianity*, p. 156. But cf. Frederick Temple, 'The Relations between Religion and Science', in Cockshut, *Religious Controversies*, pp. 254–65.
40. Knighton, *Forest Life in Ceylon*, II:388–9.
41. *Journal of Sacred Literature*, 1865, p. 290.
42. Ibid., p. 290. See also *Dublin University Magazine*, 1873, p. 215.
43. Huxley, *Evolution and Ethics*, p. 61. See also Griffin, 'The Burman', pp. 662–3.
44. Cobbold, *Religion in Japan*, pp. 44–5.
45. Amberley, 'Recent Publications on Buddhism', p. 316. See also Dods, *Mohammed, Buddha, and Christ*, pp. 161–2.
46. Davids, *Buddhism*, p. 106.

47. Eitel, *Buddhism*, p. 84.
48. Hardy, *Legends*, p. 165.
49. Knighton, *Forest Life in Ceylon*, II:412 – 13.
50. Benn, review of Copleston, *Buddhism*, p. 145.
51. Alabaster, *The Wheel of the Law*, p.xl. See also Collins, 'Buddhism and "The Light of Asia"', p. 186.
52. Clarke, 'Buddhism', pp. 725 – 6. See also Titcomb, *Short Chapters on Buddhism*, p. 50.
53. Berry, *Christianity and Buddhism*, p. 79.
54. Ellinwood, *Oriental Religions and Christianity*, p. 150.
55. Schumann, *Buddhism*, p. 65.
56. *The Westminster Review*, 1856, p. 317.
57. Hardy, *Legends*, p. 168. Cf. Schumann, *Buddhism*, p. 59 for the distinction between *causa* and *conditio*, the latter of which pertains to *paticcasamuppāda*.
58. Bigandet, *The Life, or Legend of Gaudama*, p. 86.
59. See Gogerly, 'An Outline of Buddhism', p. 41; Oldenberg, *Buddha: His Life, His Doctrine, His Order*, p. 226; Titcomb, *Short Chapters on Buddhism*, p. 55; Monier-Williams, *Buddhism*, p. 102; Bettany, *The Great Indian Religions*, p. 149; Beames, 'A Plain Account of Buddhism', 1896, p. 155; *The Christian Remembrancer*, 1858, pp. 101 – 2.
60. Goodwin, 'Mosaic Cosmogony', pp. 138 – 9.
61. Hardy, *Legends*, p 114.
62. See ibid., pp. 96, 101.
63. See ibid., p. 219. See also Neale, 'Buddha and Buddhism', p. 446.
64. Hardy, *A Manual of Buddhism*, p. 35n. See also Hardy, *Legends*, pp. 108, 161, 197 – 8.
65. *The Intellectual Observer*, 1867, p. 426.
66. *The Christian Remembrancer*, 1858, p. 98.
67. Alwis, 'Buddhism', p. 34.
68. Edkins, *Religion in China*, pp. 80 – 1. See also pp. 81 – 2; Edkins, *The Religious Condition*, p. 95.
69. Bigandet, *The Life, or Legend of Gaudama*, pp. 11, 25. See also Titcomb, *Short Chapters on Buddhism*, pp. 33 – 4.
70. Eitel, *Buddhism*, p. 62. Cf. Dubose, *The Dragon, Image and Demon*, p. 209.
71. Eitel, *Buddhism*, p. 63. See also Copleston, *Buddhism*, p. 248.
72. See, e.g., Buchanan, 'On the Religion'; Joinville, 'On the Religion and Manners'; Davy, *An Account of the Interior of Ceylon*; Sangermano, *A Description of the Burmese Empire*.
73. See, e.g., Davids, *Buddhism*.
74. Monier-Williams, *Buddhism*, pp. 117 – 22.
75. Gogerly, 'An Introductory Sketch', p. 2. See also Hardwick, *Christ and other Masters*, p. 154.

76. Beal, *A Catena of Buddhist Scriptures*, p. 147.
77. See, e.g., Beal, *Buddhism in China*, pp. 98, 114.
78. Müller, 'A Bishop on Buddhism', p. 109; Claughton, 'Buddhism', p. 139; Edkins, *Religion in China*, p. 139; Berry, *Christianity and Buddhism*, pp. 94 – 5.
79. Müller, 'A Bishop on Buddhism', p. 109.
80. See Söderblom, 'Holiness', Otto, 'Buddhism and Christianity'.
81. Davids, *Buddhism*, pp. 208, 203, 209.
82. Monier-Williams, *Buddhism*, pp. vii, 305.
83. Dods, *Mohammed, Buddha, and Christ*, p. 177.
84. Eitel, *Buddhism*, pp. 50 – 1. See also Cobbold, *Religion in Japan*, p. 51.
85. De Harlez, 'The Buddhistic Schools', pp. 53 – 4. See also Ball, *Is Buddism a Preparation*, p. 12; Gerhart, 'Original Buddhism', p. 305.
86. Loubère, *A New Historical Relation*, pp. 130, 61.
87. Ward, *History, Literature, and Religion of the Hindoos*, I:civ.
88. Ersch and Gruber, 'Buddha, Buddhaismus', p. 332.
89. Edkins, 'Notices of Buddhism in China'; Wilson, 'On Buddha and Buddhism', p. 255.
90. *London Quarterly Review*, 1858, p. 522.
91. *The Christian Remembrancer*, 1858, p. 95. See also Knighton, *The History of Ceylon*, p. 67.
92. *The London Encyclopaedia*, 1829, IV:694.
93. *Allgemeine Deutsche Real-Encyclopädie*, 1833, II:296; 1843, III:7; 1851, III:405; 1864, III:830.
94. *The Penny Cyclopaedia*, 1836, p. 530.
95. Maurice, *The Religions of the World*, pp. 81 – 2, 72 – 4. See also *The Saturday Review*, 1884, p. 249.
96. *The Calcutta Review*, 1845, p. 251.
97. Simpson, *The Hindu Pantheon*, p. 160. See also Cunningham, *The Bhilsa Topes*, p. 23.
98. See, e.g., Lillie, *The Popular Life of Buddha*; Lillie, *Buddha and Early Buddhism*.
99. Gogerly, 'An Outline of Buddhism', p. 31.
100. Clarke, 'Buddhism', p. 728. His source for the Voltairean phraseology was probably Barthélemy St Hilaire, *The Buddha and His Religion*, p. 176.
101. Titcomb, *Short Chapters on Buddhism*, p. 172. See also, e.g., Müller, 'Lecture on Buddhist Nihilism', p. 139; Armstrong, 'Buddhism and Christianity', p. 177; *London Quarterly Review*, 1888 – 9, pp. 329 – 30.
102. Eitel, *Buddhism*, p. 66.
103. Watters, 'Mr. Eitel's Three Lectures', pp. 65 – 6.
104. Eitel, *Buddhism*, pp. 2 – 3.
105. Dubose, *The Dragon, Image and Demon*, p. 208.

106. Watters, 'Mr. Eitel's Three Lectures', p. 65.
107. *London Quarterly Review*, 1888 – 9, p. 330.
108. Scott, *Buddhism and Christianity*, p. 16.
109. See Huxley (ed.), *Life and Letters*, I:319 – 20.
110. Davids, 'The Ancient Buddhist Belief', pp. 222 – 3.
111. Davids, *Lectures*, p. 90.
112. Kellogg, *The Light of Asia*, p. 11.
113. Green, 'Christianity and Buddhism', p. 312.
114. Scott, *Buddhism and Christianity*, p. 14.
115. See, e.g., Calvin, *Institutes*, I:3.
116. Armstrong, 'Buddhism and Christianity', pp. 197 – 8. See also Barthélemy St Hilaire, *The Buddha and His Religion*, pp. 164 – 5; *Chambers's Encyclopaedia*, 1874, II:405; 1861, II:405.
117. Edkins, *The Religious Condition*, p. 122; See also Edkins, *Religion in China*, p. 97.
118. *The Saturday Review*, 1883, p. 695.
119. Dods, *Mohammed, Buddha, and Christ*, p. 180. See also Grant, *The Religions of the World*, p. 149.
120. Bigandet, *The Life, or Legend of Gautama*, p. 73.
121. Beal, *Buddhism in China*, p. 107.
122. Müller, 'The Meaning of Nirvana', p. 285. See also Müller, 'Buddhist Pilgrims', pp. 253 – 4.
123. Yule, *A Narrative*, p. 233.
124. Claughton, 'Buddhism', p. 145. See also Ball, *Is Buddhism a Preparation*, p. 16.
125. Eitel, *Buddhism*, pp. 102 – 3. See also Adams, *Curiosities of Superstition*, p. 26; Kellogg, *The Light of Asia*, pp. 358 – 9.
126. Grosier, *A General Description*, II:222.
127. *Encyclopaedia Britannica*, 1810, VI:29.
128. Judson, *An Account of the American Baptist Mission*, p. 3.
129. Medhurst, *China*, p. 215. See also Francklin, *Researches*, pp. 11 – 12; and Knighton, *The History of Ceylon*, p. 73.
130. Davids, *Buddhism*, IV:434. See Alwis, 'Buddhism', p. 30; Gogerly, 'An Outline of Buddhism', p. 43; Gogerly, 'An Introductory Sketch', p. 10; Childers, *Dictionary*, pp. 265, 267; Childers, 'Notes on Dhammapada', p. 220; Hardy, *Legends*, p. 174; Bigandet, *The Life, or Legend of Gaudama*, pp. viii, 21, 323; Burnouf and Lassen, *Essai sur le Pali*, p. 196; Burnouf, *Introduction*, p. 588. Burnouf was convinced that etymologically, 'Nirvana' meant 'extinction'. But he was less certain what the Buddha meant by it. See Welbon, *The Buddhist Nirvāna*, pp. 53 – 63.
131. Barthélemy St Hilaire, *The Buddha and His Religion*, p. 140. His insertion of Foucaux as a supporter of the annihilationist interpretation is doubtful. See Welbon, *The Buddhist Nirvāna*, pp. 89 – 100.

132. Wilson, 'On Buddha and Buddhism', p. 256. See also Burnouf, *Introduction*, p. 590.
133. Hardwick, *Christ and Other Masters*, p. 165. See also Dods, *Mohammed, Buddha, and Christ*, p. 155; Gerhart, 'Original Buddhism', p. 305; *London Quarterly Review*, 1858, p. 541.
134. Arnold, *The Light of Asia*, viii.
135. Kellogg, *The Light of Asia*, pp. 221 – 2.
136. Wilkinson, *Edwin Arnold*, p. 93.
137. See, e.g., Rowell, *Hell and the Victorians*.
138. Davy, *An Account of the Interior of Ceylon*, pp. 160 – 1.
139. Armstrong, 'Buddhism and Christianity', p. 187.
140. Barthélemy St Hilaire, *The Buddha and His Religion*, p. 175.
141. Bigandet, *The Life, or Legend of Gaudama*, p. 347.
142. Ward, *History, Literature, and Religion of the Hindoos*, II:213.
143. *Asiatic Journal and Monthly Register*, 1831, p. 262.
144. *Allgemeine Deutsche Real-Encyclopädie*, 1833, II:296 – 7; 1851, III:405; 1864, III:830.
145. *The Penny Cyclopaedia*, 1836, p. 530. See also *The Calcutta Review*, 1845, p. 251.
146. *The Prospective Review*, 1850, p. 477.
147. Prinsep, *Tibet*, pp. 139 – 40; Cunningham, *The Bhilsa Topes*, p. 23.
148. Barham, 'Buddha and his Critics'. See also Müller, 'The Meaning of Nirvana', p. 281.
149. See, e.g., *Journal of Sacred Literature*, 1865, p. 290; Edkins, review of S. Beal, *The Romantic Legend*, p. 376; Bettany, *The Great Indian Religions*, p. 147.
150. Culbertson, *Darkness*, p. 77; See also Simpson, *The Hindu Pantheon*, p. 161.
151. Jersey, 'Buddhism and Christianity', p. 586.
152. Müller, 'Buddhist Pilgrims', p. 249. See also p. 246.
153. Müller, 'Lecture on Buddhist Nihilism', p. 143.
154. Childers, *Dictionary*, p. 265.
155. Beal, *A Catena of Buddhist Scriptures*, p. 173. See also Amberely, 'Recent Publications on Buddhism', p. 313.
156. *Dublin University Magazine*, 1873, p. 213.
157. *The Westminster Review*, 1878, p. 340. See also Machar, 'Buddha and Buddhism', p. 167; Burnouf, 'Le Bouddhisme en Occident', p. 343; and cf. Berry, *Christianity and Buddhism*, p. 91.
158. Oldenberg, *Buddha: His Life, His Doctrine, His Order*, p. 266.
159. Ibid., p. 284. See also Welbon, *The Buddhist Nirvāna*, pp. 194 – 208.
160. Titcomb, *Short Chapters on Buddhism*, p. 80.
161. Colinet, 'Recent Works on Primitive Buddhism', p. 278; Scott,

Buddhism and Christianity, p. 217; Beames, 'A Plain Account of Buddhism', pp. 155–56.

162. Buchanan, 'On the Religion', p. 266. See also p. 180, where he rejected both annihilationist and absorptionist interpretations.
163. Sangermano, *A Description of the Burmese Empire*, pp. 102–3.
164. Yule, *A Narrative*, p. 236. 'Unreality' is an incorrect translation for 'anatta' or 'anātman'. It would be better translated as 'non-soul' or 'non-self'.
165. Clarke, 'Buddhism', p. 726.
166. Davies, 'The Religion of Gotama Buddha', p. 335. See also Beal, *Buddhism in China*, pp. 199–200; Collins, 'Buddhism and "The Light of Asia"', pp. 163, 165; Grant, *The Religion of the World* p. 135; Copleston, 'Buddhism', pp. 134–5, though Copleston tends to the annihilationist position.
167. See, e.g., *Asiatic Journal and Monthly Register*, 1832, pp. 315–16; *The Edinburgh Review*, 1862, p. 408 (written in fact by Max Müller).
168. *The Christian Remembrancer*, 1858, p. 97.
169. Edkins, *The Religious Condition*, p. 207. See also Amberley, 'Recent Publications on Buddhism', pp. 312–13; Machar, 'Buddha and Buddhism', p. 169.
170. Adams, *Curiosities and Superstition*, p. 22.
171. Eitel, *Buddhism*, p. 122. See also Copleston, *Buddhism*, p. 152; Scott, *Buddhism and Christianity*, p. 218; *The Quarterly Review*, 1890, p. 339; Barth, *The Religions of India*, pp. 113–14; Ellinwood, *Oriental Religions and Christianity*, p. 153.

5 VICTORIAN PRECEPTS AND BUDDHIST PRACTICE

1. *The Nineteenth Century*, 1877, p. 331.
2. Chadwick, *The Victorian Church*, II:122.
3. *Encyclopaedia Britannica*, 1842, V:637.
4. Roer, review of Burnouf, *Introduction*, p. 789.
5. Ware, 'The Development of Buddhism', p. 802. See also Monier-Williams, 'Literary Admirers of Buddhism', pp. 218–19.
6. Caird, *Buddhism*, p. 20.
7. Huxley, *Evolution and Ethics*, p. 68.
8. Buchanan, 'On the Religion', p. 255.
9. Tennent, *Christianity in Ceylon*, p. 219. See also Hardy, *A Manual of Buddhism*, p. 358.
10. Sirr, *Ceylon and the Cingalese*, p. 79. See also pp. 114–15.
11. *The Westminster Review*, 1856, p. 325. See also Knighton, *Forest Life in Ceylon*, II:53; Knighton, *The History of Ceylon*, 1845, pp. 80–1.
12. Eitel, *Buddhism*, p. 64.

13. Caird, *Buddhism*, pp. 15–16; Alwis, 'Buddhism', p. 4; Kellogg, *The Light of Asia*, p. 270.
14. *The Church Quarterly Review*, 1882, p. 105.
15. Gogerly, 'On Transmigration', pp. 221–2.
16. Eitel, *Buddhism*, p. 84. But cf. Alabaster, *The Wheel of the Law*, pp. xix-xx.
17. Copleston, 'Buddhism', p. 130.
18. *The Quarterly Review*, 1890, p. 345.
19. Beal, *Buddhism in China*, p. 200.
20. Adler, 'A Prophet of the People', p. 687.
21. *The Saturday Review*, 1883, p. 695.
22. Dods, *Mohammed, Buddha, and Christ*, pp. 168–9. See also Benn, review of Copleston, *Buddhism*, p. 145.
23. Claughton, 'Buddhism', p. 144.
24. *London Quarterly Review*, 1888–9, p. 330. See also p. 341.
25. Galton, 'The Morality of Buddhism', p. 6. See also Copleston, *Buddhism*, p. 63; Monier-Williams, *Buddhism*, p. 14; Hardwick, *Christ and Other Masters*, p. 169.
26. Kellogg, *The Light of Asia*, pp. 14–15.
27. Claughton, 'Buddhism', p. 151.
28. *The Nineteenth Century*, 1877, p. 347.
29. Barthélemy St Hilaire, *The Buddha and His Religion*, p. 152.
30. Brockett, 'Buddhism', p. 226.
31. Clarke, 'Buddhism', p. 727.
32. Hardy, *Legends*, p. 214.
33. Titcomb, *Short Chapters on Buddhism*, p. 175; Eitel, *Buddhism*, p. 79.
34. *London Quarterly Review*, 1886, p. 291.
35. Dods, *Mohammed, Buddha, and Christ*, p. 169.
36. Scott, *Buddhism and Christianity*, p. 221. See also pp. 223–4.
37. Ibid., p. 234.
38. Berry, *Christianity and Buddhism*, pp. 106, 109.
39. Beames, 'A Plain Account of Buddhism', p. 157.
40. Armstrong, 'Buddhism and Christianity', p. 185.
41. Alabaster, *The Wheel of the Law*, p. xx. See also Watters, 'Mr. Eitel's Three Lectures', p. 68.
42. Ware, 'The Development of Buddhism', p. 805. See also Caird, *Buddhism*, p. 7.
43. Dunlap, 'Buddhist Priests of Siam', p. 425. See also Berry, *Christianity and Buddhism*, pp. 102–3.
44. Dennis, *Christian Missions*, I:382. See also Sheffield, 'Christianity and the Ethnic Religions', p. 111.
45. Ball, *Is Buddism a Preparation*, p. 22.
46. Davy, *An Account of the Interior of Ceylon*, p. 168.
47. Tennent, *Christianity in Ceylon*, p. 228.

48. Knighton, *Forest Life in Ceylon*, II:417–19.
49. Claughton, 'Buddhism', p. 153.
50. *Encyclopaedia Metropolitana*, 1845, XVI:60. See also Buchanan, 'On the Religion', p. 256.
51. Yule, *A Narrative*, p. 241.
52. Gutzlaff, 'Journal of a Residence', p. 18. But cf. Feudge, 'The Mammoth Religion', p. 347.
53. Gilmour, *Among the Mongols*, p. 255. See also Dods, *Mohammed, Buddha, and Christ*, p. 175.
54. *The Quarterly Review*, 1890, p. 345.
55. Houghton, *The Victorian Frame of Mind*, p. 189.
56. Sargant, *Buddha*, p. 17.
57. Eitel, *Buddhism*, p. 82.
58. Titcomb, *Short Chapters on Buddhism*, p. 175.
59. Hume, *An Inquiry*, p. 91.
60. Grosier, *A General Description*, II:232.
61. Le Comte, *Memoirs*, See also Marshall and Williams, *The Great Map of Mankind*, p. 108, to whom I am indebted for this reference.
62. *Encyclopaedia Britannica*, 1797, III:363.
63. *The English Encyclopaedia*, 1802, I:820; *Encyclopaedia Perthensis*, 1807, IV:130; *Pantologia*, 1813, II:n.p.; Platts, *Manners and Customs*, p. 538; *The London Encyclopaedia*, 1829, pp. 303–4.
64. Gutzlaff, *China Opened*, II:225–6. See also Hardwick, *Christ and Other Masters*, p. 341.
65. Philosinensis, 'Remarks on Budhism', p. 217.
66. Kesson, *The Cross and the Dragon*, p. 186.
67. Davis, *China*, II:47; Culbertson, *Darkness*, p. 89.
68. Culbertson, *Darkness*, p. 79. See also p. 74.
69. Davis, *China*, II:48.
70. Neale, 'Buddha and Buddhism', p. 447.
71. Balfour, 'Buddhism', p. 10.
72. Barrow, *Travels in China*, p. 422; *Encyclopaedia Britannica*, 1842, VI:560.
73. Cobbold, *Religion in Japan*, p. 73.
74. Sirr, *Ceylon and the Cingalese*, p. 113.
75. Knighton, *Forest Life in Ceylon*, II:33–5.
76. *The Prospective Review*, 1850, p. 484.
77. *London Quarterly Review*, 1854–5, p. 455. See also Benn, review of Copleston, *Buddhism*, p. 146.
78. Buchanan, 'On the Religion', p. 276.
79. *The London Encyclopaedia*, 1829, IV:695; *The Edinburgh Encyclopaedia*, 1830, III:pt. 2, 531.
80. Bigandet, *The Life, or Legend of Gaudama*, p. 534.
81. Ibid., pp. 531–2. See also Colquhoun, *Amongst the Shans*, p. 153; Yoe,

'Buddhists and Buddhism', p. 731; and cf. Sangermano, *A Description of the Burmese Empire*, p. 153.

82. Müller, 'Buddhist Pilgrims', p. 252.
83. Gogerly, 'An Outline of Buddhism', p. 17.
84. *The Christian Remembrancer*, 1858, p. 98.
85. Sandberg, 'Philosophical Buddhism', p. 266.
86. Beal, *A Catena of Buddhist Scriptures*, p. 150; Titcomb, *Short Chapters on Buddhism*, p. 147; Alabaster, *The Wheel of the Law*, p. xliv; Monier-Williams, *Buddhism*, pp. 210 – 11.
87. Beal, *A Catena of Buddhist Scriptures*, p. 151; Barthélemy St Hilaire, *The Buddha and His Religion*, pp. 141 – 4; Bigandet, *The Life, or Legend of Gaudama*, p. 104; *London Quarterly Review*, 1888 – 9, p. 341.
88. Stewart, 'An Account of the Kingdom of Thibet', p. 476.
89. Cranmer-Byng (ed.), *An Embassy to China*, p. 135. See also p. 233.
90. Barrow, *Travels in China*, p. 449.
91. *The Encyclopaedia Edinensis*, 1827, I:678.
92. Platts, *Manners and Customs*, p. 538; *The London Encyclopaedia*, 1829, IV:304. See also Philosinensis, 'Remarks on Budhism', pp. 217 – 18.
93. Medhurst, *China*, pp. 217 – 18. See also *The National Cyclopaedia*, 1847, III:911 – 12; 1857, III:911 – 12.
94. Clarke, 'Buddhism', p. 713; *The Westminster Review*, 1878, p. 348.
95. Davis, *China*, II:41.
96. Culbertson, *Darkness*, p. 121; Davids, 'Buddhism', p. 438; Green, 'Christianity and Buddhism', p. 321. See also Müller, 'Christianity and Buddhism', p. 68.
97. *The Westminster Review*, 1856, p. 329.
98. Alabaster, *The Wheel of the Law*, p. xxxvi.
99. Dubose, *The Dragon, Image and Demon*, p. 290.
100. Anderson, *The Buddha of Christendom*, p. 73. See also pp. vi – vii; but cf. Torrens, *Travels*, p. 179.
101. Clarke, 'Buddhism', p. 719.
102. Kellogg, *The Light of Asia*, p. 358. See also Beal, *Buddhism in China*, pp. 103, 217.
103. Gilmour, *Among the Mongols*, pp. 253 – 4. See also Monier-Williams, *Buddhism*, pp. 156, 469.
104. Claughton, 'Buddhism', p. 145.
105. Titcomb, *Short Chapters on Buddhism*, p. 109.
106. Müller, 'Christianity and Buddhism', p. 68.
107. Ibid., p. 68.
108. *The Penny Cyclopaedia*, 1836, p. 532.
109. Eitel, *Buddhism*, p. 30. But cf. Watters, 'Mr. Eitel's Three Lectures', p. 65.
110. Machar, 'Buddha and Buddhism', pp. 41 – 2.

111. Kellogg, *The Light of Asia*, pp. 159–60.
112. Prinsep, *Tibet*, p. 163.
113. Bigandet, *The Life, or Legend of Gaudama*, p. 493.
114. Ibid., p. 163; Speir, *Life in Ancient India*, pp. 368–9.
115. *Literature*, 1901, pp. 243–4. See also *The Church Quarterly Review*, 1882, pp. 106–7.
116. But cf. Strong, *The Metaphysic of Christianity and Buddhism*, p. 2.
117. Davids, *Lectures*, p. 151. See also Scott, *Buddhism and Christianity*, pp. 24–5.
118. Davids, 'Buddhism and Christianity', pp. 11–12. See also Carpenter, 'The Obligations of the New Testament', pp. 975–9; *The Church Quarterly Review*, 1882, p. 107.
119. Buchanan, 'On the Religion', p. 278.
120. *The Prospective Review*, 1850, p. 489. See also Forbes, *Eleven Years in Ceylon*, p. 206; *The Westminster Review*, 1856, p. 308.
121. Neale, 'Buddha and Buddhism', p. 440. See also Sargant, *Buddha*, p. 23.
122. *Journal of Sacred Literature*, 1865, p. 299.
123. Clarke, 'Buddhism', p. 722. See also, Armstrong, 'Buddhism and Christianity', p. 186.
124. *Dublin University Magazine*, 1873, p. 206. See also Adler, 'A Prophet of the People', p. 688; Eitel, *Buddhism*, pp. 6–7; Jersey, 'Buddhism and Christianity', p. 580; *London Quarterly Review*, 1886, pp. 291–2; Bettany, *The Great Indian Religions*, p. 232.
125. Philosinensis, 'Remarks on Budhism', p. 216.
126. Tennent, *Christianity in Ceylon*, p. 191.
127. Scott, *Buddhism and Christianity*, p. 280.
128. Kellogg, *The Light of Asia*, p. 376. See also Kesson, *The Cross and the Dragon*, p. 186.
129. Bryant, 'Buddhism and Christianity', pp. 378–9.
130. Crawfurd, *Journal of an Embassy*, II:98.
131. Upham, *The Mahāvansi*, I:xxxii.
132. Roer, review of Burnouf, *Introduction*, p. 785.
133. Knighton, *Forest Life in Ceylon*, II:2; Alwis, 'Buddhism', p. 4. See also Clarke, 'Buddhism', p. 718.
134. Hardwick, *Christ and Other Masters*, pp. 168–9.
135. Kellogg, *The Light of Asia*, p. 356; Barthélemy St Hilaire, *The Buddha and His Religion*, p. 14. See also Tennent, *Christianity in Ceylon*, p. 204. But cf. p. 205.
136. Chadwick, *The Victorian Church*, II:466.

6 'THE HEATHEN IN HIS BLINDNESS'?

1. Kesson, *The Cross and the Dragon*, p. 180.
2. *The Christian Remembrancer*, 1858, p. 93.
3. Upham, *The History and Doctrine of Budhism*, p. vii.
4. Philosinensis, 'Remarks on Budhism', p. 219. See also Benevolens, 'Burmah', p. 554.
5. Gutzlaff, *China Opened*, II:216 – 17.
6. Kesson, *The Cross and the Dragon*, p. 179.
7. Gogerly, 'On Transmigration', pp. 224 – 25.
8. *London Quarterly Review*, 1854 – 5, p. 439.
9. Hardy, *The British Government and the Idolatry of Ceylon*, p. 9.
10. Hardy, *Legends*, p. ix. See also p. xiii; Carus, *Buddhism*, pp. 263 – 5.
11. Monier-Williams, *The Holy Bible and the Sacred Books of the East*, pp. 12 – 13. See also Monier-Williams, 'Literary Admirers of Buddhism', p. 217. But cf. Carus, *Buddhism*, pp. 306 – 7.
12. *The Church Quarterly Review*, 1891, p. 84. See also Sheffield, 'Christianity and the Ethnic Religions', pp. 108 – 9.
13. Clarke, 'Buddhism', p. 720.
14. *Chambers's Encyclopaedia*, 1874, II:409. But cf. *London Quarterly Review*, 1886, p. 297.
15. Cobbold, *Religion in Japan*, pp. 79 – 80.
16. Knighton, *The History of Ceylon*, p. 86.
17. Scott, *Buddhism and Christianity*, pp. 12 – 13.
18. Culbertson, *Darkness*, p. 70.
19. Claughton, 'Buddhism', p. 141. See also Jersey, 'Buddhism and Christianity', p. 577; Griffin, 'The Burman', p. 659; Rattigan, 'Three Great Asiatic Reformers', p. 312.
20. Titcomb, *Short Chapters on Buddhism*, p. 1.
21. *The Westminster Review*, 1856, p. 326.
22. Ibid., p. 331.
23. Prinsep, *Tibet*, p. 168.
24. *The Westminster Review*, 1878, p. 354. See also Jersey, 'Buddhism and Christianity', p. 591.
25. *The Church Quarterly Review*, 1882, p. 91.
26. Kellogg, *The Light of Asia*, p. 171. See also Johnston, 'Christ and Buddha', pp. 39 – 40.
27. *The Prospective Review*, 1850, p. 492.
28. Maurice, *The Religions of the World*, p. xx. See also Hardwick, *Christ and Other Masters*, p. xii.
29. Grant, *The Religions of the World*, p. 134.
30. Berry, *Christianity and Buddhism*, p. 9.
31. Carpenter, review of Copleston, *Buddhism*, p. 367.
32. Copleston, *Buddhism*, p. x.

33. Beal, *A Catena of Buddhist Scriptures*, p. 8. But cf. Amberley, 'Recent Publications on Buddhism', p. 298, who suggests Beal's conjectures are no less wild and fanciful than the cosmogonical speculations of the Buddhists themselves.
34. Martin, 'Is Buddhism a Preparation', p. 203.
35. Ball, *Is Buddism a Preparation*, p. 9.

Bibliography

Articles by 'Anon', 'Various', and the like are here listed alphabetically according to the title of the journal or periodical in which they appeared.

Abel-Rémusat, Jean P. 'Note sur quelques Epithètes descriptives de Bouddha'. *Journal des Savans* (1819): 625–33.

Adams, W. H. Davenport. *Curiosities of Superstition and Sketches of Some Unrevealed Religions*. London: J. Masters and Co., 1882.

Adler, Felix. 'A Prophet of the People'. *The Atlantic Monthly* 37 (1876): 674–89.

Alabaster, Henry. *The Wheel of the Law*. London: Trübner & Co., 1871.

Alexander, Sidney A. *Sakya-Muni: The Story of Buddha*. Oxford: A. Thomas Shrimpton & Son, 1887.

Allgemeine Deutsche Real-Encyclopädie, Leipzig: Brockhaus, 1833–7; 1843–8; 1851–5; 1864–73.

Allibone, Samuel A. *A Critical Dictionary of English Literature and British and American Authors Living and Deceased* ... 3 vols. Pennsylvania: Lippincott, 1880.

Almond, Philip C. 'The Buddha of Christendom: A Review of the Legend of Barlaam and Josaphat'. *Religious Studies* (forthcoming).

'Buddhism in the West: 300 B.C.–A.D. 400'. *The Journal of Religious History* (forthcoming).

'The Medieval West and Buddhism'. *Eastern Buddhist* 19 (1986), 85–101.

Altick, Richard D. *The English Common Reader: A Social History of the Mass Reading Public 1800–1900*. Chicago: University of Chicago Press, 1957.

Alwis, James. 'Buddhism: Its Origin; History; and Doctrines'. *Journal of the Pali Text Society* 1 (1883): 1–37.

Ambereley, John R. 'Recent Publications on Buddhism'. *The Theological Review* 9 (1872): 293–317.

Bibliography

Anderson, Robert. *The Buddha of Christendom*. London: Hodder & Stoughton, 1899.

Armstrong, Richard A. 'Buddhism and Christianity'. *The Theological Review* 7 (1870):176–200.

Arnold, Edwin. *The Light of Asia*. New York: Crowell & Co., 1884.

Anon. 'Chinese Buddhism'. *Asiatic Journal and Monthly Register* 6 (1831): 260–6.

Anon. 'Colossal Statue of Buddha'. *Asiatic Journal and Monthly Register* 23 (1827):252.

Anon. 'On the Three Principal Religions in China'. *Asiatic Journal and Monthly Register* 9 (1832):302–16.

Baker, Samuel W. *Eight Years in Ceylon*. London: Longmans, Green & Co., 1891.

Balfour, D. M. 'Buddhism'. *The Universalist Quarterly and General Review* 31 (1874):5–6.

Ball, J. Dyer. *Is Buddism a Preparation or Hindrance to Christianity in China?* Hong Kong: St Paul's College, 1907.

Barham, Francis. 'Buddha and his Critics'. *The Times*, 24 April 1857.

Barrow, John. *Travels in China, Containing Descriptions, Observations, and Comparisons, Made and Collected in the Course of a Short Residence at the Imperial Palace of Yuen-Min-Yuen* ... London: T. Cadell & W. Davies, 1804.

Barth, Auguste, *The Religions of India*. London: Kegan Paul, Trench, Trübner, & Co., 1891.

Barthélemy St Hilaire, Jules. *The Buddha and His Religion*. London: George Routledge, 1895.

Beal, Samuel. *A Catena of Buddhist Scriptures from the Chinese*. London: Trübner & Co., 1871.

Buddhism in China. London: S.P.C.K., 1884.

The Romantic Legend of Sakya Buddha. London: Trübner & Co., 1875.

Beames, John. 'A Plain Account of Buddhism', *The Imperial and Asiatic Quarterly Review* 2 (1896):145–61; 3 (1897):144–58.

Benevolens. 'Burmah: Doctrines and Practices of the Budhists; their Geography, Astronomy, and Upper Regions; Rewards and Punishments ...' *The Chinese Repository* 2 (1834):554–63.

'Burmah: – its Situation, Extent, Population, Productions and Trade ...' *The Chinese Repository* 2 (1834):500–6.

Benn, Alfred W. Review of Copleston, *Buddhism*. *The Academy* 43 (1893): 145–6.

Bennett, John W. *Ceylon and its Capabilities; an Account of its Natural Resources, Indigenous Productions, and Commercial Facilities* ... London: W.H. Allen & Co., 1843.

Berry, Thomas S. *Christianity and Buddhism*. London: S.P.C.K., 1891.

Bibliography

Best, Geoffrey. *Mid-Victorian Britain: 1851–1875*. London: Weidenfeld and Nicolson, 1971.

Bettany, George T. *The Great Indian Religions*. London: Ward, Lock, Bowden & Co., 1892.

Bigandet, Paul A. *The Life, or Legend of Gaudama, the Budha of the Burmese*. Rangoon: American Mission Press, 1866.

Bird, James. *Historical Researches on the Origin and Principles of the Bauddha and Jaina Religions* ... Bombay: American Mission Press, 1847.

Bixby, James T. 'Buddhism in the New Testament'. *Arena* 3 (1890): 555–6.

Bloomfield, Maurice. 'The Essentials of Buddhist Doctrine and Ethics'. *International Journal of Ethics* 2 (1891–2): 313–26.

Brandon, Ruth. *The Spiritualists*. London: Weidenfeld and Nicolson, 1983.

Brear, Douglas, 'Early Assumptions in Western Buddhist Studies'. *Religion* 5 (1975): 136–59.

The British Cyclopaedia of Literature, History, Geography, Law, and Politics. London: Orr & Smith, 1835–8.

Anon. Review of Lillie, *The Popular Life of Buddha*. *British Quarterly Review* 80 (1884): 175.

Brockett, Linus P. 'Buddhism: Its Origins and Results'. *Methodist Quarterly Review* 21 (1861): 219–27.

Bryant, William M. 'Buddhism and Christianity'. *Andover Review* 2 (1884): 255–68, 365–81.

Buchanan, Francis. 'On the Religion and Literature of the Burmas'. *Asiatick Researches* 6 (1799): 163–308.

de Bunsen, Ernest. *The Angel-Messiah of Buddhists, Essenes, and Christians*. London: Longmans, Green & Co., 1880.

Burnouf, Emile. 'Le Bouddhisme en Occident'. *Revue des Deux Mondes* 88 (1888): 340–72.

Burnouf, Eugène. *Introduction à l'histoire du Buddhisme indien*. Paris: Imprimerie Royale, 1844.

Burnouf, Eugène and Lassen, Christian. *Essai sur le Pali, ou Langue sacrée de la presqu'île au-delà du Gange*. Paris: Librairie Orientale de Dondey-Dupré Père et Fils, 1826.

Caird, John. *Buddhism*. New York: J. B. Alden, 1883.

Anon. 'Indian Buddhism – Its Origin and Diffusion'. *The Calcutta Review* 4 (1845): 241–81.

Calvin, John. *Institutes of the Christian Religion*. London: S.C.M. Press, 1961.

Campbell, Bruce F. *Ancient Wisdom Revived: A History of the Theosophical Movement*. Berkeley: University of California Press, 1980.

Candlin, George T. 'What should be our Attitude toward the False Religions?' *The Chinese Recorder* 23 (1892): 99–110.

Carpenter, J. Estlin. 'The Obligations of the New Testament to Buddhism'. *The Nineteenth Century* 8 (1880): 971–84.

Bibliography

Carus, Paul. *Buddhism and its Christian Critics*. Chicago: Open Court Publishing Co., 1897.

Chadwick, Owen. *The Victorian Church*. 2 vols. London: A. & C. Black, 1970.

Chambers, William. 'Some Account of the Sculptures and Ruins at Mavalipuram, a Place a few Miles North of Sadras ...' *Asiatick Researches* 1 (1788): 145 – 70.

Chambers's Encyclopaedia. London: W. & R. Chambers, 1860 – 8; 1874.

Child, Lydia M. 'Resemblances between the Buddhist and Roman Catholic Religions'. *The Atlantic Monthly* 26 (1870): 660 – 5.

Childers, Robert C. *A Dictionary of the Pali Language*. London: Kegan Paul, Trench, Trübner & Co., 1909.

'Notes on Dhammapada, with Special Reference to the Question of Nirvāna'. *The Journal of the Royal Asiatic Society* 5 (1871): 219 – 30.

Anon. Review of *Paraméswara-jnyána-góshthí. A Dialogue of the Knowledge of the Supreme Lord* ... Cambridge: Deighton, Bell & Co., 1856. *The Christian Remembrancer* 35 (1858): 81 – 129.

Anon. 'Buddhism'. *The Church Quarterly Review* 31 (1891): 70 – 85.

Anon. 'The Rise of Buddhism'. *The Church Quarterly Review* 14 (1882): 88 – 107.

Clarke, James F. 'Buddhism: or, the Protestantism of the East'. *The Atlantic Monthly* 23 (1869): 713 – 28.

Claughton, Peter C. 'Buddhism'. *Journal of the Transactions of the Victoria Institute* 8 (1874): 138 – 66.

Clausen, Christopher. 'Victorian Buddhism and the Origins of Comparative Religion'. *Religion* 5 (1973): 1 – 15.

Cobbold, George A. *Religion in Japan: Shintoism, Buddhism, Christianity*. London: S.P.C.K., 1894.

Cockshut, Anthony, O.J., ed. *Religious Controversies of the Nineteenth Century: Selected Documents*. London: Methuen, 1966.

Coleman, Charles. *The Mythology of the Hindus*. London: Parbury, Allen & Co., 1832.

Colinet, Ph. 'Recent works on Primitive Buddhism'. *The Dublin Review* 19 (1888): 121 – 39; 23 (1890): 256 – 85.

Collins, Richard et alii. 'Buddhism, and "The Light of Asia"'. *Journal of the Transactions of the Victoria Institute* 28 (1897): 153 – 89.

Copleston, Reginald S. 'Buddhism'. *The Nineteenth Century* 24 (1888): 119 – 35.

Buddhism; Primitive & Present in Magadha and in Ceylon. London: Longmans, 1892.

Colquhoun, Archibald R. *Amongst the Shans*. London: Field and Tuer, conjointly with Simpkin, Marshall & Co. and Hamilton, Adams & Co., 1885.

Cox, Hiram. *Journal of a Residence in the Burmhan Empire, and more particularly at the Court of Amarapoorah.* London: Warren & Whittaker, 1821.

Cranmer-Byng, J.L., ed. *An Embassy to China. Being the Journal kept by Lord Macartney during his Embassy to the Emperor Ch'ien Lung 1793 –1794.* Hamden, Connecticut: Archon Books, 1963.

Crawfurd, John. *History of the Indian Archipelago: Containing an Account of the Manners, Arts, Languages, Religions, Institutions, and Commerce of its Inhabitants.* 3 vols. Edinburgh: Archibald Constable & Co., 1820.

Journal of an Embassy from the Governor-General of India to the Courts of Siam and Cochin China. 2 vols. London: Colburn & Bentley, 1830.

Creuzer, Friedrich. *Symbolik und Mythologie der alten Völker, besonders der Griechen im Auszuge von Dr. Georg Heinrich Moser.* Leipzig: Carl Wilhelm Leske, 1822.

Culbertson, Michael S. *Darkness in the Flowery Land.* New York: Charles Scribner, 1857.

Cunningham, Alexander. *The Bhilsa Topes; or, Buddhist Monuments of Central India: Comprising a brief historical Sketch of the Rise, Progress, and Decline of Buddhism* ... Varanasi: Indological Book House, 1966.

Davids, T.W. Rhys. 'The Ancient Buddhist Belief Concerning God'. *Modern Review* 1 (1880): 219 – 23.

'Buddha's First Sermon'. *Fortnightly Review* 32 (1879): 899 – 911.

'Buddhism'. *The Encyclopaedia Britannica,* IV:424 – 38. Edinburgh: A. & C. Black, 1876.

Buddhism. London: S.P.C.K., 1877.

'Buddhism and Christianity'. *The International Quarterly* 7 (1903): 1 – 13.

Lectures on the Origin and Growth of Religion as Illustrated by some Points in the History of Indian Buddhism. London: Williams and Norgate, 1881.

Davies, William. 'The Religion of Gotama Buddha'. *The Atlantic Monthly* 74 (1894): 334 – 40.

Davis, John F. *China: A General Description of that Empire and its Inhabitants, &c.* 2 vols. London: John Murray, 1857.

Davy, John. *An Account of the Interior of Ceylon and of its Inhabitants, with Travels in that Island.* Reprinted in *Ceylon Historical Journal* 16 (1969).

Dennis, James S. *Christian Missions and Social Progress.* 3 vols. Edinburgh: Oliphant, Anderson & Ferrier, 1897, 1899, n.d.

Dods, Marcus. *Mohammed, Buddha, and Christ.* London: Hodder and Stoughton, 1888.

Anon. 'Buddhism and its Founder'. *Dublin University Magazine* 82 (1873): 206 – 18.

Dubose, Hampden C. *The Dragon, Image and Demon, or the Three Religions of China.* London: S.W. Partridge & Co., 1886.

Dunlap, Eugene P. 'Buddhist Priests of Siam'. *Church at Home and Abroad* 11 (1892): 423 – 6.

Bibliography

The Edinburgh Encyclopaedia. Edinburgh: William Blackwood, 1830.

Anon. *'Asiatic Researches: or, Transactions of the Society instituted in Bengal, for inquiring into the History and Antiquities, the Arts, Sciences and Literature of Asia,* vol. VI. 1801'. *The Edinburgh Review* 1 (1803): 26–43.

Anon. *'Asiatic Researches: or, Transactions of the Society instituted in Bengal, for inquiring into the History and Antiquities, the Arts, Sciences and Literature of Asia.* Volume the Second. London, 1804'. *The Edinburgh Review* 9 (1807): 92–101, 278–304.

Anon. Review of Taylor, J., *Prabodh Chandrodaya* ... London, 1812. *The Edinburgh Review* 22 (1813–14): 400–9.

Anon. 'Recent Researches on Buddhism'. *The Edinburgh Review* 115 (1862): 379–408.

Edkins, Joseph. 'Notices of Buddhism in China'. *North China Herald,* no. 196, 29 April 1854.

The Religious Condition of the Chinese. London: Routledge, Warnes, & Routledge, 1859.

Review of Beal, *The Romantic Legend. The Academy* 10 (1876–7): 376–7.

Chinese Buddhism. London: K. Paul, Trench, Trübner & Co., 1893.

Religion in China. London: Kegan Paul, Trench, Trübner & Co., 1893.

Eitel, Ernest J. *Buddhism: Its Historical, Theoretical and Popular Aspects.* London: Trübner & Co., 1884.

Ellinwood, Frank F. *Oriental Religions and Christianity.* New York: Charles Scribner's Sons, 1892.

Encyclopaedia Britannica. Edinburgh: Bell & MacFarquhar, 1797; Edinburgh: Constable, Vernor, Hood, & Sharpe, 1810; Edinburgh: Constable, Gale & Fenner, Wilson & Sons, 1817; Edinburgh: A. & C. Black, 1842.

The Encyclopaedia Britannica. Edinburgh: A. & C. Black, 1853–60.

The Encyclopaedia Edinensis. Edinburgh: John Anderson, 1827.

Encyclopaedia Metropolitana. London: B. Fellowes, etc., 1845.

Encyclopaedia Perthensis. Perth: C. Mitchel & Co., *c.* 1807.

The English Encyclopaedia. London: G. Kearsley, 1802.

Ersch, Johann S., and Gruber, J.G., eds. 'Buddha, Buddhaismus'. *Allgemeine Encyclopädie der Wissenschaften und Künste* ... Leipzig: 1818–89.

Erskine, William H. 'Observations on the Remains of the Bouddhists in India'. *Transactions of the Asiatic Society of Bombay* 3 (1823): 494–537.

Everett, Charles C. 'Recent Studies in Buddhism'. *The Unitarian Review* 18 (1882): 421–36.

Faber, George S. *The Origin of Pagan Idolatry Ascertained from Historical Testimony and Circumstantial Evidence.* 3 vols. London: F. & C. Rivingtons, 1816.

Fairbairn, Andrew M. 'History of Religions'. *The Contemporary Review* 47 (1885): 436 – 43.

Fergusson, James. *Tree and Serpent Worship: Or Illustrations of Mythology and Art in India.* London: W. H. Allen, 1868.

Feudge, Fannie R. 'The Mammoth Religion of the World'. *Galaxy* 16 (1873): 342 – 54.

Filliozat, Jean. *Studies in Asokan Inscriptions.* Calcutta: Indian Studies Past and Present, 1967.

Forbes, Jonathan. *Eleven Years in Ceylon, comprising Sketches of the Field Sports and Natural History and an Account of its History and Antiquities.* 2 vols. London: Richard Bentley, 1841.

'Notes on the Buddhas from Ceylonese Authorities ...'. *The Journal of the Asiatic Society of Bengal* 5 (1836): 321 – 30.

Francklin, William. *Researches on the Tenets and Doctrines of the Jeynes and Buddhists Conjectured to be the Brahmans of Ancient India, with Discussion on Serpent Worship.* London: Francklin, 1827.

Frazer, Robert W. *A Literary History of India.* London: T. Fisher Unwin, 1898.

Froude, James A. *Short Studies on Great Subjects.* Vol. IV. London: Longmans, Green, & Co., 1899.

Galton, Charles. 'The Founder of Buddhism', *The Month* 79 (1893): 153 – 60.

'The Morality of Buddhism'. *The Month* 78 (1892 – 3): 4 – 15.

Gerhart, Emanuel V. 'Original Buddhism'. *Reformed Quarterly Review* 39 (1892): 291 – 308.

Gilmour, James. *Among the Mongols.* London: The Religious Tract Society, 1888.

Glacken, Clarence J. *Traces on the Rhodian Shore.* Berkeley: University of California Press, 1976.

Gmeiner, John. 'The Light of Asia and the Light of the World'. *The Catholic World* 42 (1885): 1 – 9.

Gogerly, Daniel J. 'An Introductory Sketch of Buddhism'. In Gogerly, *Ceylon Buddhism,* 1 – 14.

'An Outline of Buddhism'. In Gogerly, *Ceylon Buddhism,* 15 – 44. *Ceylon Buddhism.* 2 vols. Colombo: Wesleyan Methodist Book Room, 1908.

'On Transmigration'. In Gogerly, *Ceylon Buddhism,* 211 – 48.

Goodwin, Charles W. 'Mosaic Cosmogony'. In *Religious Controversies,* edited by Anthony Cockshut, pp. 136 – 69.

Grant, George M. *The Religions of the World.* London: A. & C. Black, 1895.

Green, Robert F. 'Christianity and Buddhism'. *Proceedings of the Literary and Philosophical Society of Liverpool* 44 (1890): 299 – 322.

Bibliography

Griffin, Lepel H. 'The Burman and his Creed'. *The Fortnightly Review* 54 (1890): 657–73.

Grosier. *A General Description of China: Containing the Topography of the Fifteen provinces which Compose this Vast Empire* ... 2 vols. London: G. G. & J. Robinson, 1795.

Gutzlaff, Charles F. *China Opened.* 2 vols. London: Smith, Elder & Co., 1838.

'Journal of a Residence in Siam, and of a Voyage along the Coast of China to Mantchou Tartary'. *The Chinese Repository* 1 (1832–3): 16–25, 274–6.

'Remarks on the Present State of Buddhism in China'. *The Journal of the Royal Asiatic Society of Bengal* 16 (1856): 73–92.

Hardwick, Charles. *Christ and other Masters. An Historical Inquiry into Some of the Chief Parallelisms and Contrasts between Christianity and the Religious Systems of the Ancient World.* London: Macmillan & Co., 1875.

Hardy, R. Spence. *The British Government and the Idolatry of Ceylon.* London: Crofts & Blenkarn, 1841.

Christianity and Buddhism Compared. Colombo: Wesleyan Mission Press, 1874.

Legends and Theories of the Buddhists. London: Williams & Norgate, 1881.

A Manual of Buddhism. Varanasi: Chowkhamba Sanskrit Series Office, 1967.

de Harlez, Charles. 'The Buddhistic Schools'. *The Dublin Review* 43 (1889): 47–71.

Harrison, Frederic, ed. *The New Calendar of Great Men: Biographies of the 558 Worthies of All Ages and Nations in the Positivist Calendar of Auguste Comte.* London: Macmillan, 1892.

Heyck, Thomas W. *The Transformation of Intellectual Life in Victorian England.* London: Croom Helm, 1982.

Hibbert, Christopher. *The Dragon Wakes.* London: Longman, 1970.

Hodgson, Brian H. *Essays on the Languages, Literature and Religion of Nepal and Tibet.* 2 vols. in one. London: Trübner & Co., 1874.

'European Speculations on Buddhism'. In Hodgson, *Essays*, I: 96–101.

'Notices of the Languages, Literature, and Religion of Nepal and Tibet'. In Hodgson, *Essays*, I: 1–35.

'Quotations from Original Sanskrit Authorities in Proof and Illustration of the Preceding Article'. In Hodgson, *Essays*, I: 65–96.

Holbrook, Silas P. *Sketches by a Traveller.* Boston: Carter & Hendee, 1830.

Houghton, Walter E. *The Victorian Frame of Mind, 1830–1870.* New Haven: Yale University Press, 1957.

Huc, Eviariste-Regis. *Travels in Tartary, Thibet and China, 1844–1849.* 2 vols. London: Routledge & Sons, 1928.

Hume, David. *An Inquiry Concerning the Principles of Morals.* New York: Liberal Arts Press, 1957.

173

Humphreys, T. Christmas. *The Development of Buddhism in England*. London: The Buddhist Lodge, 1937.

Sixty Years of Buddhism in England. London: The Buddhist Society, 1968.

Huxley, Leonard. *Life and Letters of Thomas Henry Huxley*. 2 vols. London: Macmillan, 1900.

Huxley, Thomas H. *Evolution and Ethics and Other Essays*. London: Macmillan, 1911.

Anon. 'Buddhism and its Legends'. *The Intellectual Observer* 10 (1867): 421–8.

Jersey, Margaret Child-Villiers, Countess of. 'Buddhism and Christianity'. *The National Review* 4 (1884–5): 577–91.

J.M.M. 'Buddhism'. *Journal of Sacred Literature* 35 (1865): 281–300.

Johnston, J. Wesley. 'Christ and Buddha: Resemblances and Contrasts'. *Methodist Review* 58 (1898): 32–40.

Joinville, ?Pierre. 'On the Religion and Manners of the People of Ceylon'. *Asiatick Researches* 7 (1801): 399–446.

Jones, William. 'On the Chronology of the Hindus'. *Asiatick Researches* 2 (1790): 111–47.

'Dissertation 111. On the Hindu's, being the Third Anniversary Discourse Delivered to the Society, Feb. 2, 1786'. In Jones, William, et alii. *Dissertations and Miscellaneous Pieces Relating to the History and Antiquities, the Arts, Sciences, and Literature, of Asia*. Dublin: P. Byrne & W. Jones, 1793.

'A Supplement to the Essay on Indian Chronology'. *Asiatick Researches* 2 (1790): 389–403.

de Jong, J.W. 'A Brief History of Buddhist Studies in Europe and America'. *The Eastern Buddhist* 7 (1974): i:55–106, ii:49–82.

Judson, Ann H. *An Account of the American Baptist Mission to the Burman Empire. In a Series of Letters addressed to a Gentleman in London*. London: Joseph Butterworth & Son, 1827.

Kaempfer, Engelbert. *The History of Japan together with a Description of the Kingdom of Siam, 1690–1692*. 3 vols. Glasgow: James MacLehose & Sons, 1906.

Kellogg, Samuel H. *The Light of Asia and the Light of the World*. London: Macmillan, 1885.

Kennedy, Vans. *Researches into the Nature and Affinity of Ancient and Hindu Mythology*. London: Longman, Rees, Orme, Brown & Green, 1831.

Kesson, John. *The Cross and the Dragon*. London: Smith, Elder, & Co., 1854.

Kistner, Otto. *Buddha and his Doctrine: A Bibliographical Essay*. London: Trübner & Co., 1869.

Bibliography

Knighton, William. *Forest Life in Ceylon (With Four Dialogues between a Buddhist and a Christian).* 2 vols. London: Hurst & Blackett, 1854.

The History of Ceylon from the Earliest Period to the Present Time. London: Longman, Brown, Green & Longmans, etc., 1845.

Knox, Robert. *An Historical Relation of Ceylone.* Ceylon: Tisara Prakasakayo, 1966.

Koeppen, Carl F. *Die Religion des Buddha und ihre Entstehung.* 2 vols. Berlin: Ferdinand Schneider, 1857–9.

Lassen, Christian. *Indische Alterthumskunde.* 4 vols. Bonn: H.B. König, 1847–62.

Le Comte, Louis. *Memoirs and Observations … Made in a late Journey Through the Empire of China.* London: Benjamin Tooke, 1699.

Lillie, Arthur. *Buddha and Early Buddhism.* London: Trübner & Co., 1881.

The Influence of Buddhism on Primitive Christianity. London: Sonnenschein, 1893.

The Popular Life of Buddha. London: Kegan Paul, Trench & Co., 1883.

Anon. Review of Lillie, Arthur, *Buddha and Buddhism.* Edinburgh: T. & T. Clark, 1900. *Literature* 8 (1901): 243–4.

The London Encyclopaedia. London: Thomas Tegg, 1829.

Anon. 'Buddhism'. *London Quarterly Review* 10 (1858): 513–44.

Anon. 'Modern Buddhism'. *London Quarterly Review* 72 (1888–9): 325–46.

Anon. 'The British Government and Buddhism', *London Quarterly Review* 3 (1854–5): 436–56.

Anon. 'The Religion of Burmah'. *London Quarterly Review* 67 (1886): 283–97.

Loubère, Simon de la. *A New Historical Relation of the Kingdom of Siam.* London: no publisher, 1693.

Low, J. 'General Observations on the Contending Claims to Antiquity of Brahmans and Buddhists'. *The Journal of the Asiatic Society of Bengal* 18 (1849): 89–130.

Lubac, Henri de. *La Rencontre du Bouddhisme et de l'Occident.* Paris: Aubier, 1952.

MacDonald, Frederika. 'Buddha and Buddhism'. *Religious Systems of the World.* London: Swan Sonnenschein, 1890.

Machar, Agnes M. 'Buddha and Buddhism'. *The Canadian Monthly* 13 (1877–8): 35–42, 165–71.

Mahony, Capt. ?William C. 'On *Singhala*, or *Ceylon*, and the Doctrines of BHOODHA, from the Books of the *Singhalais*'. *Asiatick Researches* 7 (1801): 32–56.

Malalasekera, G.P. *Encyclopaedia of Buddhism.* Ceylon: Government of Ceylon, 1961.

Manuel, Frank E. *Isaac Newton Historian.* Cambridge, Mass.: Belknap Press, 1963.

Bibliography

The Eighteenth Century Confronts the Gods. Cambridge, Mass.: Harvard University Press, 1959.

Marshall, Peter J., ed. *The British Discovery of Hinduism in the Eighteenth Century.* Cambridge: Cambridge University Press, 1970.

Marshall, Peter J. and Williams, Glyndwr. *The Great Map of Mankind: British Perceptions of the World in the Age of Enlightenment.* London: J.M. Dent & Sons, 1982.

Martin, William A.P. 'Is Buddhism a Preparation for Christianity?' *The Chinese Recorder* 20 (1889): 193–203.

Maurice, Frederick D. *The Religions of the World and their Relation to Christianity.* London: Macmillan, 1861.

Medhurst, Walter H. *China: Its State and Prospects.* London: John Snow, 1838.

Mill, James. 'Religion and Character of the Hindus'. *The Edinburgh Review* 29 (1817–18): 377–403.

The History of British India. London: Baldwin, Craddock, & Joy, 1817; London: James Madden & Co., 1840–8; London: James Madden & Co., 1858.

Monier-Williams, Monier. *Buddhism, in its Connexion with Brahmanism & Hinduism, and in its Contrast with Christianity.* London: John Murray, 1889.

The Holy Bible and the Sacred Books of the East. London: Seeley & Co., 1887.

'Literary Admirers of Buddhism', *Our Day* 3 (1888–9): 215–21.

Anon. Review of Upham, *The History and Doctrine of Budhism. Monthly Review* 118 (1829): 577–91.

Moor, Edward. *The Hindu Pantheon.* London: J. Johnson, 1810.

Müller, F. Max. 'A Bishop on Buddhism'. *The New Review* 8 (1893): 107–15.

'Buddhist Pilgrims'. In Müller, *Selected Essays*, II:234–79.

'Christianity and Buddhism'. *The New Review* 4 (1891): 67–74.

The Dhammapada. Oxford: Clarendon, 1898.

'Lecture on Buddhist Nihilism'. In Müller, F. Max, *Lectures on the Science of Religion.* New York: Scribner & Co., 1872, 129–47.

'The Meaning of Nirvana'. In Müller, *Selected Essays*, II:280–91.

Selected Essays on Language, Mythology, and Religion. Vol. II. London: Longmans, Green, & Co., 1881.

The National Cyclopaedia of Useful Knowledge. London: Charles Knight, 1847–51; London: Routledge & Co., 1856–9.

The National Encyclopaedia: A Dictionary of Useful Knowledge. London: William Mackenzie, 1867–8.

Neale, Edward V. 'Buddha and Buddhism'. *Macmillan's Magazine* 1 (1860): 439–48.

Neumann, Ch. F. 'Buddhism and Shamanism'. *Asiatic Journal and Monthly Register* 16 (1835): 124–6.

Bibliography

Anon. 'Buddhism'. *New Englander* 3 (1845):182-91.

Various. 'The Influence upon Morality of a Decline in Religious Belief'. *The Nineteenth Century* 1 (1877):331-58, 531-46.

Oldenberg, Hermann. *Buddha: His Life, His Doctrine, His Order*. London: Williams & Norgate, 1882.

Anon. 'The History and Doctrine of Budhism'. *Oriental Herald and Journal of General Literature* 21 (1829):93-103.

Otto, Rudolf. 'Parallelen und Wertunterschiede im Christentum und Buddatum'. Rudolf Otto Archive, University of Marburg.

Pals, Daniel L. *The Victorian 'Lives' of Jesus*. San Antonio: Trinity University Press, 1982.

Pantologia. A New Cyclopaedia. London: G. Kearsley, 1813.

The Penny Cyclopaedia. London: Charles Knight, 1833- .

Percival, Robert. *An Account of the Island of Ceylon containing its History, Geography, Natural History, with the Manners and Customs of its Various Inhabitants* ... Reprinted in *The Ceylon Historical Journal* 22 (1975).

Philips, Richard. *The Story of Gautama Buddha and his Creed: An Epic*. London: Longmans, Green, & Co., 1871.

Philosinensis, 'Remarks on Budhism; together with Brief Notices of the Island of Poo-to and of the Numerous Priests who Inhabit it'. *The Chinese Repository* 2 (1834):214-25.

Platts, John. *The Manners and Customs of All Nations*. London: Henry Fisher, Son, & Co., 1827.

Prinsep, Henry T., and Prinsep, James. *Tibet, Tartary, and Mongolia: Their Social and Political Condition and the Religion of Boodh, as there Existing*. London: W. H. Allen, 1851.

Anon. 'Eastern Monachism'. *The Prospective Review* 6 (1850):473-93.

Anon. Review of Monier-Williams, *Buddhism*, and Oldenberg, *Buddha: His Life, His Doctrine, His Order. The Quarterly Review* 170 (1890): 318-46.

Rattigan, William H. 'Three Great Asiatic Reformers: A Study and a Contrast'. *London Quarterly Review* 92 (1899):291-312.

Roer, Eduard. Review of Burnouf, *Introduction. The Journal of the Asiatic Society of Bengal* 16 (1845):783-809.

Rowell, Geoffrey. *Hell and the Victorians*. Oxford: Clarendon Press, 1974.

Said, Edward. *Orientalism*. London: Routledge and Kegan Paul, 1978.

Salisbury, Edward E. 'M. Burnouf on the History of Buddhism in India'. *Journal of the American Oriental Society* 1 (1849):275-98.

'Memoir on the History of Buddhism, read before the American Oriental Society, at their Annual Meeting, in Boston, May 28, 1844'. *Journal of the American Oriental Society* 1 (1849):79-135.

Sandberg, Graham. 'Philosophical Buddhism in Tibet'. *The Contemporary Review* 57 (1890):256-71.

Bibliography

Sangermano. *A Description of the Burmese Empire. Compiled chiefly from Burmese Documents*. London: Susil Gupta, 1966.

Sargant, William L. *Buddha and His Religion*. Birmingham: William Hodgetts, 1864.

Anon. 'Attractions of Modern Buddhism'. *The Saturday Review* 58 (1884): 248–9.

Anon. 'Buddha's Doctrine'. *The Saturday Review* 54 (1882): 765–6.

Anon. 'Buddhism and Christianity'. *The Saturday Review* 55 (1883): 694–5.

Schumann, Hans W. *Buddhism: An Outline of its Teachings and Schools*. Wheaton, Illinois: Theosophical Publishing House, 1974.

Scott, Archibald. *Buddhism and Christianity: A Parallel and a Contrast*. Edinburgh: David Douglas, 1890.

Scott, Patrick. 'The Business of Belief: The Emergence of "Religious" Publishing'. In *Sanctity and Secularity: The Church and the World*, edited by Derek Baker, pp. 213–24. Oxford: Blackwell, 1973.

Anon. 'Mr. Fielding on Buddhism'. *Scottish Review* 33 (1899): 286–301.

Sheffield, D. Z. 'Christianity and the Ethnic Religions'. *The Chinese Recorder* 34 (1903): 106–18.

'Dr. Kellogg's "Light of Asia and Light of the World"'. *New Englander* 49 (1888): 24–34.

Simpson, William O., ed. *The Hindu Pantheon by Edward Moor*. Madras: J. Higginbotham, 1864.

Sirr, Henry C. *Ceylon and the Cingalese; Their History, Government, and Religion, the Antiquities, Institutions, Produce, Revenue, and Capabilities of the Island ...* 2 vols. London: William Shoberl, 1850.

Söderblom, Nathan. 'Holiness'. In *Encyclopaedia of Religion and Ethics*, edited by James Hastings, VI: 731–41. Edinburgh: T. & T. Clark, 1913.

Speir, Charlotte. *Life in Ancient India*. London: Smith, Elder, & Co., 1856.

Stewart, John. 'An Account of the Kingdom of Thibet. In a letter from John Stewart, Esquire, F.R.S., to Sir John Pringle, Bart., P.R.S.' *Philosophical Transactions* 67 (1777): 465–89.

Strong, Dawsonne M. *The Metaphysic of Christianity and Buddhism: A Symphony*. London: Watts & Co., 1899.

'The Revival of Buddhism in India'. *The Westminster Review* 153 (1900): 271–82.

Symes, Michael. *An Account of an Embassy to the Kingdom of Ava in the year 1795*. 2 vols. Edinburgh: Constable & Co., 1827.

Tennent, James E. *Christianity in Ceylon; Its Introduction and Progress under the Portuguese, the Dutch, the British, and American Missions: With an Historical Sketch of the Brahmanical and Buddhist Superstitions*. London: John Murray, 1850.

Bibliography

Anon. 'The Oriental Collections at the British Museum'. *The Times*, 12 April 1886, p. 12.

Titcomb, Jonathan H. *Short Chapters on Buddhism, Past and Present*. London: Religious Tract Society, 1883.

Torrens, Henry D. *Travels in Ladák, Tartary, and Kashmir*. London: Saunders, Otley, & Co., 1862.

Anon. 'Announcement of Illustrated Edition of Arnold's *The Light of Asia*'. *Trübner's American, European & Oriental Literary Record* 5 (1884): 90.

Turnour, George. *The First Twenty Chapters of the Mahawanso: and a Prefatory Essay on Pali Buddhistical Literature* ... Ceylon: Cotta Church Mission Press, 1836.

Upham, Edward. *The History and Doctrine of Budhism*. London: R. Ackermann, 1829.

The Mahávansi, the Rájá-Ratnácari, and the Rájá-Vali, forming the Sacred and Historical Books of Ceylon; also a collection of Tracts Illustrative of the Doctrines and Literature of Buddhism. 3 vols. London: Parbury, Allen & Co., 1833.

Ward, William. *A View of the History, Literature, and Religion of the Hindoos: Including a Minute Description of their Manners and Customs and Translations from their Principal Works*. 2 vols. London: Black, Parbury, & Allen, 1817.

Ware, Edgar J. 'The Development of Buddhism in India'. *The Fortnightly Review* 33 (1879–80): 801–21.

Watters, Thomas. 'Mr. Eitel's Three Lectures on Buddhism'. *The Chinese Recorder* 4 (1871): 64–8.

Welbon, Guy R. *The Buddhist Nirvāna and Its Western Interpreters*. Chicago: University of Chicago Press, 1968.

The Wellesley Index to Victorian Periodicals 1824–1900. 3 vols. Toronto: University of Toronto Press, 1966–

Anon. 'Buddhism: Mythical and Historical'. *The Westminster Review* 66 (1856): 296–331.

Anon. Review of Beal, *The Buddhist Tipitaka*, 1876; *A Letter to Dr. R. Rost, Librarian, India Office, London*, 1874; *A Catena of Buddhist Scriptures*, 1871; *The Romantic History of Buddha*, 1875. *The Westminster Review* 53 (1878): 328–54.

Wilford, Francis. 'An Essay on the Sacred Isles in the West with other Essays connected with that Work'. *Asiatic Researches* 8 (1805): 245–368.

Wilkinson, William C. *Edwin Arnold as Poetizer and as Paganizer*. New York: Funk and Wagnalls, 1884.

Wilson, Horace H. 'On Buddha and Buddhism'. *The Journal of the Royal Asiatic Society of Great Britain and Ireland* 16 (1856): 229–65.

Bibliography

Wright, Brooks. *Sir Edwin Arnold: The Interpreter of Buddhism to the West.* New York: Bookman Associates Inc., 1957.

Yoe, Shway. 'Buddhists and Buddhism in Burma'. *The Cornhill Magazine* 42 (1880): 721–31.

Yule, Henry. *A Narrative of the Mission sent by the Governor-General of India to the Court of Ava in 1855, with Notices of the Country, Government, and People.* London: Smith, Elder, & Co., 1858.

Index

Index

Buchanan, Francis, 11, 23, 57, 61, 70, 108, 112, 118, 122, 128
Buddha: an avatar, 15–16, 30, 59; a god, 9, 10, 15–16, 39, 56, 57, 58, 61, 64; a heretic, 15, 17, 20; historical, 2, 17–20, 55, 56, 60–4, 65; lives of, 48, 66–9, 126; mythological, 55, 56, 139; a reformer, 3, 17, 18, 29, 30, 60, 72, 73, 74, 75, 76; statuary, 9, 20, 21, 24, 125; 'two Buddhas' theory, 17–19; *see also* Gautama, Sakya Muni, Sommona-Codom, Siddhartha
Buddhist hell, 44
Buddhist monks, *see* Buddhist priests
Buddhist priests, 10–11, 38, 80, 85, 108, 119–23; *see also* bonzes, Ho-Chang, lamas, monasticism, Poonghees, Talapoins
Bunsen, Ernest de, 127, 128; *The Angel-Messiah of Buddhists, Essenes, and Christians* 127
Burnouf, Eugène, 19, 24, 25, 26, 27, 28, 32, 34, 58, 63, 97, 103; *Introduction à l'histoire du Buddhisme indien*, 19, 24, 25, 28, 32, 58, 97; *Essai sur le Pali*, 27, 63

Caird, John, 78, 81, 112, 113
Carlyle, Thomas, 69, 73
Carpenter, Joseph Estlin, 68, 137
caste system (Hindu), 72, 74, 75, 76
Catholicism, 73, 74, 75, 76, 119, 141; and Buddhism, 73–6, 123–6, 127, 131; Victorian attitudes towards, 73–6, 119, 127, 131
Chadwick, Owen, 111, 130
Chandler, Henry, 115
Chandragupta, Maurya, 64
Chambers, William, 9, 14, 26, 57
Child-Villiers, Margaret, 39, 106
Childers, Robert C., 28, 103, 107; *A Dictionary of the Pali Language*, 28
Chrishna, *see* Krishna
Christendom, 73, 99
Christianity, 35, 36, 40, 41, 42, 47, 48, 67, 84, 90, 92, 93, 107, 116, 125, 139; and Buddhism, 2, 3, 12, 35, 38, 40, 41, 47, 48, 68, 69, 82, 83, 89, 107, 112, 113, 116, 122, 123, 125, 126–8, 129, 130, 132–8
Clarke, James Freeman, 74, 89, 98,

115, 124, 125, 129; *Ten Great Religions*, 74
Claughton, Bishop Piers, 94, 101, 114, 115, 117–18, 125, 136
Clausen, Christopher, 1
climate, as cultural determinant, 43, 44, 46, 49, 51, 81, 85
Clough, Benjamin, 26, 103
Cobbold, George, 2, 87, 121, 135
Coleman, Charles, 30
Colinet, P., 45, 108
Collins, Revd Richard, 2, 39, 109
communism, 75
comparative chronology, 55, 62, 63
comparative mythology: *see* mythology
Comte, Auguste, 98
Comtism: *see also* positivism, 94, 99
Condorcet, Marquis de, 115
Confucianism, 37, 132, 138
Confucius, 115
Copernicus, Nicholas, 91, 93
Copleston, Bishop Reginald, 34, 43, 69, 88, 109, 118, 137; *Buddhism*, 6, 88, 137
cosmology, 56, 90–3, 110, 140; Buddhist, 44, 46, 91, 92, 93; Christian, 92, 93; Hindu, 92, 93; scientific, 46, 91, 92; Western, 92
Couplet, Philippe, 62
Cousin, M., 133
Cox, Hiram, 21; *Journal of a Residence in the Burmhan Empire*, 21
Crawfurd, John, 11, 14, 18, 21, 41, 130; *History of the Indian Archipelago*, 14
Creuzer, Friedrich, 17; *Symbolik und Mythologie*, 17
Csoma, Alexander, 25
Culbertson, Michael, 63, 85, 106, 120, 124, 136; *Darkness in the Flowery Land*, 63
Cunningham, Brevet-Major Alexander, 19, 38, 57, 72, 97, 106

Darwin, Charles, 86, 90, 93, 98; *The Origin of Species*, 86, 98
Davids, T. W. Rhys, 26, 34, 46, 55, 66, 72, 77, 82–3, 84, 86, 88, 97, 99, 103, 124, 128; *Lectures on the Origin and Growth of Religion*, 97
Davies, William, 109
Davis, Sir John, 63, 120, 124; *China*, 63
Davis, Samuel, 63

182

Index

Printed in the United Kingdom
by Lightning Source UK Ltd.
99509UKS00001B/3